THE GREAT EVIL

(WOSICE TANKA KIN)

CHRISTIANITY, THE BIBLE
AND THE
NATIVE AMERICAN
GENOCIDE

BY

CHRIS MATO NUNPA, PhD

SEE SHARP PRESS ◆ TUCSON, ARIZONA

See Sharp Press
P.O. Box 1731
Tucson, AZ 85702

www.seesharppress.com

Mato Nunpa, Chris.
    The Great Evil / Chris Mato Nunpa ; Tucson, Ariz. : See Sharp Press, 2020.
    Includes bibliographical references and index.
    200 p. ; 23 cm.
    ISBN 978-1-947071-36-0

    1. Columbus, Christopher--Influence. 2. America--Discovery and exploration-
-Spanish. 3. Indians, Treatment of. 4. Indians--First contact with Eoropeans. 5. Indi-
ans-- Population. 6. Genocide--History. 7. Christianity--Congroversial literature. 8.
Indians--Religion and mythology. 9. Indians, Treatment of--North America--History.
10. Indians of North America--Government Relations. 11. Indians of North America-
-Government Policy. 12. Genocide--North America--History. 13. United States--Race
Relations. 14. Indians--Religion and Mythology..
    I. Title.

CONTENTS

*To all the survivors of the Indigenous
Holocaust of the United States,
and to my wife, Mary Beth Faimon,
for her support and encouragement*

Introduction

"Train up a child in the way he should go, and when he is old
he will not depart from it."
(Proverbs 22:6)

I was born in an "Indian" hospital in Pipestone, Minnesota on September 3, 1940, and I was raised in a small Dakota community in southwestern Minnesota, Pezihuta Zizi Otunwe, "Yellow Medicine Community." Back then, a Dakota baby could not be born in Granite Falls, Minnesota, our border town which was four miles away. It had to be in Pipestone in the Indian Hospital, 75 miles away. A Dakota could not be sick in Granite Falls, s/he had to be sick in Pipestone. This was a legalized form of segregation and of racial discrimination. And, of course, we—the Dakota (the "segregated,"), and the Wasicu folk of Granite Falls, MN (the segregationists)—thought this was OK, that it was normal, like the warmth of the sunshine or the air that we breathe.

Continuing on, the full name of my community is, actually, Pezihuta Zizi K'api Makoce, "Land Where The Yellow Medicine is Dug," the ancient Dakota name for this area. The name applied to my community by the federal government, through the Bureau of Indian Affairs (BIA), is the "Upper Sioux Community." Another incidental note—this is something that a colonizing power does: the colonizer (in this case, the U.S. and its Euro-American citizenry) renames places. Hence, we have "Upper Sioux Community" instead of the ancient Dakota name for the area, "Yellow Medicine Community." As Linda Tuhiwai Smith, a noted Maori scholar writes, "They (the Colonizer) Came, They Saw, They Named, They Claimed," with emphasis upon "They Named"![1]

The examples provided in the preceding paragraph are concrete examples of imperialism and colonialism.[2] What I mean by the term imperialism is a total system of foreign power which penetrates, transforms, and defines a land, its peoples, and its resources for purposes of domination and exploitation.[3] When I think of the term "penetrate" or "penetration," I think of the coming of the first western Europeans and the subsequent invasion, land theft, the occupation, and the transformation of the Americas. Of course, this refers to Columbus and the Spanish, initially, then the French, the Dutch, and the English, et. al.

The "penetration" process of Indigenous lands began in the islands of the Caribbean, then spread to the East Coast of the United States. Then, the process crossed the Appalachian mountains into the lands of the Native Peoples living in the Ohio River Valley; then, the Mississippi River Valley—from Minnesota down to Louisiana; then further west into the land of the Aboriginal Peoples of the Great Plains, extending from North and South Dakota down to Oklahoma and Texas; then through the Rocky Mountains and Southwest deserts; and, finally into the West Coast, from the states of Washington and Oregon, down to California. This invasion took about four centuries (the 1500s, the 1600s, the 1700s, and the 1800s); during that time the colonizers, invaders, exploiters, and land-grabbers stole the approximately three billion acres of land within the continental United States. By the end of the 19th century, the massive land theft was complete; the conquest was complete.

As was the genocide project. It was a time of mass killing. The killing fields were the entire expanse of what is now known as the United States of America. About 98.5 percent of the 16 million Indigenous Peoples of the U.S. at the time of contact (1500)[4] had been systematically killed off. By 1900, there were only 237,000 or so Aboriginal Peoples left, according to the U.S. Bureau of Census.[5]

Another aspect of this imperialistic process was the "transformation" of the land: the cutting down of the trees, the clearing of brush, the building of houses and towns, schools and churches, the plowing up of fields with metal/steel plows, the fencing off of the lands with barbed wire, the damming of rivers, the building of roads over Native trails, etc. "Transformation" also refers to the transformation of culture: imposition of the conquerors' languages (primarily Spanish, French, and English), their religious ideology (viz., Christianity, with its "subduing the earth," "dominion," "cursed earth," and religious imperialism), their economic ideology (viz., capitalism, with its foundation of greed, selfishness, and materialism), and forcing their customs and traditions, their values, and their world view upon the First Nations Peoples. Keep in mind one of Kurt Jonassohn's and Frank Chalk's four motives for Genocide, specifically, "imposing an ideology (e.g., Christianity, etc.) or belief upon the victim group." This imposition of ideologies, beliefs, and values upon a victim group is a component of genocide.

Another component is calling the Native Peoples "Indian(s)," an inaccurate term which has stuck with us (i.e., the Indigenous Peoples) since 1492. The conquerors, whether they were French, Spanish, Dutch, or English, defined us as "savages" or pagans, as "uncivilized," as "sub-human," or as "animals."

Then, because we, the Aboriginal Peoples, were so bad, so evil, in their eyes, they felt few or no twinges of conscience about invading and stealing our lands, killing us, exploiting us, removing us, enslaving us, and oppressing us. They used their Bible, their Christian beliefs, and other rationales to justify the killing and other appalling criminal acts perpetrated against the Aboriginal Peoples of the U.S.

Influence of Christianity

There were, approximately, 140 people on the "rez" when I grew up (the 1940s and the 1950s): men, women, children, babies, and elders. However, in spite of our small numbers, we had three Christian mission churches on our reservation—the Presbyterian, the Episcopal, and the Assemblies of God. "They" (the white Christians from the three denominations) must have thought we were desperately in need of "salvation." White missionaries used to come and be pastors, conduct church services, hymn singing, Sunday School, Bible Studies, etc., to evangelize us. The Assemblies of God conducted Bible-verse-memorization contests, from which I learned many Bible verses. At one point in my school years, the Assemblies of God used to send to our reservation white students from North Central Bible College in Minneapolis (now known as North Central University). They came on weekends and held a church service on Saturday night and Sunday school classes and a church service on Sunday morning. The college students would either sleep in the church or in homes of the Dakota people. Then, the Dakota who attended the church services and Sunday schools (e.g., my mother, family members, and relatives) would bring food and we would all eat the Sunday noon meal together. I really enjoyed those times – the good music, the good food, and the good fellowship (not so much the preaching and the "saving").

When I was growing up in Yellow Medicine, I used to go to Sunday School and Vacation Bible School in the summer at all three churches at different times during my youth. Since we were a thoroughly Christianized

Dakota community, the churches were our social centers. Our traditional ceremonies and traditions, by the time I was growing up, had been not only suppressed but also supplanted. Thus, we engaged in Christian activities such as Sunday services, baptisms, funerals, and the white man's holidays. Some of my most pleasant memories of my childhood were centered around the churches.

At one point, in my teens, I sang in the choir at the Pezihuta Zizi ("Yellow Medicine") Presbyterian church. I used to go to all three Christmas programs and services because all three churches gave a lot of apples, oranges, and bags of candies, not just to the children but also to the adults. From a Dakota child's perspective, it was wonderful. It was truly a time of great joy and glad tidings.

A further note: Since we were so Christianized and colonized, I did not experience or participate in most of our traditional Dakota ceremonies when I was growing up. Such ceremonies included the Canduhupa (the Pipe); the Inipi, the "Make-Alive" Ceremony (involving rocks, fire, steam, etc.), a purification ceremony; the Hanbde Ceyapi, the "Crying for a Vision" ceremony, or Vision Quest; the Wiwanyag Wacipi, lit., "Dancing While Watching the Sun," or the Sun Dance, etc. We were taught by the missionaries to look upon these traditional Dakota sacred ceremonies as sinful, heathenish, and definitely un-Christian. I did not learn, participate in, or practice these ceremonies until I was an adult. I did participate, though, in permitted ceremonies. One was the Ituhan, the "Gift-Giving" Ceremony. Another was the Wokiksuye Wotapi, the "Remembrance Feast," held one year after the death of a family member or a loved one.

A third traditional ceremony was the name-giving ceremony. For example, I received my name from my maternal great-grandfather, Inyang Mani Hoksida, "Running Walker Boy." My great-grandfather's Wasicu name was John Roberts. I had an older brother who died in infancy. So, when I was born in 1940, my great-grandfather took me in his arms and declared, "Detanhan Ed Hdi Nazin eciyapikte." "From this time, he shall be called 'One who stands in his brother's place.'" So, I took the place in the family of the brother who had left this time and place. I consider myself fortunate that my family and our community still had these few ceremonies.

Hurtful Incidents

When I was I was eight or nine years old (1948 or 1949), several incidents occurred with the missionaries and their Christian teachings. One incident, which I vividly remember, involved my cousin asking one of the young Assemblies of God missionaries the following question: "Some of our grandmothers and grandfathers, who have died, didn't know Jesus as their savior. What happened to them?" The missionary, a young man from Texas, replied, "If they didn't know Jesus Christ as their personal savior, they are burning in hell right now." I remember this like it was yesterday, even though this happened over seventy years ago. The missionary's words seared my heart and became indelibly etched in my memory.

Now that I am in my elderly years, and as I look back upon this and similar incidents, I have questions. One is this: What kind of God did this young missionary have who would cause him to say, "they [the grand-parents and great grand-parents] are burning in hell right now"? Another question is: Why would this missionary tell young children such a hurt-ful thing? Our grandparents were good people, kind and generous people. They cared for others, and they helped people in need. A final question: The Assemblies of God missionaries taught us that God is love, that God is a loving God. Why would this supposedly "loving God" punish or ban-ish people who never heard of Jesus Christ to eternal torment in hell? In my end-time years, I still don't know any good answers to these questions.

It was upsetting and bewildering for our young minds to hear and grasp this notion—that our loving grandparents, long gone, were "burning in hell." We wanted to believe that our relatives, kind, and generous people, were now in "heaven" because, according to these missionaries, "Heaven" was the place where good people go. And "hell," according to the mission-aries, was the bad place, a terribly hot place, where bad people went .

The transition from Christianity to traditional spirituality began then, in my early childhood, with such hurtful and disrespectful statements, teachings, and actions, though I didn't know it at that time. (In our Dakota religious thought and spirituality, there is no "heaven" or "hell.") I decided, eventually, as an adult, that I didn't like the concepts of "heaven" and "hell," especially "hell," which had such final and painful implications for follow-ers of other religions.

Thus, such Christian teaching and such hurtful, insensitive, and disre-spectful statements have left emotional scars on our people, including this writer. The Christian Church has wreaked much havoc through these cruel statements and suppression of religious ceremonies and practices upon not only the Dakota People of Minnesota but also upon all other Indigenous Peoples of the United States and the Americas. This incident along with other such hurtful and disrespectful statements and incidents contributed to my eventual withdrawal from Christianity and my return to traditional Dakota spirituality and to our ancient ceremonies. However, at the time, we all still liked the baloney sandwiches, the cookies, and the Kool-Aid that the missionaries gave us. So, I, and other Dakota youths, kept going to the churches. We continued to listen to, and eat, their baloney.

It was the missionaries of the Assemblies of God who taught us a Bible verse from the book of Proverbs 22:6, "Train up a child in the way he should go: and when he is old he will not depart from it." Another verse, which was drilled into my mind, was in the book of Psalms, chapter 119, verse 11, "Thy word have I hid in mine heart, that I might not sin against thee." (KJV) The Bible, with verses such as the preceding, was part of my ongoing indoctrination, part of my childhood training, or to put it more bluntly, part of my brainwashing. We were taught that that the white man's Bible was the word of God, the standard for truth, and that it contained the necessary values for living our lives. Wakan Tanka, the "Great Mystery," or the God of the Dakota People, was a false god, like Baal, a semitic deity in the Old Testament. Our ceremonies were from the devil, and the Dakota People had no truth. Our ancient Dakota beliefs and values were to be abandoned, and our customs and traditions were to be suppressed and then supplanted by Christianity. Of course, at this time in my childhood, I didn't know how to articulate this.

Christianity, as I learned later, was a colonialist religious ideology, and the Bible was a tool of the colonization process. Or one could say, the Church (Christianity) and the State (the colonizer), worked hand-in-hand in the exploitation, subjugation, and continued oppression of the Indigenous Peoples of the U.S. (Capitalism could be added, thus creating an unholy trinity.)

Another incident which I vividly remember, from when I was growing up in the late 1940s, concerned two Dakota women who went to the Pezihuta Zizi Presbyterian Church ("The Yellow Medicine Presbyterian Church"). I remember them saying that our traditional gift-giving ceremony, "Ituhan kin he Wakan Sica etanhan" (gift-giving or give-away), is from the Devil.

That was very confusing to me, because my family and relatives, and other Dakota families in the community, practiced this beautiful tradition. Also, I thought of the Assemblies of God pastor who would say before taking the offering, "Jesus said, 'It is more blessed to give than to receive.'" Even then I thought that our give-aways were good, and that even Jesus would like this because we were giving, not taking. In retrospect, I can now see that I was right. What would fit in more with the spirit of Jesus' teaching that it is "more blessed to give than to receive" than our Dakota gift-giving ceremonies? Also, in retrospect, it was painful to see our own Dakota People (viz., these two Dakota women) now evangelizing (or self-colonizing, if you will) their own people in a judgmental, non-compassionate, and disrespectful manner, similar to the attitudes and actions of their white Presbyterian counterparts.

I sensed and saw that something was wrong. I didn't know until my graduate school years that we, the Dakota People of Yellow Medicine, were a thoroughly colonized and Christianized people. In addition, I didn't know then that the Dakota People turning away from their own beliefs and ways was one of the many hurtful and harmful effects of Christianity upon Dakota society, upon our culture, customs and traditions, and upon our spirituality.

A third incident that I remember from my teenage years involved a new Presbyterian pastor who wished to have bingo in the church basement as a means of raising revenue for church and youth activities. One of the male Dakota Presbyterians replied "that's gambling and a sin." Some of our Dakota Christians were stricter than our white teachers and ministers, and had become just as self-righteous and judgmental as their white Christian counterparts. Roy Meyer in his book, *The History of the Santee Sioux*, refers to the conflict between those Dakota who wished "to preserve many of the heathen customs" and the "church party" made up of "those Dakota who had been most strongly under missionary influence on the old reservation and who often surpassed their teachers in moralistic rigidity, . . ."[6] He was right. Some of us surpassed the missionaries, our white Christian teachers, in that "moralistic rigidity."

The colonizer, in using his religion (Christianity) as an instrument of exploitation and oppression, was extremely successful. One teaching that came across loud and clear to the Dakota People of Yellow Medicine, from the missionaries of the Presbyterian and the Assemblies of God denominations, was how to be rigid, judgmental, and dogmatic.

Thus, when I took courses from the American Indian Studies Program at the University of Minnesota, Twin Cities campus, one of the things which surprised and really amazed me was the use of the Bible by Euro-Americans in their destructive and murderous interactions with Indigenous Peoples.

A Simple Question

About half a century ago, a friend and classmate of mine asked me the following question (this is a paraphrase): "Why would any Native person want to be a Christian or be associated with the Christian church since Christianity had done so many terrible things to the Indigenous Peoples in the name of Christ and Christianity?" I think that I, at that time, and because I was so colonized and Christianized, offered a rather lame explanation about the history of our people in Minnesota, something about the Dakota-U.S. War of 1862, and how, out of hopelessness and despair because of this tragic and traumatic event, many of our Dakota people converted to Christianity. Also, I said something to the effect that I was a product of my background and circumstances (like we all are, as humans), that many of my relatives were Christian, that my father was an Episcopal lay-reader in the Diocese of Minnesota, that I was baptized as an Episcopalian, and that I even went to an Episcopal seminary with the idea that I was going to be an Episcopal priest. In addition, I would now add that many Dakota people, back in the 1850s and 1860s, accepted Christianity as a means of survival—they wanted to live, rather than starve or be killed.

I graduated in 1959 from Granite Falls Public Schools, went to Bemidji State University, and received my Baccalaureate Degree in 1964 from St. Cloud State University; then I went to graduate school at the University of Minnesota (Twin Cities campus) and took many American Indian Studies courses as part of my academic preparation for my Masters degree in 1971 and Ph.D. in 1974. My collateral field for the Ph.D. was in American Indian Studies, as it was called then (1968–1974) at the U of M. I learned many things about the experiences of our Indigenous Peoples with Christianity and its missionaries, things which my teachers at Granite Falls Public Schools never taught me (and, as far as I know, still don't), things which my professors at Bemidji State and St. Cloud State University never told me, and things which made me ponder deeply my friend's question.

My own initial question back then was, "If these killers of Native Peoples used Bible verses to justify killing us, then is their killing of us 'holy murder' and thus justified?" That and friend's question about why any Native person would want to embrace Christianity, my personal and academic experiences, and my own evolving thoughts, all contributed to my withdrawing from Christianity and the Christian Church.

Music and Indoctrination

The Assemblies of God taught us a lot of lively and catchy choir tunes, and these helped to indoctrinate, to program, and to condition us into believing their Christian message.

Of course, at the time, I didn't know there were English words such as "indoctrinate," "program," and "condition." Also, we would sing "Onward Christian Soldiers," and would march in time and in place. Another song was "I'm in the Lord's Army," and we would make motions with our hands like we were shooting off artillery or gallop with our feet like we were galloping in the cavalry. The idea that we were in a "war" became impressed in our young minds. If we were in a "war," then we were to kill our enemies.

The Presbyterian missionaries had their hymns translated into the Dakota Language, and had the Bible translated into Dakota. In addition, two of the missionaries compiled dictionaries. Rev. Riggs did the *Dakota English Dictionary,* and Rev. Williamson did the *English Dakota Dictionary.* (Riggs and the Williamsons did not credit previous work of the Pond brothers, also missionaries to the Dakota People, for their work with the Dakota Language.) Some of our Christian Dakota, from Pezihuta Zizi ("Yellow Medicine") helped Riggs and Williamson with these written works. However, neither Riggs nor Williamson bothered to mention the names or give credit to the Dakota individuals who helped them. This speaks for itself.

The Episcopal Church not only had their hymnbooks translated into Dakota, but also their 1928 Book of Common Prayer. These two churches used these written works as instruments to implement their imperialistic agenda, that is, the conversion of and the leading of the Dakota People out of their heathen "darkness" and into the "light" of Christianity.

Bible Verse Memorization

The Assemblies of God were a fundamentalist and evangelical Christian denomination. They were "Bible Thumpers" and their missionaries taught and had us memorize Bible verses. Some of the first verses I memorized were: "For God so loved the world that he gave his only begotten Son that whosoever believeth in Him would not perish but have everlasting life" (John 3:16, KJV); "For all have sinned, and come short of the glory of God" (Romans 3:23, KJV); " . . . There is none righteous, no, not one"

(Romans 3:10, KJV), and so many more verses. I found out, then, that we, as humans, including white people, were bad people, or "sinners," as they taught us. However, later on, I learned that although white people were sinners, too, the Dakota People were worse sinners, and thus below the white Christians. It was during this time that I also learned and memorized the verse quoted at the beginning of this chapter (Proverbs 22:6). Already, in my teen years, I was beginning to think some of these white Christians were racist (i.e., had prejudice toward the Dakota and had the power to act upon their prejudice).

The Assemblies of God missionaries even had Bible verse-memorization contests, of which I won my share. When I won a contest, I liked it when the missionaries would pat me on the head and says things like, "nice little Indian boy" (similar to what I say now to our cat, "nice little cat"). I liked it even better when they would give me a baloney sandwich, Kool-Aid, and a cookie. I really liked the eating part, nourishing the inner man, so to speak.

Religious Ideology and Indoctrination

The Assemblies of God also believed in "saving" people. If one believed that s/he was a sinner, believed that Jesus died for their sins, and if they accepted Jesus Christ as their personal savior, then they were, basically, "saved." Thus, I was "saved" three summers in a row by the Assemblies of God missionaries at their summer Bible camp at Lake Geneva in Alexandria, Minnesota. I think I was ages 8, 9, and 10 in those three summers in the late 1940s.

As I look back at these experiences, one of the topics about which I now think is child abuse. Why do I say this? At these Bible camps, I most certainly enjoyed the day-time activities such as swimming, playing softball, and playing volleyball. Also, we ate very well there, and, so, I really liked the food!

However, I didn't enjoy the night-time activities in which we had to go to the chapel and listen to the preacher talk about hell, sinners, being saved, and accepting Jesus. They would talk about hell-fire, and about how if we didn't accept Jesus Christ as our personal savior we were not going to heaven. Instead, we would be left behind when Jesus returns, and we, then, would go straight to hell and suffer being burned forever and ever. This caused a great deal of fear and terror. They scared the hell out of me (and I'm sure, many others). Or, I should say, they scared the hell *into* me.

They had a song which contained the words, "He's coming soon, He's coming soon . . . " to the tune of a Hawaiian melody. With the fear of hell-fire and eternal torment instilled in us by the preacher, the song that Jesus is coming soon added to our terror a new fear: being left behind when Jesus returns.

I ask myself now, "Was this emotional and psychological child abuse?" We were children, anywhere from seven to twelve years old, and as Richard Dawkins asks in *The God Delusion*, can "a six-year-old child [in my case, a seven-year-old child] . . . properly be said to have a religion at all, whether it is Jewish or Christian or anything else?" We had been taken from our homes and we were separated from our parents and family as small children. We were a captive audience, and terror induced in childhood can and does carry over to adulthood. Dawkins writes of a Jill Mytton who "was brought up to be terrified of hell" and "eternal damnation," "escaped from Christianity as an adult, and now counsels and helps others similarly traumatized in childhood."[7]

If a person and people are stripped of their traditional religion, this could amount to more than just child-abuse. According to two genocide scholars, "Imposing an ideology [Christianity, a religious ideology] or a belief upon [a] victim group" is one of the four common motives of Genocide.[8] Thus, my experiences as a child in this Summer Bible Camp fulfilled this fourth criterion of genocide.

I was baptized three times, at least, at different times in my life. As one Lakota buddy of mine, who had a similar experience on his reservation, says, "I was sprinkled, sprayed, and dunked." Each church had to give me the "correct" baptism. Looking back now at my childhood experiences with the Christian Church, I ask myself, "Self, how stupid was that?" And, Self would respond, "that is very stupid!" I would say, sometimes facetiously, and sometimes seriously, that "when my time comes to leave this time and place, I have all the bases covered." On the one hand, I was saved and baptized multiple times by the Christian missionaries, and on the other hand I am now following the ancient spiritual ways and ceremonies of our Dakota People, given to us by Tunkansida Wakan Tanka, "Grandfather Great Mystery." Thus, when it's time go, I will find out who's right.

Biblical Injunctions

Biblical injunctions were used to justify the destruction of Indigenous Peoples and the razing and burning to the ground (or holocausts, "great destruction by fire") their homes and communities, and to the dispossession and expropriation of their lands and resources. Commonly used Biblical notions that serve to justify the slaughter of Native Peoples and destruction of their communities include passages such as the genocidal commands of the Old Testament God ("kill everything that hath breath," "leave alive nothing that breatheth," etc.); the chosen people/promised land notions; the "Canaan, land of milk and honey" idea; "subduing the earth" and "dominion" over it; and "the Lord hath given us our inheritance" teaching.

Two ideas from the New Testament that were used to justify genocidal and destructive behaviors against the Indigenous Peoples and their communities include, first, "the Great Commission," in which Christ tells his followers to proselytize and to "make disciples of all the nations," found in the books of Matthew (28:19, NKJV) and Mark (16:15, KJV). This was, and is, religious imperialism.

It appears that Jesus Christ was an advocate of establishing a religious empire, was an apologist for religious imperialism, which meant, and means to hold no respect for the religious beliefs, values, and practices of the other peoples of the world. The second idea was Christ and Christianity as the only truth and way, as stated in the Gospel of John 14:6, in which Christ says, " I am the way, the truth, and the life: no one comes to the Father except through Me." (NKJV) Since Christ declared himself the Truth, then, this meant that other religious beliefs and systems of spirituality were false, were not the truth. This is incredibly arrogant and disrespectful of other religions and spiritual beliefs, of which some were much older than Christianity. One can see in this why Christianity has been involved in many, many wars and conflicts since its inception.

In addition to the genocidal commands of the Old Testament God and the imperialistic and arrogant assertions of Jesus Christ, several papal bulls of the Roman Catholic Church incorporated these ideas. This allowed the Western European kings, explorers, and missionaries to perpetrate genocide, to subdue, to kill, to steal, to enslave, and to exploit Indigenous Peoples. (We'll discuss three papal bulls in particular later in this book—*Romanus Pontifex*, from Nicholas V in 1455; *Inter Caetera*, from Alexander VI in 1493; and *Sublimus Dei*, from Paul III, in 1537.) The "Doctrine of

Discovery" was based on these papal bulls and the above-mentioned as-sertions of Jesus Christ.

In conclusion, the influence of the Christian Church upon me was pro-found, particularly the Bible teaching and the Bible-verse memorization contests of the Assemblies of God, various hurtful and disrespectful inci-dents over the years, and my experience with other Christian denomina-tions. In large part, these things led directly to the writing of this book.

The Genesis of *The Great Evil*

Western Europeans, who eventually became U.S. Euro-Americans, used many rationales for perpetrating genocide on the Indigenous Peoples of what is now the United States of America. One rationale came from the Bible to justify not only the killing of First Nations peoples but also to justify massive land theft, suppression and criminalization of Native cer-emonies, suppression of indigenous languages, and enslavement of Native Peoples. During my academic work in American Indian Studies, which was the collateral field for my Ph.D., at the University of Minnesota, Twin Cities campus, under Professor Roger Buffalohead, and during my 45-plus teaching years, I discovered that there were numerous historical events in which the killers quoted Bible verses before, during, or after a genocidal event in order to justify the murdering and slaughtering of our First Na-tions peoples. I refer to this as Wosice Tanka Kin, the Dakota phrase for "The Great Evil." This Great Evil began in 1492, when the first white men came to the shores of the Americas.

The Great Evil also had disastrous effects on our relatives, such as the animal peoples, the bird peoples, the fish peoples, and all other forms of life, not only here in Minnesota and in the rest of the United States, but also in the rest of the Americas. In the more than 500 years since The Great Evil began, the lands have been contaminated, the air polluted, the rivers and lakes defiled, and animals poisoned and slaughtered. Some animals and plants are now extinct, as are some Native Peoples of the U.S., in par-ticular those Native Peoples who lived on the Atlantic Coast. Beyond these crimes, this Great Evil, wrought by the western Europeans, has brought the United States, the rest of the Americas, and the world to the brink of ecological destruction.

The historical events that I came across were not the result of an orga-nized and systematic research process on my part, but the consequence of the following: listening to the oral tradition in my own home while growing up; reading books; taking Indigenous Nations and Dakota Studies courses; and listening to my fellow Indigenous academic writers and other scholars and researchers over my 45-year-plus professional teaching career. In particular, my graduate school courses on Indigenous Nations Studies and History had the most influence on my thinking and writing. These courses provided a basis for understanding the cornucopia of graphic and relevant historical events and Biblical allusions used in justifying the genocide of the Indigenous Peoples of the United States.

While reading about genocidal massacres and other atrocities I came across language which I recognized as Bible verses or language which sounded like biblical phraseology. Then, I would use concordances to see if these words, or phrases, were in the Bible, and if they were I referenced them.

As well, I'll discuss Manifest Destiny (which was not, as is commonly believed, an entirely secular matter). Manifest Destiny was a belief system and policy based upon the chosen people and promised land notions of the Old Testament, and upon the genocidal commands of the Old Testament God. It was a policy of and justification for imperialistic, God-ordained expansion of the United States.

I do not claim to be writing a definitive study of these matters, nor am I writing for academics. I am writing for those who are interested in Indigenous Peoples and their history, those who are interested in the genocide of the Indigenous Peoples, and in particular for those who are interested in biblical studies as related to Native Peoples. My goal is to alert people to the fact that the Holy Bible was used to justify the slaughter of millions upon millions of Indigenous People, not only here in the United States, but also in all of the Americas. (I disavow the term "definitive," because I have observed over my 80 "winters" on *Ina Maka* [Mother Earth] that most Euro-American academics strive to write the definitive account or the definitive book on any given subject, person, or event. This is not my intention. For example, it is OK, from my perspective, if someone else writes the definitive work on the genocidal commands of the Old Testament God as related to the ensuing genocidal events in the Americas. However, I do wish to help set in motion conversations and dialogues concerning the Bible and its relation to the genocide of the Indigenous Peoples of the Americas.)

Since knowledge of the genocide has been suppressed, "hidden," ever since the Western Europeans first came here and began mass murdering in 1492, it is indeed time for this truth to finally be told and taught in the schools, both public and private. It's also time for truth telling as regards the massive land theft; the breaking of treaties and the promises therein; the suppression of aboriginal languages; the criminalizing of Indigenous spirituality and ceremonies; the enslavement and exploitation of First Nations Peoples; and the continued oppression of the Indigenous Peoples of the United States.

Perspective

Since I am a Dakota man, I will be coming from the point of view of an Indigenous person. For example, I come from a people whose lands were stolen. Thus, I will look at history differently than the descendants of the people who stole the lands. The Dakota perspective says that the white man "stole" the land. Most Euro-Americans and Euro-Minnesotans will say "our ancestors settled the land." Another example: I come from a people whose treaties were broken by others. So, I will say that the white man "violated" or "broke" the treaties, that the United States and the various states are "promise breakers." Most of the Wasicu (the Dakota term for the white man) will not talk about the treaties nor will they say, "we violated the treaties," because it would reflect unfavorably upon white people, and upon the United States of America, and it would conflict with the conceited concept of "American exceptionalism."

One more example: the Indigenous person will say, "The U.S. and its Euro-American citizenry perpetrated genocide upon the Indigenous Peoples of the U.S." Or, the Dakota writer will say, "The State of Minnesota and its Euro-Minnesotan citizenry perpetrated genocide upon the Dakota People of Minnesota." Most white people do not talk about genocide, except when it regards another people or nation committing it (e.g., the Nazis mass murdering the Jews and Romanis, et. al., or the Turkish nation perpetrating genocide against the Armenians). Instead, white academics tend to talk about the "population decline" (a nicer phrase than the term, genocide, don't you think?) of the Indigenous Peoples, and Euro-American scholars will often say, further, that disease was the main factor in this decline, but they won't mention bio-terrorism.

Practical Matters

Terminology

Before I go any further, I should define and explain some of the terminology that I'll use. First of all, I despise the term "Indian" and will use this term only when I have to use it. I consider it demeaning and inaccurate. The term "Indian" obscures the rich diversity and beauty of Indigenous cultures, societies, values, and world views. "Indian" is a term that was forced upon all of us by the colonizers. This term has now been with us for over half a millennium, and was first used by a lost Italian who stumbled upon one of the Caribbean islands back in 1492 and thought he was someplace else. Thus, the term "Indian" is a colonial imposition, and I reject this term for this reason alone. According to the white supremacist mentality of U.S. Euro-American society, Indigenous Peoples are insignificant and unimportant. So, it really doesn't make any difference what "we," i.e., they—the white supremacists—call these savages. It's okay to call them any name as long as everybody understands whom "we" are talking about. Even though the Dakota have their own name for themselves (viz., "Dakota" as opposed to "Sioux," etc.), "we" can call them whatever we please, simply because we can.

And of course the term "Indian" refers properly only to people from the country of India. They are the real Indians. So, use of the term Indian in regard to Native peoples is not only a colonial imposition, but also grossly inaccurate.

So, what term(s) will be used in this book to substitute for the term "Indian"? The terms "Indigenous", "Native," "Aboriginal," and "First Nations," "First Americans," "Original Americans," etc., will be used interchangeably. Secondly, in addition to using the phrase "white man" for the invaders, stealers, destroyers, and exploiters who came to the Americas in 1492, I will use the following terms: "Western European," "Euro-American," and "Caucasian." I will use the Dakota term, "Wasicu," for these white people.

Thirdly, instead of using the term "Sioux" for my people, I will use our term, "Dakota. For example, "Damakota," "I am Dakota"; or "Daunkotapi," "We are Dakota." The term "Sioux," like "Indian," is another term which I loathe. "Sioux" generally means "snake" or "enemy." I have heard many of my Dakota, Lakota, and Nakota colleagues from both South Dakota and

North Dakota say, "I am not a Sioux—a snake or enemy. I am a Dakota (or Lakota, or Nakota, a "friend" or "ally."

Another term I will not use is "tribe." I find this term demeaning and disparaging of the Indigenous Peoples. Winona LaDuke, an Anishinabe writer and activist, uses the term "denigrated" to refer to the application of "tribe" to the Native Nations of the United States. LaDuke writes, "North America is similarly comprised of a series of nations known as "First Nations" in Canada, and, with few exceptions, denigrated in the United States with the term 'tribes.'"[9] Instead, I will use either the term "People" or "Nation" for the word "tribe." Also, independent and autonomous Peoples and/or Nations make treaties with other autonomous peoples. "Tribes" do not make treaties with other sovereign nations or peoples.

References and Study Aids

The various reference works and study aids which were helpful in the writing of this book include:

1) Various translations of the Bible:

These translations include the King James Version, which shall be listed, from this point on, as KJV, and the New King James Version, or NKJV, which are the main translations I've used for this work. Other translations which will be used, at various times, include the New American Bible (1970), a Catholic version; the Torah (1962, 1967), a translation of the five books of Moses by the Jewish Publishing Society (JPS); and the Tanakh (1985), also from the JPS, which will be used for Old Testament references not found in the Torah.

These various translations are helpful to the reader in showing that the meaning of a given Bible verse is fairly uniform. Some of the verses used in this study are so clear that the use of alternative translations, concordances, and commentaries of theologians is unnecessary. For instance, Deuteronomy 20:16 says, "But of the cities of these people, which the Lord thy God doth give thee for an inheritance, thou shalt save alive nothing that breatheth," (KJV) and the meaning of the command given by the Old Testament God is quite clear. Anyone who has a modicum of common sense can easily understand that Yahweh, the Old Testament God, is telling his people to kill all human and animal life in those cities ("save alive nothing that breatheth"). This means killing all the men, women, children, babies, young people, elders, and animals, in addition, to destroying the cities. The Catholic version (NAB) reads, " . . . you shall not leave a single soul alive." The Torah says, " . . . you shall not let a soul remain alive." Thus, as one can see, one doesn't need to go to a seminary, or to know Hebrew or Greek, to understand this particular verse.

2) Concordances:

The first concordance is Abingdon's *Strong Exhaustive Concordance of the Bible* and the second is Young's *Analytical Concordance*. These reference books show every word in the text of the King James Version and the books, the chapters, and the verses in which a word or phrase is used, and were extremely useful in identifying relevant Bible verses when a particular scriptural allusion or a suspected biblical reference was used in a quotation.

3) Commentaries:

One commentary is *The Bethany Parallel Commentary on the Old Testament* (1983) and the second is *The Bethany Parallel Commentary on the New Testament* (1983).

They feature the commentaries of five theologians: Matthew Henry (Presbyterian); and Robert Jamieson (Presbyterian), Andrew Fausset (Church of England), and David Brown (Presbyterian); and Adam Clarke (Methodist). Even though the commentators are all Protestants, the reader will still get a clear, definite picture of what is being said and what is meant. These commentaries present "a wide spectrum of evangelical thought."[10] (Also, in the majority of historical genocidal events that this book will be discussing, the killers were WASPs—White Anglo-Saxon Protestants.) Other commentaries will be referred to occasionally because of their thought-provoking and sometimes outrageous content. These additional commentaries will be clearly identified.

Again, the reason for the use of these commentaries is to illustrate the contrast (and sometimes agreement) between what the theologians say Bible verses mean and how Euro-American murderers used these same verses to justify genocide and other crimes against humanity.

In regard to the phrase "a wide spectrum of evangelical thought," I wish to make the following comments. The term "evangelical" comes from the word "evangelize," which according to the dictionary means "to preach the gospel to" and "to convert to Christianity."[11] The term "evangelicalism," according to the Church of England, is "applied to the school which lays special stress on personal conversion and salvation by faith in the atoning death of Christ."[12] This concept is related to and is derived from what Christianity calls the Great Commission as found in Matthew 28:19-20, "Go therefore and make disciples of all nations, baptizing them in the name of the Father, and of the Son, and of the Holy Spirit, Teaching them to observe all things that I have commanded you: and, lo, I am with you always, even to the end of the age. Amen." (NKJV). (Several papal bulls, which will be discussed later, refer to these evangelical and imperialistic religious commands in the Bible.)

To reiterate, the use of the commentaries is to compare how the theologians interpret particular Bible verses with how the perpetrators/killers interpreted and applied these verses to justify murdering Indigenous Peoples, in addition to using these verses to rationalize the stealing of Native lands, the breaking of treaties, the suppressing of Indigenous religions, ceremonies, and spirituality; the prohibiting and suppressing of aboriginal languages, and the enslavement of the Native Peoples of the U.S.

Genocidal Acts and the Bible

This book will focus on selected and specific historical events from four different centuries of genocidal acts against the Indigenous Peoples by Western Europeans and Euro-Americans, and how they then used Bible verses to justify such acts. I'll also quote and apply the UN Genocide Convention of 1948 (Appendix D) and its five criteria to these various genocidal events, atrocities, and massacres discussed here. I'll do the same with the "Four Common Motives For Genocide," as identified by Frank Chalk and Kurt Jonassohn.

I'll pay particular attention to Columbus and his fellow conquerors slaughtering eight million Indigenous People in only twenty-one years, circa 1500, the Pequot Holocaust of 1637, and 19th-century genocidal acts, such as the genocide of the Dakota People of Minnesota 1862–1863, the Sand Creek Massacre of the Cheyenne and Arapaho, 1864, and other similar events, and to the use of Bible verses by the perpetrators. The actions and attitudes of the Christian English, especially the Puritans, expressed a mindset informed by biblical concepts: notions of chosen people and promised land, the genocidal commands of Jehovah/Yahweh, the biblical God, which became the basis of the Manifest Destiny doctrine, and so on.

This biblically informed mindset established a pattern (invasion, occupation, extermination, removal, massive land theft, etc.), the legacy of which continues to this day.

The Scope and Magnitude of the Genocide

It's helpful to make a few general comments to indicate the purpose, scope, and magnitude of the genocide against the Indigenous Peoples of the U.S. For example, Frank Chalk and Kurt Jonassohn identify four common motives of genocide:

1.) to eliminate groups of people who the perpetrators imagine are threats;

2.) to spread terror among enemies;

3.) to acquire economic wealth;

4.) to impose an ideology or belief upon the victim group.[13]

All four of these motives are evident in the Indigenous Holocaust. Colonial settlers in Virginia and New England in the seventeenth century attempted to obliterate the "heathens" and "savages" in the name of Christianity and civilization.

In the colonies and in various states such as Minnesota, Colorado, Texas, and California, the colonial and state governments offered bounties for Indigenous scalps in order to kill First Nations Peoples and to spread terror among these Peoples, whose land they wanted to steal.[14]

Across the U.S., governors made it state policy to address and implement a Final Solution of their local "Indian Problem"; presidents celebrated massacres of entire villages, and Peoples; and, then, governors and presidents alike, characterized these policies as wise and just decisions. Newspaper editorials encouraged genocide: in Minnesota papers advocated "Extermination or Removal" of the Dakota People; there were similar newspaper editorials in other states including California, Kansas, Colorado. (We will see specific examples when the subject of the genocide of the Dakota People is discussed later in the book.)

In a book which she edited, *The State of Native America*, M. Annette Jaimes points out that recent studies have established that there were somewhere between nine and eighteen million Native people living north of the Rio Grande at the time of first contact. The data from these studies reveal the actual rate of extermination pertaining to Native North America during the period of conquest as having been 98 to 99 percent overall. Jaimes goes on to say that it is plain that the killing stopped only when there was almost no one in the targeted population left to kill, and the killing process leading to this result was sustained without interruption, generation after generation, century after century, "with a stamina even the Nazis cannot be said to have mustered."[15] Jaimes, then, says, "Not only does the rate of extermination suffered by the Indigenous Peoples of North America vastly exceed that experienced by the Jews of Europe under the Nazis, it represents a scale and scope of genocide without parallel in recorded human history."[16]

Lenore Stiff Arm and Phil Lane, Jr. in their essay, "The Demography of Native North America," use the figure of 16 million Indigenous people living within the continental United States at the time of contact, and I will use this figure as well. Stiff Arm and Lane go on to mention that by 1900, four centuries after Columbus, there were only approximately 237,000 Native Peoples left.[17] This corresponds to a depopulation rate, or extermination rate, of 98.5%.

What happened? What happened to decrease the population of the many Native Nations of the United States from 16 million to less than a quarter million in 400 years? The answer is genocide, the deliberate and systematic killing of a racial, political, or cultural group by another group. It was a genocide that was so breathtakingly monstrous that it caused David Stannard, in his book, *American Holocaust*, to write, "the destruction of the Indians of the Americas was, far and away, the most massive act of genocide in the history of the world."[18] This statement is so significant that it is worth repeating, "the destruction of the Indians of the Americas was, far and away, the most massive act of genocide in the history of the world."

Endnotes

1. *Decolonizing Methodologie: Research and Indigenous Peoples,* by Linda Tuhiwai Smith. London: Zed Books, 1999, pp. 80–81.

2, *From a Native Daughter: Colonialism and Sovereignty in Hawai'i,* by Haunani-Kay Trask. University of Hawaii, 1999, p. 251.

3. Ibid.

4. Lenore Stiff Arm and Phil Lane, Jr. "The Demography of Native North America: A Question of American Indian Survival," in *The State of Native America,* 1992, p. 27.

5. Ibid., pp. 36–37.

6. *History of the Santee Sioux: United States Indian Policy on Trial,* by Roy W. Meyer. Lincoln, NE: University of Nebraska Press, 1993, p. 204.

7. *The God Delusion.* London: Black Swan, 2006, pp. 361–362.

8. *The History and Sociology of Genocide*, by Frank Chalk and Kurt Jonassohn. New Haven, CT: Yale University Press, 1990.

9. "Indigenous Environmental Perspectives: A North American Primer," by Winona Laduke, in *Native American Voices: A Reader, Second Edition.* Akwekon Press, 2001, p. 353.

10. *The Bethany Parallel Commentary On the Old Testament.* Nashville: Bethany House Publishers, 1985, from "Publishers Preface."

11. Merriam-Webster's Collegiate Dictionary Eleventh Edition, 2012, p. 432.

12. *The Oxford Dictionary of the Christian Church*, F. L. Cross, ed. Oxford: Oxford University Press, 1974, p.486.

13. Chalk and Jonassohn, op. cit., p. 29.

14. *A Little Matter of Genocide: Holocaust and Denial in the Americas 1492 to the Present*, by Ward Churchill. San Francisco: City Lights Books, 1997, pp. 180.

15. "Introduction: Sand Creek," by M. Annette Jaimes, in *The State of Native America.* South End Press, 1992, p. 7.

16. Ibid.

17. "The Demography of Native North America: A Question of American Indian Survival," by Lenore Stiff Arm and Phil Lane, Jr., in *The State of Native America,* 1992, p.27.

18. *American Holocaust: The Conquest of the New World*, by David E. Stannard. Oxford: Oxford University Press, 1992, p. x.

ACKNOWLEDGMENTS

I wish to acknowledge my father, Christian H. Cavender, and my mother, Elsie M. Two Bear Cavender, for their teachings and values, and providing a safe, encouraging, and supportive environment in which I grew up. I know that if there is anything good which I have done, it is because of my parents' love and support. And I miss them dearly!!

I wish to thank the Yellow Medicine Community, the Pezihuta Zizi Otunwe, for providing a haven in which to play, learn, and grow up. And, who helped me to be a proud Dakota!

I wish to thank Professor Roger BuffaloHead, a Ponca man, and a trained historian who was my primary Professor in American Indian Studies at the University of Minnesota, Twin Cities campus, and who had a profound impact on my teaching career.

I wish to acknowledge some of the writers/scholars/academics, both Native and non-Native, who have shaped and influenced my thinking and world-view: Vine Deloria, Jr.; Charles Eastman, Elizabeth Cook-Lynn; Linda Tuhiwai Smith; Waziyatawin, Ph.D.; Roy W. Meyer; Richard Drinnon; Haunani -Kay Trask; George Tinker; M. Annette Jaimes; Edward H. Spicer

In the area of Genocide Studies, I wish to acknowledge: Ward Churchill; David Stannard; Russell Thornton; Eric Markusen; Stephen C. Feinstein; Yael Danieli

In the area of Biblical Studies, I wish to acknowledge: the Assemblies of God missionaries who taught me Bible stories and verses; the Inter-Varsity Fellowship, at Bemidji State University, who conducted systematic Bible Studies; Seabury-Western Theological Seminary, Evanston, Illinois, at which I studied for a year-and-a-half.

1

RELIGIOUS/HISTORICAL FOUNDATIONS

of Genocide, Land Theft, Slavery, and Religious Suppression

"And when the Lord your God shall deliver them [7 Canaanite Nations] over to you, you shall conquer them and utterly destroy them; you shall make no covenant with them, nor show mercy to them . . . Also you shall destroy all the peoples whom the Lord your God delivers over to you; your eye shall have no pity on them . . ." (Deuteronomy 7:2, 16, NKJV)

There were three main religious factors which underlay and contributed to the genocide of the Indigenous Peoples of the Americas, and more specifically of the Native Peoples in what is now known as the United States of America.

These three factors were 1) the Old Testament God's genocidal commands; 2) the imperialistic pronouncements of Jesus Christ from the New Testament, specifically, the Great Commission, and his assertion that He is the Truth; and 3) the papal bulls of the Roman Catholic Church. We'll discuss these in turn and see how they relate to the genocide, the land theft, slavery, and the religious suppression of the Indigenous Peoples of the Americas.

Genocidal Commands of the Old Testament God

The Lord is a man of war; the LORD is His name (Exodus 15:3, NKJV)

The LORD, the Warrior—LORD is His name! (Torah)

The main purpose of this chapter is to give the reader a flavor of the brutality and horror of the genocidal commands of Yahweh, the Old Testament God. Thus, we will look at a number of Old Testament commands from the New King James Version. We'll also look at the same verses from the Torah and the Tanakh. Occasionally, we'll look at the same verses from the New American Bible, a Catholic translation,

First a few comments about the name Yahweh: Yahweh is an abbreviation of the longer name "Yahweh Sabaoth."[1] This name means "He who musters armies." The name "Yahweh" identifies the Jewish God as the military leader of His chosen people, the Israelites. It is thus no wonder that the God named Yahweh is a killer God. As well, it is no surprise that Yahweh is called "a man of war" (NKJV) and a "Warrior" (Torah) in Exodus 15:3.

Yet it's difficult to understand why Yahweh calls himself a warrior. As I understand the teaching of the missionaries, who came to our little Dakota community back in the late 1940s and early1950s, God is omnipotent, all-powerful. If this God is all-powerful, then, He will always win a fight or a battle. When this God kills someone, it cannot be called war, or combat, it must be called what it is: murder. The omnipotent Yahweh, by this inescapable logic, is not a warrior but a murderer. We'll shortly see this murderous and brutal Jewish God of war at work.

We'll also look at what five theologians from the Bethany Parallel Commentaries have to say about particular verses and passages, and we'll discuss selected chapters and/or verses, or one could say "texts of terror",[2] to use Dr. Philip Jenkins' term, from Psalms, Numbers, Deuteronomy, Joshua, and I Samuel, chapter 15.[3] Thus, the reader will have a baseline with which to contrast or compare what the theologians say about a particular verse, the killers' understanding and actions based upon the same verse(s), and the author's commentary.

> By the rivers of Babylon, there we sat down, yea, we wept, when we remembered Zion . . . Happy is the one who takes and dashes your little ones against the rock! (Psalms 137: 1 & 9, NKJV)

> By the rivers of Babylon, there we sat, sat and wept, as we thought of Zion . . . a blessing on him who seizes your babies and dashes them against the rocks! (Tanakh)

The New American Bible (NAB), a Catholic version, has a footnote regarding Psalm 137:9: "According to the ruthless custom of ancient warfare, children were indeed thus cruelly killed." The footnote says, "But it seems more probable that here the psalmist is personifying 'the daughter of Babylon' as a mother whose little ones are the adult citizens, not the infants, of the city."[4] I will leave it to the reader to determine if it is probable that the "little ones," or "babies," are the adult citizens and not the infants of the city.

Phillip Jenkins, in *Laying Down the Sword*, states that "the Bible overflows with 'texts of terror,' . . . and biblical violence is often marked by indiscriminate savagery."[5] Jenkins mentions the above Psalm (Psalm 137), and, comments upon it as a "text of terror" marked "by indiscriminate savagery," and which ends with "blessing anyone who would seize Babylon's infants and smash their skulls against the rocks."[6]

Our five theologians cited in the Bethany Parallel Commentaries on the New and Old Testaments—Henry, Jamieson, Fausset, Brown, and Clark—say nothing condemnatory of either Yahweh or of the Israelites seizing babies and dashing them against rocks. Adam Clarke, our Methodist theologian, writes approvingly of the "total extermination of your inhabitants" [the Canaanites, which would include the "little ones," the toddlers] because the [chosen people] have "rid the world of a curse so grievous."[7] This attitude is very much like that of the genocidal Old Testament God and is much in the vein of the "Herem" warfare of the Israelites, that is, of "utter destruction."[8]

> So Israel made a vow to the Lord, and said, If You will indeed deliver this people into my hand, then I will utterly destroy their cities . . . And the Lord listened to the voice of Israel, and delivered up the Canaanites; and they utterly destroyed them and their cities. So the name of that place was called Hormah [or "utter destruction"].[9] (Numbers 21:2–3, NKJV)

The NAB's footnote for verse 3 says, "Hormah: related to the Hebrew word 'herem,' meaning 'doomed.' A reminder: 'herem' means 'utter destruction.'"[10] The Torah uses the term "proscribe" for the NKJV's "utterly destroy." The footnote, also, defines the term "proscribe" as "utterly destroy."[11]

Regarding Numbers 21:2–3, none of the theologians express any horror nor condemnation of God and the Israelites for their "utter destruction" of the Canaanites and their cities. In fact, Matthew Henry says that God "enabled the Israelites by his [God's] grace." I checked my Merriam-Webster's Collegiate Dictionary for the definition of "grace." The first meaning is, "unmerited divine assistance given humans for their regeneration or sanctification."[12] To connect the term "grace" to a blatantly genocidal event, as Matthew Henry has done, is incredible. JFB applies the phrase "vow of extermination"[13] to describe what God and the Israelites did to the Canaanites. At least, these three writers (Jamieson, Fausset, and Brown) used an accurate term, "extermination," to signify what God commanded the Israelites to do.

> And they warred against the Midianites, just as the Lord commanded Moses; and they killed all the males. (Numbers 31:7, NKJV)

It is noteworthy that the New American Bible, the Catholic version, titles Numbers Chapter 31 "Extermination of the Midianites."[14]

The Bethany theologians use terms and phrases like "God's over-ruling providence," "just vengeance," "divine order," "sinners against God," and "their cup of iniquity was full," to express God's attitude, one part "hatred of the sinners," i.e., the Canaanites, et. al., and the other part approval of the slaying and the mass-murdering of the males.[15] These theologians are saying that God's "over-ruling providence," His "divine order," and His need to "punish sin" justified all this violence and slaughter. Also, since not believing in the Old Testament God makes one a "sinner against God" and makes his "cup of iniquity full," then it is "proper"[16] for God to destroy the person or group.

> Now therefore Kill every male among the little ones and kill every woman who has known a man intimately. (Numbers 31:17, NKJV)

Note that God is commanding "the little ones" who are male to be killed, as well as every woman who has had sex with a man. How different is this from the words and actions of Pol Pot or ISIS?

As I read about the killing of the male "little ones" and about the Midianite women, I could not help but think that the Old Testament God, as well as the theologians, are judgmental and misogynistic in their attitudes toward women. Note Henry's characterization of women, "the principal criminals," "dangerous to let them live," and "they still will be tempting the Israelites to uncleanness."[17]

JFB says this about the women: "The Midianitish women had forfeited all claims to mild and merciful treatment."[18] Finally, Adam Clarke writes of the women of the Midianites, "their lives were forfeited by their personal transgressions."[19] The misogynistic statements and attitudes of these theologians, and of the Old Testament God, remind me of several passages in David Stannard's book. In one he quotes a Ioan P. Couliano saying that "woman is the blind instrument for seduction of nature, the symbol of temptation, and evil . . . Besides her face, the principal baits of her allure are the signs of her fertility, hips and breasts . . . only witches will dare to have wide hips, prominent breasts, conspicuous buttocks, long hair."[20] Stannard also describes the male world of the adventurer as "a world in which women are at best irrelevant or ineffectual, and at worse are harlots, castrators, or murderesses."[21]

That's a stark contrast to the statement by Floyd Red Crow Westerman (a Dakota) who said, "Honor and protect our women," which is a teaching of the Dakota People.[22]

One might also contrast the attitude toward women of the theologians, as mentioned in the preceding paragraph, with a statement of Dr. Charles Eastman, Wahpetunwan Dakota, "the place of our women (in Dakota society) is secure."[23]

Then let's consider the "My God, Right or Wrong" attitude. Theologian Adam Clarke says, in regard to Numbers 31:17: " . . . the principle that God, who is the Author and Supporter of life, has a right to dispose of it when and how He thinks proper; and the Judge of all the earth can do nothing but what is right.[24] I have to admit that I have trouble understanding Clarke's logic. Here is a God commanding the killing of women and children, vulnerable members of any society, and yet this God "has a right," is "proper," and the Judge (God) "can do nothing but what is right"—in killing women and children. Such dissonance! Adam Clarke is, indeed, a true believer in "my God, right or wrong." It makes me wonder if most Christians have this same belief. If they did (or still do) it would go a long way toward explaining why they didn't (and in many cases still don't) have a more respectful, loving, and caring attitude not only toward their own women and children, let alone toward Indigenous women and their children.

The repugnant commands of the Old Testament God to kill women and children are not the type of commands that we would expect from an all-good, all-perfect God. These commands are what we would expect from a Hitler, a George Washington, a Saddam Hussein, an Andrew Jackson, a Josef Stalin, or from current and recent U.S. Presidents and military commanders who bomb and kill ("shock and awe," etc.), and who use drones to slaughter non-combatant civilians, including women, children, and elders—in Iraq, Afghanistan, Pakistan, Yemen, etc. Of course, it is likely that if Christians can say, "My God, right or wrong," then they will, no doubt, also, say, "My country, right or wrong."

And when the Lord your God delivers them over to you, you shall conqueror them [the Canaanites, the Hittites, et. al.] and utterly destroy them. You shall make no covenant with them nor show mercy to them. (Deuteronomy 7:2, NKJV).

Let us see what the theologians have to say about this "text of terror." Henry, JFB, and Clarke agree that the "people of these abominations" (Henry),[25] the "incorrigible sinners" (JFB),[26] the "idolatrous nations" (Clarke),[27] must be utterly destroyed, in other words, subjected to genocide.

I was somewhat confused by Matthew Henry's comment, that "after-ages were not to draw this into a precedent; this will not serve to justify those barbarous laws which give no quarter."[28] Henry calls those laws which "give no quarter" "barbarous," yet God commanded the Israelites to not "show mercy to them" (NKJV), that is, to the seven nations indigenous to the Old Testament "promised land.

(Contrast this with Deuteronomy 4:31, "God is a merciful God," or, with Psalms 103:8, "The LORD is merciful and gracious," or with Jeremiah 3:12, in which God says, "I am "merciful.")

Jamieson, Fausset, and Brown (JFB) further state, "This relentless doom of extermination which God pronounced, or declared, against those tribes of Canaan cannot be reconciled with the attributes of the divine character . . . ."[29] I agree. It is difficult to reconcile a supposedly "loving God," or a "merciful God," with a God who commanded the total destruction of the seven Native Peoples of Canaan.

Then, we have Adam Clarke's comments about the "true faith" and "true religion" and that peoples who do not accept the "true faith" were to be "utterly destroyed . . . provided they did not renounce their idolatry and receive the true faith."[30]

How morally different is the Protestant, Adam Clarke, a Methodist, from a Muslim Imam, or from a Catholic priest, or from ISIS, or from a fundamentalist and evangelical Christian who thinks that their beliefs constitute the true religion? Clarke says "idolatrous nations" are to be "utterly destroyed" or to be "cut off." And Christian settlers and governments relentlessly fulfilled that divine command. It's no surprise that many Native Peoples of the Americas saw the western Europeans and the U.S. Euro-Americans as having a Bible in one hand and a sword in the other.

And thou shalt consume [or, "destroy"] all the people which the LORD thy God shall deliver thee; thine eye shall have no pity upon them . . . . (Deuteronomy 7:16, KJV)

Jamieson, Faussett, and Brown (JFB, their comments are lumped together in the Bethany commentaries) say nothing specific about the term "consume" or the clause, "thine eye shall have no pity upon them." Instead, Henry says, "we cannot question the constancy of God's mercy,[31] and JFB speak of the "infinite perfections"[32] of Yahweh. Adam Clarke writes, the Israelites' "continuance in the state of favour was to depend on their faithfulness to the grace of God."[33] One pertinent question here is, how can this "God of mercy" or this God who says "I am merciful," also, say at the same time, "destroy the people" and "have no pity upon them"? How can the theologians say we cannot question "the constancy of God's mercy" or doubt the "infinite perfections" of Yahweh while, at the same time, God is ordering the genocide of the Canaanites and the other Indigenous Peoples of the "promised land"? Bugliosi talks about the "unfathomable horror"[34] of God's wanton murder sprees and, then, quotes Thomas Paine, who wrote, "the Bible tells us" that all the murders in the Old Testament "were done by the express command of God."[35] Bugliosi further states, "To believe, therefore, the bible to be true, we must unbelieve all our belief in the moral justice of God: for wherein could crying or smiling infants offend?"[36]

But the Lord your God will deliver them [the enemies] over to you, and will inflict defeat upon them until they are destroyed. And He will deliver their kings into your hand, and you will destroy their name from under heaven; no one shall be able to stand against you until you have destroyed them. (Deuteronomy 7:23–24, NKJV)

Matthew Henry, JFB, and Adam Clark say nothing specific regarding the mass killing and destruction reflected in these two verses. They are silent. And they are not alone. The national and state governments, the historical societies, and the colleges and universities, including those in Minnesota, suppress the truth of the Dakota and other Indigenous genocides, just as the theologians excuse the genocides perpetrated by the Israelites on the Canaanites, the Hittites, and the other Indigenous Peoples of Canaan.

But of the cities of these peoples which the LORD your God gives you as an inheritance, you shall let nothing that breathes remain alive . . . But you shall utterly destroy them: namely, the Hittites, and the Amorites, the Canaanites, and the Perizzites, the Hivites, and the Jebusites; as the Lord your God has commanded you. (Deuteronomy 20:16–17, NKJV).

All five theologians say that entire peoples must be killed, or as the New King James Version states, "you shall let nothing that breathes remain alive."

Matthew Henry admits, regarding verses 16 and 17: " . . . but of the cities which were given to Israel for an inheritance, no remnants must be left of their inhabitants.[37] In other words, the Old Testament God gave, as an inheritance, the lands of the Canaanites to the Israelites, which led to the belief that this same God also gave the lands of the U.S. Indigenous Peoples as an "inheritance" to the Western Europeans. None of the theologians express any horror, outrage, or condemnation of the genocidal commands of Yahweh, or of the genocidal actions of the Israelites. In fact, the theologians basically approve of both Yahweh's genocidal commands and the Israelites' perpetration of genocide.

I appreciate Clarke's statement that the commands of the Old Testament God are very clear in Deuteronomy 20:16–17 ("save alive nothing that breatheth," and "thou shalt utterly destroy them"). No one with a modicum of common sense will have a problem understanding these genocidal commands. Clarke and the other theologians seem to have no problem with the commands to "save alive nothing that breatheth" and to "utterly destroy," since they believe that their God is a just God, and therefore it is moral and just to kill women, children, and babies.

It is telling that during the centuries in which the Native American genocide took place, to the best of my knowledge, no high authority in the Catholic Church nor in any of the Protestant denominations condemned the near-continual atrocities. They either stayed silent or actively encouraged the genocide of Native Peoples.

In the book of Joshua, there are many instances of genocidal commands from the Old Testament God and resultant atrocities. Here are only a few.

Joshua 10:1–43 describes the commandments of the Old Testament God and the horrific slaughter of the five Amorite kings (of Jerusalem, Hebron, Jarmuth, Lachish, and Eglon) by the Israelites.

. . . while Joshua . . . had made an end of slaying them with a very great slaughter till they were finished . . . . (Joshua 10:20, NKJV)

When Joshua and the Israelites had finished dealing them a deadly blow, they were wiped out. (Tanakh)

Matthew Henry writes that "The result of this vigorous pursuit was, 1. That a 'very great slaughter' was made of the enemies of God and Israel.'" [38] JFB & Adam Clarke say nothing about verse 20.

Then Horam king of Gezer came up to help Lachish; and Joshua smote (overcome) him and his people, until he had left him none remaining. (Joshua 10:33, KJV)

. . . but Joshua defeated him and his army, letting none of them escape. (Tanakh)

Matthew Henry, Jamieson, Fausset, Brown, and Clarke say nothing negative about Joshua and the Israelites mass-murdering Horam and his men and "letting none of them escape."

. . . he (Joshua) left none remaining, but utterly destroyed all that breathed, as the Lord God of Israel commanded. (Joshua 10:40, KJV)

Thus Joshua conquered the whole country . . . he let none escape, but proscribed everything that breathed—as the Lord, the God of Israel, had commanded. (Tanakh)

"All that breathed" would, again, include the women, the children, and the elders, the most vulnerable groups in any society. Again the theologians offer no condemnation of either Yahweh's genocidal command, or the perpetration of the genocide.

If a person delights in genocide, and in killing, in exterminating, in utterly destroying, etc., then chapter 10 of the Book of Joshua, will fill the bill. All of its killing, putting to the sword, utterly destroying, leaving no survivors, all of its blood and gore are reminiscent of several comments by the Rev. Colonel John M. Chivington who perpetrated the Sand Creek Massacre in 1864 in Colorado. Chivington said, "My intention is to kill all Indians I may come across," and "I long to be wading in gore." [39] Well, both Joshua and his Israelites, and Chivington and his troops, were "wading" in a whole lot of "gore," as they killed "all that breathed."

Ward Churchill makes another pertinent comment about the killing of children and elders: "Chivington's comment above about 'killing all Indians' strongly implies he killed 'everyone from the most elderly and infirm to newborn infants.'"[40] Thus, even if Chivington did not say that he was following, specifically, the example of the Old Testament God, of Joshua, and of the Israelites, in Chapter 10 of the Book of Joshua, Chivington was most certainly killing toddlers, babies, women, and elders of the Cheyenne and Arapaho Peoples, just as Joshua had done to the Canaanites.

Joshua 11 contains yet more genocidal commandments of the Old Testament God and outlines the horrific slaughter of the Canaanites, the Amorites, the Hittites, the Perizzites, the Jebusites, and the Hivites that ensued.

> And the Lord delivered them into the hand of Israel, who smote them, . . . , and they smote them, . . . until they left none remaining. (Joshua 11:8–9, KJV)

> And Joshua did unto them as the Lord bade him . . . they crushed them, letting none escape. (Tanakh)

The two translations clearly indicate that Yahweh had commanded the killing and the extermination of the Canaanites, the Amorites, the Hittites, the Perizzites, the Jebusites and the Hivites.

Matthew Henry, JFB, and Adam Clarke say nothing about the annihilation, the extermination described in verses 8 and 9. In fact, these theologians were less concerned with the people being killed but with how the horses were treated in verse 9, in which the Israelites hamstrung the horses of their enemies.[41]

Of course, humans, particularly the chosen people, have license to do anything they wish to animals because of this command:

> God blessed them and God said to them, "Be fertile and increase, fill the earth and master it; and rule the fish of the sea, the birds of the sky, and all the living things that creep on earth." (Genesis 1:28, Torah)

They, the Israelites, and by extension humans, are "masters" of the earth, have "rule" and dominion over all living things, and so can do whatever they want to do to animals because they have God's approval.

How different this teaching—dominion over the animals—is from the teaching of the Dakota People. Our phrase, "Mitakuye Owasin," or "All my relatives," includes the animals. For example, the traditional Dakota refer to the Sunktanka Oyate, which means the "Horse People." Since animals are "people" and since they are our relatives, then we, as humans, are to show respect and care for not only Ina Maka, or Mother Earth, but also for the animal peoples. Certainly, if the U.S. Supreme Court can declare that corporations are people, then it is perfectly appropriate for the Dakota and other Indigenous Peoples to regard animals as people and, thus, as relatives.

Still, I am disgusted that theologians Henry, JFB, and Clarke focus upon horses and chariots and not upon the Lord's human victims.

> And they struck all the people who were in it with the edge of the sword, utterly destroying them. There was none left breathing. Then he (Joshua) burned Hazor with fire. (Tanakh, Joshua 11:11)

> They proscribed and put to the sword every person in it. not a soul survived, and Hazor itself was burned down. (NKJV)

Note the phrases, "all the people," "utterly destroying them," "none left breathing," and "put to the sword every person in it." To reiterate: This means that everyone, including all the women, all the children, and all the elders were murdered.

Matthew Henry, and Adam Clarke, basically, write nothing specifically about this herem (extermination) warfare.

> And all the spoil of these cities, and the cattle, the children of Israel took for a prey unto themselves; but every man they smote with the edge of the sword, until they had destroyed them, neither left they any to breathe. (Joshua 11:14, Tanakh)

> The Israelites kept all the spoil . . . But they cut down their populations with the sword until they exterminated them; they did not spare a soul. (KJV)

Matthew Henry says nothing about Joshua 11:14, "leaving alive none to breath," and neither does JFB or Adam Clarke. There there's Joshua 11:23:

> So Joshua took the whole land, according to all that the LORD said unto Moses; and Joshua gave it for an inheritance unto Israel according to their divisions by their tribes. And the land rested from war."   Tanakh - "Thus Joshua conquered the whole country, just as the Lord had promised Moses; and Joshua assigned it to Israel to share according to their tribal divisions. (Joshua 11:23)

It will be good for the reader to remember this verse, Joshua 11:23. Why? In a later chapter, the Christian English, the Puritans, in particular, will talk about their "inheritance," given to them by God. This "inheritance," in their minds, refers to the "promised lands," i.e., to the lands belonging to the Indigenous Peoples. Of course, these Western European Christians, soon to be Euro-American Christians, considered themselves as "chosen people," and they thought that God was helping them to take aboriginal lands, their rightful "inheritance," and so were justified, indeed divinely sanctioned, in murdering the First Nations Peoples in what eventually would become the United States of America.

In Joshua 12, we see the slaughter and destruction of 31 kings, their cities, and their peoples. This genocide, or ethnic cleansing, which included the killing of all men, women, children, and elders, was very similar to the atrocities, massacres, and genocidal events in North America and the Caribbean commencing in 1492.

> . . . in the hill country, in the lowlands, in the Arabah, in the slopes, in the wilderness, and in the Negeb [in the land of] the Hittites, the Amorites, the Canaanites, the Perizzites, the Hivites, and the Jebusites.
> (Joshua 12:8, Tanakh)

Note the phrase, "in the land of," which indicates to whom the "promised land," originally belonged, just as the lands of what is now the United States originally belonged to the Indigenous Peoples.

The KJV version of Joshua 12:9–24 repeatedly mention "their land," as in Joshua 12:1. The possessive pronoun "their" refers to the peoples who were already there—the Amorites, Canaanites, et. al. The Tanakh uses the phrase "whose territories." However, whether the terminology is "their land" or "whose territories," these passages clearly refer to the lands of the Canaanites, Hivites, et. al.

Both the Christian Euro-Americans, as we will see in later chapters, and the Israelites regarded themselves as "chosen people." Both believed in a God who instructed them to invade, steal, occupy, and exploit the lands of the Indigenous Peoples for their exclusive benefit. Both thought the lands of the Indigenous Peoples were their "inheritance." Both at the command of their God, killed, slaughtered, and murdered Indigenous Peoples in order to steal and occupy indigenous lands.

It's worth noting "herem" ("utter destruction") warfare was a code of war which the Old Testament God, approved and under which Israel fought.

If the Israelites came upon a city they were to destroy, they were to destroy *everything*. "Under this code, every living thing found in the city, everything that breathes, should be slaughtered in a kind of mass human sacrifice."[42] Remember this phrase when we discuss the Pequot Holocaust of 1637 later in the book.

> Now go and attack Amalek, and utterly destroy all that they have, and do not spare them. But kill both man and woman, infant and nursing child, ox and sheep, camel and donkey. (I Samuel 15:3, NKJV)

> Now go. attack Amalek, and proscribe all that belongs to him. Spare no one, but kill alike men and women, infants, and sucklings, oxen and sheep, camels and asses. (Tanakh)

The footnote in the New American Bible on I Samuel 15:3, regarding the term and phrase "under the ban" and "in such wars of extermination, all things (men, cities, beasts, etc.) were to be blotted out; nothing could be reserved for private use," states that the interpretation of God's will attributed to Samuel is "in keeping with the abhorrent practices of blood revenge prevalent among pastoral, semi-nomadic peoples such as the Hebrews had recently been. The slaughter of the innocent has never been in conformity with the will of God."[43]

One wonders about the footnote's last statement: "the slaughter of the innocent has never been in conformity with the will of God," especially when we all can see that their own Catholic Bible, the New American Bible, shows the Old Testament God plainly commanding, "kill men and women, children and infants, and nursing child." The Catholic who wrote that footnote's final sentence was in denial. We all can see in I Samuel 15:3 that the Old Testament God not only commands the killing, but also approves the killing, of all, including women, children, infants, and elders.

The Bethany theologians—Matthew Henry, JFB, and Clarke—say nothing about Yahweh's genocidal slaughter of the innocents. Rather, we can assume that the infants and children were among the "idolaters," and were "guilty of many other sins, for which they deserved to fall under the wrath of God."[44]

Adam Clarke, alone, of the five theologians, mentions, the genocidal command, which he shortens to "Slay both man and women." Here is what Clarke writes:

Nothing could justify such an exterminating decree but the absolute authority of God. This was given. All the reasons of it we do not know; but this we
know well, the judge of all the earth doth right. This war was not for plunder,
for God commanded that the property as well as all the people should be
destroyed.[45]

The takeaway from Clarke's statement is that he cannot conceive of a
justification for this decree, but is instead taking refuge in the old rationale
for atrocities: "God moves in mysterious ways." In this case, God moved in
murderous ways.

We, too, could probably say that "nothing could justify the genocide of
the Jews, Gypsies, et. al., but the absolute authority of Hitler. This authority
was given by Hitler to himself." Or one could say, "nothing could justify
the genocide of 16 million Indigenous People in the United States but the
absolute authority of the United States. This promised land was given to
the U.S. by God."

Basically, what Adam Clarke is saying is "might makes right."

Regarding the brutality and horror of the genocidal commands and
the personality of the Old Testament God, Richard Dawkins denounces
"the carnage, the smiting, the vindictive, genocidally racist jealous monster God of the Old Testament."[46] Another writer, Vincent Bugliosi, states
that the Old Testament God is "someone who would make history's greatest villains look like very pale imitations by comparison. Would even Ad-
olf Hitler, Josef Stalin, Mao Zedong, Pol Pot, Osama bin Laden, or Tomas
de Torquemada do the things the God of Jewish and Christian scripture
did?"[47] In looking at Bugliosi's list of impressively efficient butchers, mass
murderers, and criminals, one could say that Yahweh, the Old Testament
God, "He who musters armies," is at the very top of this murderous crew.

Vine Deloria, Jr. is a Yankton Dakota, a fellow Dakota, a prolific writer,
an author, and an attorney. Also, Deloria, who has a degree in Christian
theology, has several observations on the Old Testament God. He says, regarding one of the Old Testament prophets:

[I]t suddenly occurred to me that the Judeo-Christian Deity had been a pretty rough character all along. He was always throwing fits of anger over some
real or imagined slight; he monitored every activity of His Chosen People
to see that they were obeying some rather vague instructions he had given
them; and to hear some Protestants tell it, he had a ledger book in which
he recorded all our evil thoughts and deeds. This behavior can be described

in a humorous way but it is not very funny. It suggests a Deity very closely modeled not only after a human personality but also after a personality that is unbalanced and immature."[48]

Deloria made some comparisons of the Old Testament God to some 20th century U.S. Euro-American figures whom many of you will recognize. Deloria writes,:

> The Judeo-Christian Deity, as a matter of fact, has emotional characteristics that are quite common and can be easily identified in contemporary human beings. He has the egotism of Henry Kissinger, the stability of Donald Trump, the generosity of Edwin Meese, and the military mind of George H. W. Bush. (We should remember that Yahweh killed some 185,000 Arabs in Sennacarib's army outside Jerusalem one night, Bush slaughtered almost as many in the prolonged bombing of Iraq during the winter of 1991. Both seem to have had the same motive—the Arabs had disregarded one of their warnings.) Having a 'personal relationship' with this Deity is akin to being J. Edgar Hoover's best friend—it is safe but not satisfying.[49]

One final comment from Deloria about Yahweh, the Old Testament God:

> When we step outside this cultural context (Christian) and try to understand the Bible as a literal historical document, we discover that the portrait of the Deity sketched in the Old Testament is very negative and, in fact, may describe a psychopath like Saddam Hussein . . . . We find the image of a despotic Oriental monarch determined to have his way regardless of how it affects his subjects.[50]

Speaking of Deloria's remarks about this "pretty rough character . . . one who musters armies," Richard Dawkins has an equally impressive list of scathing adjectives to describe the Old Testament God:

> The God of the Old Testament is arguably the most unpleasant character in all fiction: jealous and proud of it; a petty, unjust, unforgiving control-freak; a vindictive, bloodthirsty ethnic cleanser; a misogynistic, homophobic, racist, infanticidal, genocidal, filicidal, pestilential, megalomaniacal, sado-masochistic, capriciously malevolent bully.[51]

Also, as one can readily see from the historical incidents and biblical passages cited, there is a "hidden" Bible whose bloody and violent passages are very morally disturbing, passages which Christians very rarely if ever discuss or confront, passages which are not read, taught, nor preached in today's churches. As Philip Jenkins writes, "If Christians or Jews needed biblical texts to justify deeds of terrorism or ethnic slaughter, their main problem would be an embarrassment of riches."[52]

In the Americas, Christian killers definitely did "utterly destroy all," and slew "both man and woman, infant, and suckling." (I Samuel 15:3) Certainly, the Western European colonists, even if they weren't quoting these above-mentioned Scriptures as they were mass-murdering Indigenous Peoples, most certainly and unconsciously drew upon, and carried out, the genocidal commands of the Old Testament God.

The Bold Assertions of Jesus Christ

In this section, we'll discuss two of the bold, rather arrogant, assertions of Jesus Christ. Since the Jewish Bible does not have a New Testament, then, obviously, we won't quote from the Torah or the Tanakh, the Jewish Bible. So, we'll use two additional Protestant translations, The New Oxford Annotated Bible with the Apocryph (NOAB) and the New English Bible (NEB).

The first assertion in John 14:6 reads:

> . . . I am the way, the truth, and the life. No man cometh unto the Father, but by me. (KJV)

> . . . I am the way, and the truth, and the life; no one comes to the Father, but by me. (NOAB)

> . . . I am the way; I am the truth; and I am life; no one comes to the Father except by me. (NEB)

What did Jesus mean by this statement? Matthew Henry says that Jesus "as Truth is opposed to falsehood and error." Henry goes on to say that "when we enquire for truth, we need learn no more than the truth as it is in Jesus." Jamieson, Fausset, and Brown and Clarke also say that Jesus is the way, the truth, and the life.[53]

This is not only bold, but also arrogant. Imagine if a person were to appear on national television and proclaim that s/he was "the Way," "the Truth," and "the Life"; this person would be considered either insane, or at the least delusional, and, then, immediately transported to the nearest psychiatric ward. Vincent Bugliosi comments: ". . . the notion of Jesus Christ being the Son of God is too fantastic a thought to visit a rational mind."[54]

Needless to say, Jesus' assertion that he is the "Truth" and "the only Way to God" is insulting, offensive and disrespectful to the millions upon millions of Indigenous Peoples in the Americas who had their own religious ways and spiritual beliefs and ceremonies long before Columbus came to the Americas, long before Jesus Christ was born 2,000 years ago.

Jesus Christ and Religious Imperialism

Two more of Christ's assertions deserve consideration. Christian adherents regard these assertions as "The Great Commission. The first is found in the Gospel of Matthew:

> Go therefore and make disciples of all the nations, baptizing them in the name of the Father and of the Son and of the Holy Ghost. (Matthew 18:19, NKJV)

> Go, therefore, and make disciples of all nations. (NAB)

> Go forth therefore and make all nations my disciples; baptize men everywhere in the name of the Father and the Son and the Holy Spirit . . . (NEB)

Note that all three versions make it quite clear that Jesus commands his disciples to "make disciples of all the nations" and to baptize them.

Matthew Henry, regarding the "Great Commission," wrote the following chilling words: "Christianity should be twisted in with national constitutions, that the kingdoms of the world should become Christ's kingdoms, and their kings the church's nursing-fathers." Henry asks, what is the principal intention of this commission? Henry's answer is "to disciple all Nations." He goes on to say, "do your utmost to make the nations Christian nations."[55] This is not unlike the desires of some Muslims who wish to impose Sharia law on all nations. Is this Christian man, Matthew Henry, who wishes to make all nations Christian nations, any better, morally, than a Muslim imam who wishes to make all nations Muslim nations?

The second assertion is found in Mark, Chapter 16:15–16, which reads,

> And He said to them, Go into the world and preach the gospel to every creature. He who believes and is baptized will be saved; but he who does not believe will be damned. (Mark 16:15–16, NKJV)

> Go into all the word and preach the gospel to the whole creation. He who believes and is baptized will be saved; but he who does not believe will be condemned. (NOAB)

Matthew Henry states, regarding Mark 16:15–16, that the disciples "are now authorized to go into all the world and to preach the gospel of Christ to every creature . . . to every human creature that is capable of receiving it."[56] Henry's comment is reminiscent of comments in the Papal Bull of Pope Paul III, *Sublimus Dei*, dated May 29, 1537:

> We . . . seek with all our might to bring those sheep of His flock who are outside into the fold committed to our charge, consider, however, that the Indians are truly men and they are not only capable of understanding the Catholic Faith but, according to our information, they desire exceedingly to receive it.

Note that Pope Paul III did not say "the Gospel"; instead he said "the Catholic Faith." Such humility! But perhaps this isn't too surprising, coming as it did less than two decades after Luther nailed his 24 theses to the door in Wittenberg.

To bring it closer to home, Episcopal Bishop Henry Whipple in his work with my people, the Dakota People of Minnesota, in the 19th century, said something similar. In September of 1862, Bishop Whipple wrote, "As a Christian I take issue with anyone who claims that God has created any human being who is incapable of civilization or who cannot receive the gospel of Jesus Christ."[57] In the same paper, Bishop Whipple says of Indigenous Peoples, in general, "The North American Indian is a savage and like all other heathen men fierce, vindictive, cruel and his animal passions are unrestrained by civilization & Christianity."

I'll leave it the reader to decide whether the words "savage," "fierce," "vindictive," and "cruel" better describe Yahweh, the Old Testament God, than Native Peoples, and whether the phrase "his animal passions are unrestrained by civilization and Christianity" applies better to the Western Europeans and Euro-Americans who slaughtered millions. However, back to the capacity to receive the Gospel: the racist and white supremacist Bishop Whipple, apparently, did believe that the Dakota People, even though they were "savage," "fierce," "vindictive," "cruel," and had "animal passions," had the capacity to receive the Gospel of Jesus Christ.

There was a genocidal mentality in the early 1860s in Minnesota, exemplified by scalp bounties on Dakota people and calls for extermination of the Dakota in the newspapers of the day. Dr. Waziyatawin writes of Bishop Whipple's intent, "He wanted the rest of the population alive (viz., the Dakota People) so that he could pursue his own imperialistic path by converting heathen souls to Christianity."[58] Bishop Whipple, good Christian that he was, didn't want to exterminate *all* of the Dakota, he wanted some left alive to convert.

Note that the term "preach" is used in Mark 16:15–16 in both the KJV and the NOAB versions. Although the term seems rather innocuous, it was, and is, deadly to the Indigenous systems of spirituality and ceremony when combined with "make disciples of all nations" (Matthew 28:19-20), which implies force and coercion.

This reminds one of Chalk and Jonnassohn's four common motives of genocide, especially the fourth motive, "to impose an ideology or a belief upon the victim group."[59] In this case, the "ideology" or the "belief" to be "imposed upon" the Indigenous Peoples of the United States, and of the Americas, was and is Christianity.

Papal Bulls

[Catholic kings and princes must] invade, search out, capture, vanquish and subdue all Saracens [Muslims] and pagans whatsoever, and other enemies of Christ wheresoever placed, and . . . to reduce their persons to perpetual slavery, and to apply and appropriate . . . possessions and goods, and to convert them to their use and profit . . . .
(Pope Nicholas V, *Romanus Pontifex*, January 8, 1455)

It is obvious that several of the terms in *Romanus Pontifex* ("The Roman Pontiff"), especially "pagans" and "other enemies," apply directly to the Indigenous Peoples of the Americas. This bull helps to provide an understanding of the "why," the motives that drove the Christian invaders to do the horrific things they did and why Christians Europeans and Euro-Americans enthusiastically approved, adopted, and implemented all of the concepts it outlines.

Inter Caetera

Pope Alexander VI's bull of May 4, 1493, *Inter Caetera* ("Among Other Works"), called for propagation of Christian doctrine, for dominion, and for subjugation of non-Christian peoples and their lands. The bull called for "the Catholic faith and the Christian religion [to] be exalted and be everywhere increased and spread . . . and that barbarous nations be overthrown and brought to the faith itself." Of course, this meant that since the Indigenous Peoples of the Americas were "barbarous," the Christian

Church, and the empires in which it held sway, could legally "overthrow" the Native Nations and seize their lands, even if it meant mass murder.

In this bull we see many phrases such as "bring them to the Catholic faith"; "lead the peoples . . . to embrace the Christian religion"; "instruct the aforesaid inhabitants . . . in the Catholic faith and train them in good morals"; etc. (Apparently, invasion of other peoples' lands, killing them, and stealing their lands constitute "good morals.")

The acts of coercion and force in the Americas were prefigured in Luke 14:23, which says, "Then the master said to the servant, 'go out into the highways and hedges, and compel them to come in, that my house may be filled.'" (NKJV) Here, Jesus Christ was telling a story to his disciples about a group of people who were invited to their master's house for dinner, but didn't want to come. So, the master instructed his servant to "compel" them to "come in." This command is similar to that in Matthew 28:19, "Go therefore and make disciples of all the nations . . . . " (NKJV) In other words, force people to do something they do not want to do. This is very disrespectful at the least. Other adjectives could be applied, such as, but not limited to, dishonorable, shameful, dishonest, and criminal.

There is a teaching from the Dakota Hanbde Ceyapi "Crying For A Vision," ceremony (or vision quest). This ceremony is practiced by many other Indigenous Peoples as well. In it, a person fasts for one to four days and nights, prays, and does not drink any water. In the course of the fasting, prayer, sacred songs, and meditation, the person receives a vision, a dream, or a revelation. When he or she comes down from the hill, a spiritual leader, or elder, will help him or her to understand the vision. This vision is not forced upon anybody else—it belongs to the person who has it. He or she does not have to train missionaries to spread the revelation to others or to conduct evangelism programs to "save," "convert," or "proselytize."

The teaching, which is derived from this ceremony, is "Respect another person's vision." Forcing a belief on another person or other people is anathema to traditional Dakota and other Indigenous People who practice this ceremony. This teaching of "Respect another's vision" is diametrically opposed to Christ's command, "Make disciples of all nations."

Approximately a dozen variations of the term "discovery" appear in the *Inter Caetera*. In it, Pope Alexander VI emphasized that "true Catholic kings and princes" should "seek out and discover" new lands inhabited by non-Christians and claim the lands. However, if the lands had already been claimed by another Christian nation, then the rights of that Christian nation ought to be respected.

In the U.S., that translates to white is right, might is right, and white might is really right! And, of course, we all can see that the United States is still most certainly exercising its might in expanding its empire and extending its global domination.

Inter Caetera also established "a line from the Arctic pole to the Antarctic pole, dividing the world in half. If any lands to the west of this line were "found and to be found, discovered and to be discovered" by a Christian prince, then this land belonged to the "discoverer." This meant that islands in the Caribbean which were "discovered" by Christopher Columbus belonged to Columbus. And if the lands of the Americas, i.e., the lands of the Indigenous Peoples of the Americas, were "discovered" by Christian nations, these lands, too, would belong to the "discoverer" Christian nations.

In the following year, on June 7, 1494, the Treaty of Tordesillas was concluded, which was inspired by *Inter Caetera*, the papal bull of 1493. This treaty legally divided the world in half. Native Peoples were not consulted, nor were they were informed, nor did they give any consent or agreement Everything 370 leagues west of the Cape Verde Islands went to Spain, and everything east went to Portugal.

Because *Inter Caetera* and the Treaty of Tordesillas gave most of the western hemisphere to Spain, the colonizing Spanish affirmed that "the bulls gave them the right to use just war to convert local populations who had refused to immediately accept Christianity."[60] Spain also developed the Requerimiento (Requirement), which informed the Indigenous Peoples of the Americas "of the truth of Christianity and the necessity to swear immediate allegiance to the Pope and to the Spanish crown." If the Native Peoples refused and/or delayed, then the Requerimiento said, "I certify to you that, with the help of God, we shall powerfully enter into your country and shall make war against you in all ways and manners that we can, and shall subject you to the yoke and obedience of the Church and of their Highnesses. We shall take you and your wives and your children, and shall make slaves of them, and as such shall sell and dispose of them as their Highnesses may command."[60]

Note that the papal bulls of 1455 and 1493, the 1494 Treaty of Tordesillas, and the Requerimiento enslavement and other crimes against humanityall advocated enslavement and other crimes against humanity. The criminal acts these bulls justified included genocide of the Indigenous Peoples of the Americas, imposing/forcing Christianity upon them, making war upon them, terrorizing them, and enslaving them.

In January 2016, the United Nations declared the Holy See legally responsible and accountable to Indigenous Peoples for effects and legacy of racist colonial papal bulls and doctrines. The United Nations Convention on the Elimination of all forms of Racial Discrimination (CERD), "has recognized that "the Holy See's *Inter Caetera* and related papal bulls are within the legal scope of racial discrimination under International Law and therefore require redress."[61]

As well, CERD said it would hold "a high-level meeting between Indigenous Peoples and the Pope regarding the canonization of Juniper Serra," that dialogues between the Holy See and Indigenous Peoples "must result in genuine redress and remedy," and that there will be follow-up by the UN CERD Committee "on the progress of the Holy See at the CERD Committee's next review of the Holy See."[62]

Sublimus Dei

Pope Paul III's bull, *Sublimus Dei* ("Exalted God"), dated May 29, 1537, enabled the evangelization of the Indigenous Peoples of the Americas. Pope Paul III reiterated the "Great Commission" of Jesus Christ when he said, "Go ye and teach all nations" (Matthew 28:19, KJV), and also stated that "all (men) are capable of receiving the doctrines of faith." Pope Paul III affirmed the humanity of the Indigenous Peoples when he asserted that they are "truly men." In addition, the bull said that the Indigenous Peoples of the Americas are not only "capable of understanding the Catholic Faith" but also that they "desire exceedingly to receive it." Another statement in the bull ought to be mentioned:

> [T]he said Indians and other peoples should be converted to the faith of Jesus Christ by preaching the word of God and by the example of good and holy living.

When we observe what Columbus did in the Caribbean Islands to the Native Peoples—killing them by the millions, cutting off Native hands and heads, attacking the people with dogs trained to disembowel, hanging them, burning them alive, etc.; and when we see what the Spanish did to the Indigenous Peoples in South America, Mexico, and in what's now the U.S Southwest, (California, in particular); and when we see the killing of 16 million Native Peoples in the United States, the stealing of three billion acres of land, and the breaking of 400+ treaties by the United States, one wonders what Pope Paul III meant when he said that Native Peoples ought to be converted "by the example of good and holy living."

It is no wonder that a letter was presented to John Paul II when he visited Peru in 1988. The letter said:

John Paul II, We, Andean and American Indians, have decided to take advantage of your visit to return to you your Bible, since in five centuries it has not given us love, peace, or justice.   Please take back your Bible, and give it back to your oppressors, because they need its moral teachings more than we do. Ever since the arrival of Christopher Columbus, a culture, a language, religion and values which belong to Europe have been imposed on Latin America by force. The Bible came to us as part of the imposed colonial transformation. It was the ideological weapon of this colonialist assault. The Spanish sword which attacked and murdered the bodies of Indians by day and night became the cross which attacked the Indian soul.[63]

The authors (members of the victim groups) could have easily added the Central American and North American Native Peoples upon whom the religious ideology of Christianity had been imposed.

In a similar vein, Red Jacket, a Seneca leader, had an exchange with a missionary in the year 1805 in New York State. Here are some of Red Jacket's words:

If we had some disputes about our hunting ground, they were generally settledwithout the shedding of much blood. But an evil day came upon us. Your forefathers crossed the great water, and landed on this island.

They wanted more land; they wanted our country. Our eyes were opened, and our minds became uneasy.

You have got our country, but are not satisfied; you want to force your religion upon us.

We understand that your religion is written in a book. If it was intended for us as well as you, why has not the Great Spirit given to us, and not only to us, but why did he not give to our forefathers, the knowledge of that book, with the means of understanding it rightly? . . . We only know what you tell us about it. How shall we know when to believe, being so often deceived by the white people?

You say there is but one way to worship and serve the Great Spirit. If there is but one religion, why do you white people differ so much about it? Why not all agree, as you can all read the book?

Since He has made so great a difference between us in other things; why may we not conclude that He has given us a different religion according to our understanding? The Great Spirit does right. He knows what is best for his children: we are satisfied." We are told that you have been preaching to the white people in this place. These people are our neighbors . . . We will wait a little while, and see what effect your preaching has upon them. If we find it does them good, makes them honest and less disposed to cheat Indians; we will consider again of what you have said.[64]

The Seneca leaders, and Red Jacket, approached the missionary to shake his hand. The missionary rose from his seat and said that he could not shake their hands because "there was no fellowship between the religion of God and the works of the devil."[65]

Because of the statement of Jesus Christ, "I am the Way, the Truth, and the Life," it was inevitable that this missionary, and those missionaries who followed, would possess the same arrogance as their leader, Jesus Christ, and have the same disdain and contempt for other religious systems and beliefs.

Vine Deloria, Jr. says, regarding the discussion on the Bible, denominations, and missionaries and their attitudes:

One aspect of Christian history that is so appalling is the almost continuous warfare between Christians. Heresy hunters seem to abound in Christian history as a regular part of its religious experiences. Persecutions for religious purposes appear to dominate many periods of Christian existence.[66]

It is no wonder that one Native organization, the Indigenous Law Institute (ILI), initiated the movement to revoke the papal bulls and is providing leadership for this effort.[67]

The ILI refers to the papal bull of 1493, *Inter Caetera*, as "The Empire-Domination Model":

The empire-domination model presumes that it is justifiable for an immigrant sovereign . . . to happen upon a country inhabited by free and independent nations, and then to simply presume 'the right' to militarily take over that country by force, and to put the original inhabitants under the foreign rule of the empire-builder. The papal bull is reflective of a language system which presumes that it is permissible for one people to assume a divine right of empire and domination over another people."[68]

The ILI further states:

In an effort to deal with the foundation of the empire-domination model, we have formally called upon Pope Paul II to revoke the *Inter Caetera* bull of 1493" . . . We have also invited him to join us on the sacred path by honoring the first principle of Traditional Native Law to 'respect the Earth as Mother, and have a sacred regard for all living things.'[69]

These three bulls, issued in 1455, 1493, and 1537, along with the imperialistic statements of Jesus Christ, and the genocidal commands of the Old Testament God, helped establish the basis for white supremacy and racism in the Western Hemisphere.

An exemple of this attitude was provided by Senator Albert Beveridge. In the year 1900, Beveridge, in a speech before the U.S. Senate, said that God had marked U.S. Euro-Americans as "chosen people," just like the Israelites of the Old Testament:

We will not renounce our part in the mission of our race, trustee, under God, of the civilization of the world. And we will move forward to our work . . . with gratitude for a task worthy of our strength, and thanksgiving to Almighty God that He has marked us [Euro-Americans] as His chosen people, henceforth to lead in the regeneration of the world . . . This is the divine mission of America, and it holds for us all the profit, all the glory, all the happiness possible for man . . . .[70, 71]

The first two papal bulls (1455 and 1493) laid the foundation for the Church Doctrine of Discovery and for Conquest. The third papal bull (1537) called for spreading the gospel of Jesus Christ and proselytizing the Indigenous Peoples of the Americas. These bulls became United States government policy. The Supreme Court ruling in one of the Marshall Trilogies court cases, Johnson v. M'Intosh, in the 1830s, used these bulls as part of its argument determining the dependent sovereignty status of today's modern Indigenous Peoples as "wards" of the U.S. government.[73] The Supreme Court Ruling in Johnson v. "M'Intosh adopted the same principle of subjugation expressed in the *Inter Caetera* bull.[72]

When the "Great Commission" of Christ" ("Go therefore, and make disciples of all the nations,") and the genocidal commands of the Old Testament ("Kill everything that hath breath") were added to the papal bulls, the consequences were disastrous, and continue to be so to this day.

Vine Deloria, Jr. sums up the situation this way:

Christianity thus endorsed and advocated the rape of the North American continent [Deloria might as well have included Central America and South America], and her representatives have done their utmost to contribute to this process ever since.[73]

The suppression and supplanting of indigenous religions, ceremonies, and traditions (more precisely the eradication of and substition of Christianity for them) continues to this day.

Endnotes

1. "Yahweh—Jehovah, Brutal Jewish God of War," by Kenneth Humphreys. https://www.jesusneverexisted.com/brutal.htm.

2. *Laying down the Sword: Why We Can't Ignore the Bible's Violent Verses*, by Phillip Jenkins. New York: Harper One, 2011, p. 6.

3. Ibid., pp. 36–39.

4. New American Bible, Catholic Book Publishing Co., Psalms 137:9, p. 694.

5. Jenkins, op cit., p. 6.

6. Ibid.

7. Adam Clarke, *Bethany Parallel Commentary on the Old Testament*, Bethany House Publishers, 1985, p. 1,182.

8. Jenkins, op. cit., pp. 32-33.

9. The Holy Bible (1976), King James Version, Giant Print Reference Edition, Thomas Nelson Publishers, 1976, p. 257.

10. The New American Bible, Numbers 21:2–3, p. 155.

11. The Torah: The Five Books of Moses. The Jewish Publication Society of America, 1967, p. 287.

12. Merriam-Webster's Collegiate Dictionary Eleventh Edition, 2012, p. 542.

13. Jamieson, Fausset, & Brown (JFB), *Bethany Parallel Commentary*, 1985, p. 309.

14. New American Bible, p. 167.

15. BPCOT, pp. 324-325.

16. Ibid.

17. Ibid., p. 325.

18. Ibid.

19. Ibid.

20. Ioan P. Couliano, quoted in David Stannard's, *American Holocaust*, 1992, p. 162.

21. Ibid., p. 172.

22. Floyd Red Crow Westerman, Presentation, Southwest Minnesota State University, April, 2004.

23. *Soul of the Indian*, by Charles Eastman. Lincoln, NE: University of Nebraska Press, 1911, p. 41.

24. BPCOT, p. 325.

25. Ibid., p. 345.

26. Ibid.

27. Ibid.

28. Ibid.

29. Ibid.

30. Ibid.

31. Ibid.

32. Ibid., p. 346.

33. Ibid.

34. Ibid.

35. *Divinity of Doubt*, by Vincent Bugliosi, New York: Vanguard Press, 2011, p. 144

36. Ibid., pp. 144–145.

37. Ibid., p. 145.

38. BPCOT, p. 361.

39. Ibid., p. 416.

40. *American Holocaust: The Conquest of the New World,* by David Stannard. Xoford: Oxford University Press, 1992, p. 131.

41. *A Little Matter of Genocide: Holocaust and Denial in the Americas: 1492 to the Present,* by Ward Churchill. San Francisco: City LightsBooks, 1997, p. 229f.

42. Jenkins, op. cit., p. 7.

43. NAB, I Samuel 15:3, p. 278f.

44. BPCOT, p. 537.

45. Ibid.

46. *The God Delusion*, by Richard Dawkins, Black Swan, 2016, p. 51.

47. Bugliosi, op. cit., p. 131.

48. *God Is Red: A Native View of Religions, Second Edition*, by Vine Deloria, Jr. Golden, CO: North American Press, 1992, p. 151.

49. Ibid.,

50. Ibid., p. 151–152.

51. Dawkins, op. cit., p. 51.

52. Jenkins, op. cit., p. 6.

53. BPCOT, p. 636.

54. Bugliosi, op. cit., p.131.

55. BPCOT, p. 257.

56. Ibid., p. 343.

57. Unpublished manuscript, Minnesota Historical Society.

58. "Colonial Calibrations: the Expendability of Minnesota's Original People," by Waziyatawin, in *William Mitchell Law Review*, Vol. 39:2, p. 458.

59. *The History and Sociology of Genocide*, by Frank Chalk & Kurt Jonassohn, Yale University Press, p. 29.

60. Stannard, op. cit., pp. 65–66.

61. United Nations (UN) Committee on the Convention on the Elimination of all forms of Racial Discrimination (CERD) for the Committee's review of the Holy See., January 14, 2016.

62. Ibid.

63. *Voices From The Margin Interpreting The Bible In The Third World*, R. S..Sugirtharajah, ed. Maryknoll, NY: Orbis Books, 2006, p. 18.

64. "Red Jacket's Reply to a Missionary," Document No. 35, in Edward H. Spicer's, *A Short History of the Indians of the United States*, Van Nostrand, 1969, pp. 262–265.

65. Ibid.

66. *God Is Red: A Native View of Religion, Second Edition*, by Vine Deloria, Jr. Golden, CO: North American Press, 1992, p. 189.

67. Steven Newcomb, Indigenous Law Institute, "Background on Bulls Burning and Campaign," by Steven Newcomb, Indigenous Law Insitute, January 22, 2008, p. 3.68. Ibid., p. 2.

69. Ibid., p. 3.

68. Ibid., p. 2.

70. Senator Albert J. Beveridge, in a speech, "In Support of an American Empire," before the U.S. Senate, January 09, 1900, "Record," 56 Cong, I Sess., pp. 704–712.

71. Newcomb, op. cit., p. 2. Also, Document 11, "Cherokee Nation V. The State of Georgia," in *A Short History of the Indians of the United States*, by Edward H. Spicer, Van Nostrand Reinhold Company, 1969, p. 187.

72. "Revoke the Inter Caetera Bull," *Turle Quarterly*, by Valerie Tlaiman. *Turle Quarterly*, Fall–Winter 1994, pp. 7–8.

73. *Custer Died For Your Sins: An Indian Manifesto*, by Vine Deloria, Jr. Norman, OK: University of Oklahoma Press, 1988, p. 30.

2

THE COMING OF COLUMBUS

"Honoring Christ and the Twelve Apostles"

"That all men should honor the Son [Jesus Christ], just as they honor the Father. He who does not honor the Son does not honor the Father [God] who sent him." (John 5:23, NKJV)

Back in 1947, I entered first grade at the Granite Falls Public Schools in Granite Falls, Minnesota. That was when I first heard about the man named Christopher Columbus. As far as I can remember, my father and my mother never mentioned him. When the teacher talked about Columbus, she taught us a poem which begin, "In fourteen hundred ninety-two, Columbus sailed the ocean blue." I've remembered this line for 73 years. The teacher went on to say that Columbus "discovered" America (think "Doctrine of Discovery" from the papal bull of 1493, *Inter Caetera*). The other thing I remember about Columbus is a picture of him on the shore with a cross.

I thought, "Columbus must be a Christian, so he must be a good man." Of course, the missionaries had taught us that Christians are good people because they serve God, and that the cross is sacred, too.

Later on, I discovered that the things I heard and learned in grade school and high school were mostly lies. I learned that Columbus did not discover America, and that there were at least 16 million Indigenous People already here in what's now the continental United States when Columbus arrived. He may have been the first European to make it to the Americas, but there is some debate about that. I also discovered that Columbus was *not* a good man, and that he and the Spanish and Portuguese soldiers killed millions of our Native People on the islands of the Caribbean.

Columbus and the Bible

Columbus seemed to be at odds with the advice in Romans 12:3, not "to think of himself more highly than he ought to think" That is, Columbus appeared to have lofty illusions of his importance, especially in the sight of his God. Note his statement:

> God made me the messenger of the new heaven and new earth of which he spoke in the Apocalypse of St. John after having spoken of through the mouth of Isaiah; and he showed me the spot where to find it.[1]

Then, consider this statement of Columbus:

> It was the Lord who put it into my mind, (I could feel His hand upon me), that fact that it would be possible to sail from here to the Indies. All who heard of my project rejected it with laughter, ridiculing me. There is no question that the inspiration was from the Holy Spirit, because He comforted me with rays of marvelous inspiration from the Holy Scriptures.[2]

Apparently, Columbus had a close connection, a "hot line," if you will, to the Lord.

Historian David Stannard mentions the connection of Columbus with the Bible, and how biblical prophecies applied to Columbus, at least in his own mind. Stannard writes:

> For years to come Columbus repeatedly would insist that his expeditions and adventures in the New World had nothing to do with "mere reason, mathematics, and maps," as two scholars of the subject put it, but rather that his "execution of the affair of the Indies was a fulfillment of prophecies in Isaiah.[3]

The basis of Columbus' scriptural concerns is revealed in Kay Brigham's *Christopher Columbus's Book of Prophecies*. One was his preoccupation with the gospel of Jesus Christ and the converting of all nations to Christianity. Relevant verses include:

> And this gospel of the kingdom shall be preached in all the world for a witness unto all nations; and then shall the end come. (Matthew 24:14, KJV)

This good news of the kingdom will be proclaimed throughout the world as a witness to all the nations. Only after that will the end come. (Matthew 24:14, NAB)

. . . Go ye into the world, and preach the gospel to every creature. (Mark 16:15, KJV)

Then he told them: Go into the whole world and proclaim the good news to all creation. (Mark 16:15, NAB)

But ye shall receive power, after that the Holy Ghost is come upon you: and ye shall be witnesses unto me both in Jerusalem, and in all Judea, and in Samaria, and unto the uttermost part of the earth. (Acts 1:8, KJV)

You will receive power when the Holy Spirit comes down on you; then you are to be my witnesses in Jerusalem, throughout Judea and Samaria, yes, even to the ends of the earth. (Acts 1:8, NAB)

Of course, Columbus believed he was a divine instrument in the spreading of the "good news" to the heathens.

Matthew Henry, a Presbyterian minister and theologian, says in regard to Matthew 24:14, "the gospel is preached for a witness to all nations, that is, a faithful declaration of the mind and will of God."[4]

When one thinks of the eight million Indigenous People killed in the Caribbean islands in 21 years by Columbus and and the Spanish soldiers, one wonders if his action is "a faithful declaration of the mind and will of God." Columbus had no such doubts.

As mentioned earlier, verses such as Mark 16:15 correspond to Frank Chalk's and Kurt Jonasson's fourth motive of genocide, that is, "to impose an ideology [which can be a religious ideology, such as Christianity or Islam] or belief upon the victim group." The followers, or disciples, or missionaries with such ideologies will all too often not only become religious imperialists, but sometimes also perpetrators of genocide.

Regarding Acts 1:8, "But ye shall receive power, after that the Holy Ghost is come upon you: and ye shall be witnesses unto me both in Jerusalem, and in all Judaea, and in Samaria, and unto the uttermost [farthest] part of the earth," you don't have to read the theologians to know what this verse means: The disciples of Jesus Christ will receive power from the Holy Spirit to evangelize and proselytize the nonChristians, eventually including the Indigenous Peoples of the Americas. So, we see that the Holy Ghost (assuming it exists) is also complicit in the evangelizing and proselytizing of nonChristian peoples, and was also complicit in the perpetration of genocide.

Back to Columbus. In addition to Columbus being preoccupied with spreading the gospel to the "end of the world," he was also preoccupied with his own role in spreading it. According to his understanding of "the divine time table for the earth's history,"[5] Columbus believed that the earth had a predetermined life of 7,000 years. So, according to his understanding, all the prophecies in the Bible had to be fulfilled before that time expired.

According to Columbus' thinking, there were only 150 years left of the 7,000 years, 150 years before the end of the world. So, Columbus believed that the Great Commission of Jesus Christ had to be preached to all the peoples of the world in the remaining time, and he, Columbus, would have a significant role in this holy endeavor. If we use 1492, the year in which Columbus stumbled upon the islands of the Caribbean, we see that he was, at minimum, over 500 years off in his mathematical calculations, and, it may well be that "the end of the world" will occur because of global climate change, not because of Jesus.

Where do the prophecies of Isaiah, a prophet of the Old Testament, come in? Columbus believed that God had spoken "through the mouth of Isaiah, and he showed me the spot where to find it."[6] According to scholars, Columbus does not point to one specific Bible verse from Isaiah but mentions several, including:

> Behold my servant whom I uphold. Mine elect, in whom my soul delighteth; I have put my spirit upon him: he shall bring forth judgment to the   Gentiles. . . . He shall not cry, nor lift up, nor cause his voice to be heard in the street . . . A bruised reed shall he not break, and the smoking flax shall he not quench: he shall bring forth judgment unto truth . . . He shall not fail nor be discouraged, till he have set judgment in the earth: and the isles shall wait for his law. (Isaiah 42:1–4, KJV).

Columbus believed that the "isles" (verse 4), or "islands" spoken of in this verse, no doubt, refer to the islands in the Caribbean upon which Columbus stumbled.

Another passage, through which God had spoken to him, according to Columbus, was Isaiah 55:5:

Behold thou shalt call a nation that thou knowest not: and nations that knew
not thee shall run unto thee because of the Lord thy God, and for the Holy
One of Israel; for he hath glorified thee. (Isaiah 55:5, KJV).

Still another Bible passage important to understanding Columbus is Ia-
siah 42:1–4:

Here is my servant whom I uphold, my chosen one with whom I am pleased.
Upon whom I have put my spirit; he shall bring forth justice to the nations
. . . Not crying out, not shouting, not making his voice heard in the street . . . A
bruised reed he shall not break, and a smoldering wick he shall not quench
. . . Until he established justice on the earth; The coastlands will wait for his
teaching. (Isaiah 42:1–4, NAB)

A footnote in the NAB regarding Isaiah 42:4 reads, "'Coastlands': the
lands of the Mediterranean. In the Old Testament the word often refers to
the pagan lands of the west."[7] This phrase, "the pagan lands of the west,"
eventually would include "the lands" of the Indigenous Peoples of the
Americas.

This is My servant, whom I uphold. My chosen one, in whom I delight. I
have put My spirit upon him. He shall teach the true way to the nations . . .
Till he has established the true way on earth; And the coastlands shall await
his teaching. (Isaiah 42:1–4, Tanakh)

Here is my servant, whom I uphold, my chosen one in whom I delight. I have
bestowed my spirit upon him, and he will make justice shine on the nations .
. . he will plant justice on earth, while coasts and islands wait for
his teaching. (Isaiah 42:1–4, NEB)

The footnotes, in the NEB, say that Isaiah 42:1 through 43:7 refer to
"Israel, the servant of God." Verses 1–4 are the "First Servant Song." A
footnote says that "Some scholars argue that the servant is a particular
individual but without agreement concerning his identity."[8] Columbus, in
his narcissistic thinking, believed that he was the"servant" whom God "up-
holds" and who is the "chosen one" — "My chosen one in whom I delight"
—who "will bring it to all peoples, the coasts and islands."

Of course none of the above translations even suggest that Christopher
Columbus was the "servant."

Another relevant verse from Isaiah reads:

Behold, thou shalt call a nation that thou knowest not, and nations that knew not thee shall run into thee because of the LORD thy God, and for the Holy One of Israel; for he hath glorified thee." (Isaiah 55:5, KJV)

In this KJV version, there is a star beside this verse, which according to the publisher, Thomas Nelson, "indicates a Messianic prophecy."[9] Christians believe that the Messiah refers to Jesus Christ, though I suspect Jewish people would not consider either Columbus or Jesus Christ the Messiah. (Of course, the Dakota and other Indigenous peoples, do not have any teaching about a Messiah.)

Two other versions say essentially the same thing,:

So you shall summon a nation you did not know, And a nation that did not know you shall come running to you—For the sake of the Lord your God, The Holy One of Israel who has glorified you. (Isaiah 55:5, Tanakh)

[A]nd you in turn shall summon nations you do not know, and nations that do not know you shall come running to you, because the Lord your God, the Holy One of Israel, has glorified you. (Isaiah 55:5, NEB)

Again, and of course, the above translations do not even suggest that Columbus was the Messiah. And the theologians unanimously state that these verses apply only to Jesus Christ.

For instance, Adam Clarke says that the Gospel writer, Matthew, "has applied it [the passage in Isaiah 42: 1–4] directly to Christ, nor can it with any justice or propriety be applied to any other person or character whatever."[10] Thus, Columbus is again left out.

But Columbus even thought some verses from Psalms applied to him.

Yet have I sent my king upon my holy hill of Zion . . . I will declare the decree: the Lord hath said unto me, Thou art my Son; this day have I begotten thee . . . Ask of me, and I shall give thee the heathen for thine inheritance, and the uttermost parts of the earth for thy possession. (Psalms 2:6–8, KJV)

Thou hast delivered me from the strivings of the people; and thou hast made me the head of the heathen: a people whom I have not known shall serve me . . . As soon as they hear of Me, they shall obey Me: the strangest shall submit themselves unto Me. (Psalms 18:4, KJV)[11]

Ask of me and I will give you the nations for an inheritance and
the ends of the earth for your possession. (Psalms 2:8, NAB)

Ask it of Me, and I will make the nations your domain, your estate, the
limits of the earth. (Psalms 2:8, Tanakh)

Concerning Psalms 2:8, theologian Matthew Henry writes, ""the kingdoms of the world shall become the kingdoms of the Lord and of his
Christ."[12] The world will be a Christian empire, according to Henry. The
"king upon my holy hill of Zion" (verse 6) is the son of God. Henry de-
clares, "Jesus Christ is a King, and God is pleased to call him His King."[13]

Similarly, Jamieson, Fausset, and Brown refer to Christ's kingdom which
"is destined to be coextensive with the earth."[14] (This sounds very much
like some Muslim fundamentalists who wish to make the kingdoms and
nations of the world submit to Islam. Christianity and Islam deserve each
other. And at least some Christians and some Muslims seem to want to
establish a religious empire.)

The theologians' comments on the verses from Isaiah and from Psalms
make very clear that these passages refer to Jesus Christ, and no one else.

Columbus did not know when he arrived on the Caribbean shores in
1492 that these islands had been inhabited for thousands upon thousands
of years. His arrival began over half a millennium of great sorrow, destruction, and catastrophe. (Recall Red Jacket's comment to the missionary,
"But an evil day came upon us. Your forefathers crossed the great water,
and landed on this island.")[15] David Stannard in *American Holocaust* details the gore, horror, and terror that Columbus inflicted upon Indigenous
Peoples. When Columbus made the statement that "we shall make war
against you in all ways and manners,"[16] he was deadly serious. These "ways
and manners" included: the slaughtering of millions of Native Peoples;
mutilating and dismembering them by cutting off their heads to test the
sharpness of swords, and cutting off their hands if they didn't bring in
their three-month's tribute of gold; using ferocious armored dogs that had
been trained to kill and disembowel those who fled; and in general stealing from, killing, raping, torturing, and terrorizing Indigenous Peoples.
Stannard says that in 21 years time, nearly eight million Native People,
men, women, children, babies, and elders, almost all of whom were non-
combatants, "had been killed by violence, disease, and despair."[17]

Columbus, shortly after landing, would read a statement, the "Requerimiento," informing the Indigenous Peoples of the truth of Christianity and the necessity to swear immediate "allegiance to the Pope and to the Spanish Crown." Of course the Native Peoples did not understand Columbus since he was speaking a foreign language. (Recall Chalk's and Jonassohn's four motives for Genocide, in this case "to impose an ideology or belief upon the victim group.")[18] Columbus further read to his victims, "[W]e can, and shall subject you to the yoke and authority of the Church and of their Highnesses. We will take you and your wives and children and make them slaves [in line with the 1455 papal bull], and as such we will sell them, and will dispose of you and them as 'Their Highnesses order.'" [19, 20]

As the reader can readily see, Church and State were working hand-in-hand in this imperialistic enterprise, the imposition of a total system of foreign domination and exploitation onto another country, the peoples, their lands, and their resources, in this case the Indigenous Peoples of the Americas.

Columbus and Genocide

If we take Stannard's figure of eight million killed in the Caribbean, and, then, if we divide this figure by the 21 years following Columbus "discovery" of America, this works out to over 380,000 persons killed per year, or over 1,000 killed in an average day's "work."

Columbus wouldn't take a back seat to Hitler in terms of "efficient" killing. Or for that matter to the U.S. government. One can speculate that Hitler might have been envious of Columbus' record. However, we do know that Hitler was envious of the U.S. How do we know this? Hitler said so. Hitler said many times to his inner circle how much he admired "the efficiency" of the U.S. genocide program against the Indigenous Peoples of the U.S., "viewing it as a forerunner for his own plans and programs" against the Jews, Romanis, et. al.[21] Think what Columbus could have done if he had the military weaponry that Hitler had, or that the United States had, and does have. It is, indeed, a staggering thought. This Indigenous writer would definitely not be alive and, most certainly, would not be writing this book, given that Western Europeans and later Euro-Americans, with the weaponry they did have, nearly killed all sixteen-million-plus of us. (Only about237,000 Native People were left alive in the U.S. in 1900, according to the Census Bureau.)

Assuming that this figure of eight million Native People murdered in the Caribbean in just 21 years is accurate, this eclipses the number of Jews killed by the Nazis during world War II, and that's not even counting the approximately 16 million Native Peoples killed on the mainland in the years to come. (Some demographers estimate a higher number.)[22]

This leads me to ask, "Why does the U.S. and its Euro-American citizenry shed justifiable tears over the Jewish genocide, and say "Never again," and, at the same time, do not shed tears over the genocide of the Indigenous Peoples of what is now the United States?" One suspects that because the U.S. government and its Euro-American citizenry were the perpetrators, they do not wish to hold the U.S. government and their ancestors responsible for what they did. Those who still hail Columbus, Manifest Destiny, and American exceptionalism would have to abandon the dearly held belief that America is an exemplary moral nation, a champion of freedom and human rights. And for many their fairy-tale version of American history is too dear to abandon. Stannard also compares the millions of Indigenous People killed by Columbus and his soldiers to the dropping of the atomic bomb on Hiroshima, which killed 130,000 Japanese, almost entirely noncombatant civilians. Stannard notes, "It took a little longer, about the span of a single human generation, but what happened on Hispaniola was the equivalent of more than fifty Hiroshimas. And Hispaniola was only the beginning."[23]

Honoring Christ and the Twelve Apostles

In the course of Columbus' war-making, his campaign of terror and murder—which the Spanish called "pacification" (as did the U.S. in Vietnam)—Bartolome Las Casas, a Catholic missionary, witnessed an event in which the "Spaniards found pleasure in inventing all kinds of odd cruelties, the more cruel the better, with which to spill human blood. They built a long gibbet, low enough for the toes to touch the ground and prevent strangling, and hanged thirteen [natives] at a time in honor of Christ our Saviour and the Twelve Apostles."[24]

The title of this section of Las Casas' book is "Honoring Christ," which title is taken from this incident, which was anything but isolated.

There are a number of biblical references to Christ as "Saviour" in the New Testament. One such reference is found in Luke 2:11, and is a familiar passage because it is usually read in Christian churches at Christmas time, "for unto you is born this day in the city of David a Saviour, which is Christ the Lord." Another reference is John 4:42 which refers to "Christ, the Saviour of the world."

According to theologian Adam Clarke, the Saviour, Jesus Christ, "makes safe, delivers, preserves, to make alive."[25] Columbus and the Spanish soldiers had a most peculiar method of honoring this Saviour who made people "safe." To paraphrase Jerry Lee Lewis, instead of "A whole lot of shakin' goin' on," we could either say there was, "A whole lot of honoring going on," or, less euphemistically, "a whole lot of killin' going on."

As to the idea and action of "honouring" "Christ our Saviour," there are a number of New Testament references which refer to "honoring" Christ. One is found in the gospel of John 5:23, "That all men should honour the Son, even as they honour the Father ...." A second is in I Timothy 6:16, which says, "Who [Christ] alone has immortality . . . . to whom be honor and everlasting power. Amen." According to these scriptural references, it is Christ who should be "honoured." Apparently Columbus and his fellow murderers truly believed that they were indeed "honouring" Christ and the twelve apostles.

Burning Alive of Hatuey

Another genocidal incident perpetrated by Columbus and his men involved an Indigenous man by the name of Hatuey. The Spanish found Hatuey and his people, and killed most of them, "enslaved" the others[26] (think of the papal bull of 1455, *Romanus Pontifex*, and the Requerimiento), and condemned their leader to be burned alive. David Stannard in *American Holocaust* chronicles this event.

> Reportedly, as they were tying him to the stake, a Franciscan friar urged him to take Jesus to his heart so that his soul might go to heaven, rather than descend into hell. Hatuey replied that if heaven was where the Christians went, he would rather go to hell.[27]

Hatuey was a brave and wise man.

Here we see the interlocking relationship between Christianity, as represented by the Franciscan friar, and the military, as represented by Columbus and his soldiers, coinciding in the horrific act of burning a man alive simply because he had a different religious belief. Shades of ISIS. Columbus, his soldiers, and the Catholic missionaries saw nothing incongruous about preaching about God's loving kindness, about Jesus' love, and then torturing and murdering people if they did not accept Christianity. One wonders how this barbarous and evil act exemplified the love of God and of Jesus Christ, though it certainly did exemplify the genocidal commandments and actions of the Old Testament God, who refers to himself as a merciful God. It should not be difficult, even for the most fervent Christian, to understand why Hatuey and his people, after watching all of Columbus's and his men's murder and butchery, would not accept and, certainly, would not follow Jesus Christ.

Several comments can be made about this heinous incident. One involves the Bible verses which mention "heaven" and "hell." The term "hell," which is used in the English translations of the Bible, represents both the Jewish "Sheol," which refers to the place of the departed, and the Greek "Gehenna," which denotes the place for the wicked after death.[28] Jesus' words in Matthew 13:41–42 also refer to hell: "The Son of man will send out His angels, and they will gather out of his kingdom all things that offend, and those who practice lawlessness, And will cast them into the furnace of fire. There will be wailing and gnashing of teeth." (NKJV)

Who shall be cast into this "furnace of fire"? Those "which do iniquity" shall be sent there. The New King James Version says, "those who practice lawlessness" will be cast into the "furnace of fire." Then, we see in another verse, "And whosover was not found written in the book of life was cast into the lake of fire." (Revelation 20:15, KJV) There are a number of other verses which could be mentioned, but verses like this contribute to the popular notion of hell as a place of fire and brimstone.[29]

Theologians Henry, Jamieson, Fausset, Brown, and Clarke say nothing about these two verses. They say nothing about the "fiery furnace" or "the furnace of fire," or the "blazing furnace." Note that it is Jesus who commands his angels to throw all sinners and evil-doers into "the furnace of fire" to suffer eternal torment. Verses dealing with hell are part of what I call the "hidden Bible"—hidden at least by the mainstream denominations and churches who studiously ignore these passages. However, fundamentalists, evangelicals, and conservative Catholics love preaching about hell and the eternal torment of sinners. While their imagined hell is fictional, they have to an alarming extent managed to create hell on earth through their blood lust and cruelty.

Hopefully, the reader can understand how a group of Dakota children, ages seven to eight years, myself among them, might have felt when a fundamentalist missionary told us that if our grandmothers and grandfathers didn't know Jesus Christ as their personal savior that they (our grandparents) were "burning in hell right now."

The opposite, much more pleasant term is "heaven." The popular notion is that this is the place where all the good people go when they die. This is the place of the Christian God (who is really the Jewish God, Yahweh), and his angels, and the place of the "saved" or "redeemed" where they receive their eternal reward and "glorify God and enjoy Him for ever."[30] This, along with the concept of hell, illustrates a central dualistic aspect of Christianity: submit and be rewarded forever, or refuse and be tortured forever.

As regards the earthly application of this duality, the Franciscan who attempted to "save" Hatuey at his immolation was a member of the Order of Friars Minor, which was founded by St. Francis Assisi in 1209. The distinguishing characteristic of the order is the insistence on complete poverty, not only for individual friars but collectively for the whole order. The Friars were to live by the work of their hands or, if need be, by begging, but were forbidden to own any property or to accept money.[31] In the incident with Hatuey, the Franciscan friar was attempting to convert Hatuey, "to impose a belief," so that Hatuey might go to heaven instead of to hell. One can see that the friar was following the commands of Christ and of the papal bull of 1537,[32] *Sublimus Dei*, to "make disciples of all the nations." Apparently, this Franciscan friar forgot the part in the 1537 bull, issued by Paul III, which says "the said Indians ... should be converted to the faith of Jesus Christ by preaching the word of God and by the example of good and holy living."[33] If burning people alive is an "example of good and holy living," one shudders to think of what would constitute bad and unholy living.

Also, in this incident we see the literal and physical killing by burning of Hatuey's body, and the figurative "murdering" of the inner man, the religion and spirituality of Hatuey. It is indeed difficult to avoid characterizing not only this act but also the other genocidal acts perpetrated by Columbus and his men, with the complicity and cooperation of the Catholic Church and its missionaries, as indescribably evil, unforgivably evil. This is no exaggeration. (See the dictionary definition of evil: 1 a: the fact of suffering, misfortune, and wrongdoing, b: a cosmic evil force; 2 something that brings sorrow, distress, or calamity.")[34]

It's also worth noting the close cooperation between the state (its military) and the church in this incident. There appears to be no separation of church (the Franciscan friar) and state (Spain, and the military). The friar and the other missionaries who accompanied Columbus obviously had no qualms about participating, along with the killers, Columbus and the Spanish soldiers, in the wrongful, criminal, and genocidal acts against the Indigenous Peoples of the Caribbean.

Even though the answers are obvious, we should ask, was the friar a Christian? Was Columbus a Christian? Were Columbus's men Christians?

Yes, yes they were. And they were following the genocidal commands in the Old Testament and in the three papal bulls discussed above. Columbus, his soldiers, the missionaries, and the friar were obedient to their Lord and Savior, Jesus Christ, at least in their own minds. And the friar was being "merciful" by offering Hatuey (and many other victims) the opportunity to embrace Christ before being burned alive.

Another question is if there were any "true" or "real" Christians present at the massacres, why didn't they speak up? Did LasCasas, who provides the description of a mass hanging, protest at the time, or at *any* time? Did he ever say anything like, "Hey guys, you shouldn't be killing people. One of the ten commandments is 'Thou shalt not kill?'"[35] Did Columbus and his men even think of Indigenous People as human beings? Or did they think of them as subhuman, or even as animals? If so, they provided a pertinent example for both George Washington[36] and Andrew Jackson,[37] who used the beast metaphor and said that Indigenous People were like wolves, and, therefore, worthy of being slaughtered.

Were Columbus and his soldiers being true Christians by doing what the Bible and Catholic Church commanded?

Columbus as a Symbol

In finishing this discussion, here is a quotation by Ward Churchill regarding Columbus:

> As a symbol, Christopher Columbus vastly transcends himself. He stands before the bar of history and humanity, culpable not only for his deeds on Española, but, in spirit at least, for the carnage and cultural obliteration which attended the conquests of Mexico and Peru during the 1500s. He stands as exemplar of the massacre of Pequots at Mystic in 1637, and of Lord Jeffrey Amherst's calculated distribution of smallpox-laden blankets to the members of Pontiac's confederacy a century and a half later. His spirit informed the policies of John Evans and John Chivington as they set out to exterminate the Cheyennes in Colorado during 1864, and it rode with the 7th U.S. Cavalry to Wounded Knee in December of 1890.[38]

Certainly, most Indigenous Peoples of the Americas do not regard Christopher Columbus as a hero, no matter how many Bible verses he quoted, no matter how much he thought he was guided by God and the Holy Spirit, no matter how much he thought he was honoring Christ and the twelve Apostles. Nor does it matter how much many Euro-Americans revere Columbus. He perpetrated genocide and slaughtered eight million Native People in the Caribbean Islands. First Nations Peoples, and their allies and supporters, in the United States of America, are striving to have Columbus Day—one might as well have a holiday celebrating Hitler—changed to Indigenous Peoples' Day. Places which have already done so include Denver, Colorado, Minneapolis, St. Paul, and South Dakota as a state. Hopefully, many more cities, as well as states will follow suit.

Endnotes

1. "Christopher Columbus: A Spiritual Giant," by Glen W. Chapman. https://www.yumpu.com/en/document/view/32343281/christopher-columbus-a-spiritual-giant

2. *Diary of Christopher Columbus*, Chapter 7, "Later Years: the Book of Prophecies and the Final Voyage." BYU Religious Studies Center. Also found in *Columbus's Book of Prophecies*, by Kay Brigham, 1991,

3, *American Holocaust: The Conquest of the New World*, by David Stannard. Oxford: Oxford University Press, 1992, p. 63.

4. *Bethany Parallel Commentary On The New Testament*. Minneapolis: Bethany House Publishers, 1983, p. 203.

5. *Christopher Columbus: A Latter-Day Saint Perspective,* by Arnold K. Garr. Provo, UT: Brigham Young University Religious Studies Center, 1992, pp. 63–69.

6. Chapman, op. cit.

7. New American Bible. New York: Catholic Book Publishing Co., 1980, p. 866.

8. The New English Bible With the Apocrypha. Oxford: Oxford University Press, 1976, p. 774.

9. King James Version, Thomas Nelson Publishers, Nashville, Tennessee, 1976, "Special Features of Your Giant Print reference Bible" (following Title Page), p. 1,091 (Isaiah 55:5).

10. Bethany Parallel Commentary On The Old Testament, Minneapolis: Bethany House Publishers, 1983, 1985 p. 1,438.

11. *Book of Prophecies*, by Kay Brigham. Provo, Utah: BYU Religious Studies Center, 1991, pp. 184–185.

12. BPCOT p. 967.

13. BPCOT, p. 966.

14. BPCOT, p. 967.

15. *A Short History of the Indians of the United States*, by Edward H. Spicer. New York: Van Nostrand Reinhold Company, 1969, p. 264.

16. Stannard, op. cit., p. 66.

17. Ibid., p. x.

18. *The History and Sociology of Genocide*, by Frank Chalk and Kurt Jonassohn. New Haven, CT: Yale University Press, 1990, p. 29

19. "Requerimiento," 1514, Christopher Columbus, Untitled Document, "http://www.doctrine of discovery.org/requerimiento.htm.

20. Stannard, op. cit., p. 66.

21. Ibid., p. 153

22. "The Demography of Native North America," by Lenore A Stiffarm with Philip Lane, Jr., in *The State of Native America*, 1992, pp. 27 & 36–37.

23. Stannard, op. cit., p. x.

24. Ibid., p. 72.

25. BPCNT, p. 358.

26. Stannard, op. cit., p. 70.

27. Ibid., pp. 623–624.

28. *The Oxford Dictionary of the Christian Church, Second Edition*, F.L. Cross, and E.A. Livingstone, eds., 1974, p. 630.

29. Ibid., p. 631.

30. Ibid., pp. 623-624

31. Ibid., p. 532.

32. *Sublimus Dei*, papal bull, May 29, 1537, by Pope Paul III (Topic: the enslavement and evangelization of Indians). Also, Matthew 28:19, KJV.

33. *Sublimus Dei*, Pope Paul III, May 29, 1537,

34. Merriam-Webster's Collegiate Dictionary Eleventh Edition, 2012, p. 433.

35. The Holy Bible: Old and New Testaments in the King James Version, Giant Print Reference Edition, Nashville: Thomas Nelson Publishers, 1976, p. 120.

36. *Facing West: The Metaphysics of Indian-Hating & Empire-Building*, by Richard Drinnon. Norman, OK: University of Oklahoma Press, 1990, p. 65.

37. Stannard, op. cit., pp. 121–122.

38. *A Little Matter of Genocide: Holocaust and Denial in the Americas, 1492 to Present*, by Ward Churchill. San Francisco: City Lights Book, 1997. p. 92.

3

THE PEQUOT HOLOCAUST
"A Sweet-Smelling Sacrifice"

"And the other lamb thou shalt offer at even, and shalt do thereto according to the meat offering of the morning, and according to the drink offering thereof, for *a sweet saviour, an offering made by fire unto the Lord.*" (Exodus 29:41, KJV) (italics added)

Although the primary focus of this chapter is the Pequot Holocaust, we'll first discuss two other instances of mass killing which involved Holy Writ.

"Christ Our Victory"

The first incident occurred in the spring of 1586 in North Carolina. The key Indigenous person involved in was Wingina, the leader of the Roanoacs People; and the primary English (really, Irish) player was Ralph Lane, who discovered that Wingina planned to drive the English out by force with the help of native allies from the south who were hired as mercenaries.

Lane, a military man with experience from the British campaigns in Ireland, tried to mount a night assault on Wingina's village, but was discovered by sentries before he carried it out. Both sides now knew the other was plotting destruction.

Ralph Lane, good Christian Protestant that he was, told Wingina he would like to meet with him and his major advisors to discuss peace. When Wingina and his unarmed men come to meet in the open field, they did not suspect treachery. But as Wingina approached, Lane gave a battle cry to his musketeers having them open fire at near point-blank range. Wingina was hit, but ran into the woods. One of Lane's men chased him into the trees and returned with Wingina's head.[1]

What was the battle cry that triggered the murder of Wingina and his people? It was "Christ Our Victory!" Dr. Robert Venables, a historian from Cornell University, says of Lane and this incident, "Protestant Englishmen were no different from Catholic Spaniards. They murdered in the name of the Prince of Peace."[2]

The Biblical reference that inspired Ralph Lane to use the "Christ Our Victory!" battle cry was I Corinthians 15:57, which reads, "But thanks be to God, who gives us the victory through our Lord Jesus Christ." (NKJV). The New American Bible reads, "But thanks be to God who has given us the victory through our Lord Jesus Christ." Both translations make very clear the meaning of this particular verse: It is Christ who gives the victory.

But what is the "victory" that Jesus Christ has given? According to theologian Matthew Henry, the victory is over "the power of death."[3] Jamieson, Fausset, and Brown say the victory is over "death and Hades" as well as over "the law and sin."[4] Adam Clarke writes, "He has given us the victory over sin, Satan, death, the grave, and hell."[5]

Apparently Lane thought that Jesus Christ had given him justification to murder Wingina and his men, and to behead Wingina. Lane and, perhaps, his soldiers, believed that Christ gave them the "victory" over Wingina and the Roanoacs. Lane apparently believed he was a good Christian, one of the "chosen people," merely fulfilling the word and will of God.

It brings to mind my childhood in the late 1940s, when I was seven to ten years old, in the Sunday School of the Assemblies of God mission on the "rez" we often sang "Onward Christian Soldiers." The Sunday School teacher had us little Dakota kids stand up and march in place and in time as we sang this war hymn. We were taught that we were in a "war," and that we, as Christians, "were marching as to war." And, of course, as in war, the enemy was to be killed. Thus, in our young minds, we understood that it's okay to kill the enemy because we'd be doing it for our Savior, Jesus Christ, and for our God. We also understood that the Old Testament God wanted us to kill. Thus, by killing the enemy, we'd merely be fulfilling God's will and purpose.

Lane and his men very evidently believed the same thing.

"The Wondrous Wisedome and Love of God "

With the coming of the white man to the Americas, there came many strange diseases, such as smallpox, which caused great epidemics among the Indigenous Peoples. One such epidemic occurred early in the 17th century. About 90 percent of the Wampanoag died of an unidentified European disease, as did a comparable number of Massachusetts and nearly as many Pawtucket and eastern Abenaki.[6] Ward Churchill says that the Native Peoples "had close contact with Europeans for years without getting sick," then, "mysteriously," this epidemic broke out.[7]

This epidemic, with all the Native deaths, was a cause for holy celebration by the Christian English. William Brandon writes, "The churchly colonists exulted, with reverence, over the frightful epidemic of 1616–1619 that had cleared so many heathen from the path of the chosen people.[8] If this was the result of deliberate bio-terrorism, it calls to mind Blaise Pascal's statement, "Men never do evil so completely and cheerfully as when they do it from religious conviction."[9]

> For thou art an holy people unto the LORD thy God: the LORD thy God hath chosen thee to be a special people unto himself, above all people that are upon the face of the earth". (Deuteronomy 7:6, KJV)

It's clear that the Christian English regarded themselves as symbolic Israelites, the new "chosen people," and acted in accord with that belief. Further, the Puritans viewed the Native Peoples as "heathens," and so just as the ungodly Hittites needed to be exterminated or driven from Canaan, the "promised land," so the heathen Indigenous Peoples—the Pequot, the Wampanoag, et. al.—needed to be exterminated or cleared from the path of the new chosen people. Brandon puts it quite eloquently:

> [T]he divine leaders of the New England theocracies, who repeatedly proved by Biblical interpretations that it was the sacred duty of the Christian English to root out the godless Canaanites ... [determined that] deliberate extermination of the independent Indian nations. . . since the Pequot War (1637), was now to be carried out.[10]

The author(s) of Deuteronomy put it this way:

> When the Lord thy God shall bring thee into the land whither thou goest to possess it, and hath cast out many nations before thee, the Hittites, and the

Girgashites, and the Amorites, and the Canaanites, and the Perizzites, and the Hivites, and the Jebusites . . . And when the LORD thy God shall deliver them before thee; thou shalt smite them, and utterly destroy them; thou shalt make no covenant with them, nor shew mercy unto them:
(Deuteronomy 7:1–2).

You don't have to be a theologian to understand what the Old Testament God is commanding here. Thus, the Christian English were obeying and fulfilling the Word of the Lord when they exterminated the Native Peoples of what is now the northeastern United States. Since they were obeying the Lord God of Israel, there was no reason to feel guilty. On the contrary, they could enjoy the feeling of self-righteousness that came from what they perceived as divine approval of their actions.

One writer characterized this particular epidemic as "The Wonderful Preparation the Lord Christ by His Providence Wrought for his people's abode in the western world."[11] He went on to point out with satisfaction that the plague had swept away "chiefly young men and children, the very seeds of increase."[12] (This reminds one of criterion (d) of the 1948 UN Genocide Convention, which cites "Preventing live births within the group.")

Thomas Morton of Merry Mount said of the 17th-century killer epidemic, "this, the wondrous wisedome and love of God, is shewne, by sending to the place his Minister, to sweepe away . . . the Salvages . . . ."[13] In the view of the colonists, the epidemic was an instrument of the Lord to kill the godless Native Peoples, just as He had directly brutalized the Egyptians.

Regarding the plagues in the Exodus stories (Exodus, Chapters 7–12), Vincent Bugliosi writes that when the pharaoh refused to let the Israelites go, "our loving God, the monarch of vindictiveness, instead of just punishing the pharaoh, decide to take it out on his poor people. He proceeded to hit the people of Egypt with one plague after another . . . "[14] These plagues included turning their water into blood, "swarming them with locusts and hoards of frogs," and lice, and "blanketing Egypt with darkness." As well, the Old Testament God had his angel kill every firstborn male Egyptian child, including pharaoh's son, "at which time, pharaoh capitulated and freed the Israelites."[15] What kind of god kills babies and children? And what kind of people worship such a god?

Bugliosi also notes that these plagues are "mass murder."[16] If these Exodus plagues and the "frightful epidemic" that killed many Indigenous People are similar in their purpose, i.e. to help God's "chosen people," the Israelites and the Christian English, then, the epidemic, instead of showing the wisdom and love of God, is indeed showing God to be a "mass murderer," showing Yahweh, the Old Testament God, as the "monarch of vindictiveness."[17]

Also, it is difficult to make sense of the incongruity of the Bible-quoting Christian English on one hand proclaiming the love and mercy of their God while, on the other gloating and exulting over the mass murder of Indigenous Peoples. One could ask, "Where is the love?" (as a popular song, in the 1970s asks). Or, where is the love of God? Or, where is the love of Jesus?

Pequot Holocaust

Another historical incident from the early 17th century graphically illustrates the extensive use of the Bible to justify genocide of Indigenous Peoples, specifically, what I call the Pequot Holocaust. On May 26, 1637, the Christian English made a stealthy night attack on a stockaded Pequot town on the Mystic River in Connecticut, burned the town, and slaughtered its 700-plus inhabitants.

Ward Churchill writes that the number of Pequots fried in the fire or bayoneted was closer to 900.[18] This burning of the town was a literal holocaust. ("Holocaust" can mean "a sacrifice consumed by fire," or "a thorough destruction involving extensive loss of life, especially through fire . . . a mass slaughter of people; esp. genocide.")[19] The killers, the Christian English, regarded the killing of the Pequots by fire as a sacrifice to God, as we shall soon see. This particular genocidal incident, because it's so well documented, features an abundance of Bible verses cited as justification, "an embarrassment of riches," to use Philip Jenkins' phrase.[20]

John Mason, a troop commander in Connecticut,[21] engaged in many assaults upon Indigenous Peoples, and, as historian John Stannard notes, "more often than not Indian women and children were consumed along with everyone and everything else in the conflagrations that routinely accompanied the colonists' assaults."[22] Regarding the killing of Indigenous women and children, Stannard also points out that Mason's partner in crime, John Underhill, "reassured" his fellow killers that "sometimes the Scripture declareth women and children must perish with their parents," and that just because they were weak, helpless, and unarmed, "did not make their deaths any less a delight to the Puritans' God."[23, 24]

In Genesis 6:5–7, the Old Testament God "repent[s]" that "he had made man on the earth," "that the wickedness of man was great in the earth," and decided to "destroy man whom I have created . . . from the face of the earth." Then, we read in Genesis 7:22, "All in whose nostrils was the breath of life, of all that was in the dry land, died." Thus Yahweh, the Old Testament God, destroyed "all living creatures" by flooding the earth (Genesis 7:10, 19, 21–23).

In Genesis 7:22, we see the term "died," or we could say that all living creatures, including humans, were murdered by God. Perpetrators of genocide often use the euphemistic terms "died" or "death" as "a defense against acknowledging [their guilt] . . ."[25] Although the above-mentioned verses do not specifically say "women, "children," and "elders," we can safely assume that the phrase, "All in whose nostrils was the breath of life" (Genesis 7:22), includes them. God, instead of punishing the "wicked" and the evildoers, punished *everybody*, including the most innocent and vulnerable. What kind of God does such a thing?" This indiscriminate mass murder set a hideous example that all too many of God's "Christian soldiers" followed.

There are many more relevant passages, passages which describe the Lord murdering women and children, or ordering their murder, but we'll only mention one more, Deuteronomy 2:33–34, in which we see the destruction of King Sihon and his people, the Amorites. Verses 33–34 read, "And the Lord our God delivered him over to us; so we defeated him, his sons, and all his people. We took all his cities at that time, and we utterly destroyed the men, women, and little ones of every city; we left none remaining." (NKJV) Later we'll see that these killings of "little ones" were a "sacrifice" to the Lord God of Israel.

The Torah version of Deuteronomy 2:34 reads, "At that time we captured all his towns, and we doomed every town—men, women, and children— leaving no survivor." A footnote defines the term "doomed" to mean "place under herem, which meant the annihilation of the population."[26]

Matthew Henry makes an astounding statement about this atrocity. He says that putting all the Amorites to the sword, men, women, and children, was justified—that these "men, women, and children" were not killed as Israel's enemies, but "as sacrifices to divine justice." God employed Israel, "as a kingdom of priests,"[27] to offer these sacrifices. Jamieson, Fausset, and Brown say that the Amorites, "one of the nations doomed to destruction," were "utterly exterminated."[28] JFB also say that the country of the Amorites "fell by right of conquest into the hands of the Israelites."[29] Of course, this phrase "right of conquest" was also used by Western Europeans and U.S. Euro-Americans to justify the stealing of Native lands and the killing of Indigenous Peoples. It would be most difficult to disagree with Thomas Jefferson's description of "the God of Moses" as "a being of terrific character—cruel, vindictive, capricious and unjust."[30]

(Even some Indigenous Peoples, such as the Anishinabe, used the phrase "right of conquest" to justify stealing another Indigenous People's land, specifically, stealing lands from the Dakota People of Minnesota. In the Constitution of the Red Lake Reservation of northern Minnesota, there is the phrase the "Right of Conquest" to justify the Anishinabe's theft.[31] Like the white conquerors, they have not paid the Dakota for the stolen lands. And, like the white conquerors, they are benefiting from Dakota lands while the Dakota receive no benefit at all from their own lands.)

Philip Jenkins, in his book *Laying Down the Sword: Why we can't ignore the Bible's Violent Verses*, says that "Herem, usually interpreted as 'utter destruction', is the single most frightening term in the whole Bible."[32] The term can also mean "ban" and cities were given this status as under a "ban," which could mean either "devoted" or "accursed" to God, or "set apart for Yahweh under a ban." The phrases "destroy utterly," or "doomed to destruction," or "utterly exterminated," etc., are some of the translations, and the meaning is clear: "every living thing in the 'doomed' city must be destroyed wholly."[33] In the Hebrew tradition, there is the idea of "holy war," and Herem is part of that tradition. This sounds very much like the Muslim "Jihad," a holy war. It is telling that Christians, particularly fundamentalist and evangelical Christians, tend to self-righteously judge Muslims who engage in "holy wars"—often lumping all Muslims into that bag—and, then, smugly, and wrongly, deny that Christians didn't and don't engage in "holy wars."

Joshua 10:28, KJV, refers to another victim city, Makkedah, as being "utterly destroyed . . . and all the souls that were therein." The Tanakh says, " . . . [God commanded] put it [Makkedah] and its king to the sword, proscribing it and every person in it and leaving none that escaped."

Both Matthew Henry and Adam Clarke write nothing negative about the slaughter, the utter destruction, and leaving none "remain," or "none that escaped." At least, JFB admit that "It was a war of utter extermination."[34] However, these theologians say nothing about the horror and brutality of the slaughter, and nothing about the killing of the innocent.

Joshua 10:30 referring to Libnah, another victim city, says, " . . . and he smote it with the edge of the sword, and all the souls that were therein; he let none escape . . . " Joshua 10:35 mentions another victim-city Eglon, where God ordered that the Israelites " . . . smote it with the edge of the sword, and all the souls therein all the souls therein, he utterly destroyed that day . . . . " Regarding Hebron, Joshua 10:37 says, "And they took it, and smote it with the edge of the sword . . . and all the souls that were therein;

he left none remaining." Finally, we read in Joshua 10:39, regarding Debir, ". . . and they smote them with the edge of the sword, and utterly destroyed all the souls that were therein; he left none remaining."

In Joshua 10:28, 30, 35, 37, and 39, we see the phrases, "all the souls that were therein; he [Joshua] left none remain in it," and "[he] destroyed it utterly, and all the souls that were therein; he left none remaining." Then, in Joshua 10:40, after Joshua had nearly exterminated the Canaanites, we see the horrifying and damning words, "he [Joshua] left none remaining, but utterly destroyed all that breathed, as the Lord God of Israel commanded."

Joshua, with the help of his Lord God, was an amazingly efficient murderer. It would not be surprising if Hitler, who was impressed by U.S. genocide of Native Peoples, was not also impressed with the efficiency of the Old Testament God and Joshua.

John Underhill, infamous for the Pequot Holocaust, was an excellent Bible scholar and knew the above-mentioned verses; he could, then, confidently reassure his fellow Christian killers that "sometimes the Scripture declareth women and children must perish with their parents."[35] And, of course, these killers need not worry about feeling any remorse because they were simply emulating and obeying their Old Testament killer God, Yahweh, who himself murdered and slaughtered hundreds of thousands, perhaps millions, of women and children.

The theologians seem not to be numb from all the killing, slaughtering, "putting to the sword," "leaving none standing" that we see in this one chapter of Joshua, alone. Instead, they seem to be imbued with holy gratitude and glee. If this rejoicing in mass murder isn't evil, it's difficult to see what is.

David Stannard says in his book, *American Holocaust*, that two passages from Deuteronomy, Chapter 7, verses 2 and 16, and Chapter 20, verses 16–17, are "unremitting" in their support for "warlike zealotry."[36] Stannard says that these two verses were "cited . . . gleefully by Puritan John Mason as justification for the extermination of Indians."[37] In Deuteronomy, 7:2 and 7:16, the Old Testament God, unequivocally commands the Israelites to "smite them, and utterly destroy them; thou shalt make no covenant with them, nor shew mercy unto them . . . Thou shalt consume all the people which the Lord thy God shall deliver thee; thine eye shall have no pity upon them."

The symbolic Israelites followed that command with zeal.

The second passage, which John Mason related directly to the Pequot Holocaust, is Deuteronomy 20:16–17 (KJV), which states:

Of the cities ... which the Lord thy God doth give thee for an inheritance, thou shalt save alive nothing that breatheth ... But thou shalt utterly destroy them—the Hittites, the Canaanites, and the Perizzites, the Hivites, and the Jebusites; and the Lord thy God hath commanded thee.[38]

The Torah's translation of the passage reads:

In the towns of the latter peoples, however, which the Lord your God is giving you as a heritage, you shall not let a soul remain alive. No, you must proscribe them ["put them to death," as in Leviticus 27:29]—the Hittites and the Amorites, the Canaanites and the Perizzites, the Hivites and the Jebusites —as the Lord your God has commaned you.

To reiterate, both of these passages from Deuteronomy were quoted directly by the Christian English perpetrators of the Pequot Holocaust of 1637. According to Stannard, John Mason specifically cited Deuteronomy, 20:17, "Thou shalt save alive nothing that breatheth ... but thou shalt utterly destroy them," as justification for that Holocaust.[39]

"At the conclusion of one especially bloody combat," John Mason declared, "the Lord was pleased to smite our Enemies in the hinder parts, and to give us their Land for an Inheritance."[40]

The above scriptural references to "hinder parts" and "Inheritance" are found in at least two Old Testament verses. The "hinder parts" reference is found in Psalms 78:66, which reads, "And he smote his enemies in the hinder parts: he put them to a perpetual reproach." (KJV) Thus, God, at least in Mason's mind, "smote" the Pequots "in the hinder parts."

Matthew Henry goes further and says the "He smote them with emerods"—"emerods" being hemorrhoids.

Adam Clarke agrees, saying that the phrase "smote his enemies in the hinder parts" refers to "the hemorrhoids with which He [God] afflicted the Philistines."[41] (The term "emerods" occurs in I Samuel 6:17, 18.) I don't know if any historians record that the Pequots or any of the other Indigenous Nations were "smitten" with hemorrhoids. However, being burned alive would tend to take one's mind off the hemorrhoids, if they were "smitten" by such.

In regard to the other scriptural reference, the phrase "give us their Land for an Inheritance" can be found in a number of Old Testament verses. One such is Numbers 33:54, which reads, "And ye shall divide the land by lot for an inheritance among your families . . . ." This verse is preceded by verse 52 which reads,

Then ye shall drive out all the inhabitants of the land from before you, and destroy all their pictures, and destroy all their molten images, and quite pluck down all their high places; And ye shall dispossess the inhabitants of the land, and dwell therein: for I have given you the land to possess it.

This commands the Israelites to conquer and divide Canaan, "the Promised Land," in other words, to engage in massive land theft. God is also commanding the Israelites to engage in religious suppression and destruction of the religious practices and sacramental objects of the Canaanites and the other inhabitants of the land.

Just as God's "chosen people," the Israelites, engaged in mass murder, land theft, and religious suppression, the new self-identified chosen people, the Christian English and later Euro-Americans, emulated them in slaughtering, stealing the land from, and suppressing the spirituality, ceremonies, and practices of the Indigenous Peoples of the U.S.

It is quite clear that John Mason, the author of the Pequot Holocaust, viewed Pequot land as his land, that it was given to him, as an "inheritance," by the Lord, God, Jesus Christ, or perhaps, by the Holy Spirit (take your pick).

It was okay to either drive out or to kill all the inhabitants since God had given them, the Christian English, the land, and had told them to "dispossess" all the inhabitants of the land. The dispossession, removal, and mass killing of the Pequots and the other Indigenous Peoples later acquired a grandiose name: "Manifest Destiny."

Historian John Stannard uses the term "conflagrations" to describe what the invaders did to their native victims.[42] These burnings, or fires, "routinely accompanied," according to Stannard, the attacks of the English, Western Europeans, and Euro-Americans, upon the Indigenous Peoples in the nearly four centuries from 1492 to 1890.

One of the perpetrators was George Washington, who followed a "scorched earth" policy against the Haudenosaunee, "The People of the Long House." during the French and Indian War. Washington burned down 28 of the 30 towns of the Seneca as well as the towns of the Mohawks, Onondagas, and other First Nations peoples. It's no accident that the Senecas referred to Washington as "the Town Destroyer."[43]

Washington ordered Major General John Sullivan to carry out the "scorched earth" policy and to attack the Haudenosaunee (Iroquois), and Sullivan did as instructed. Sullivan reported to Washington that he destroyed "everything that contributes to their support" and said that he had turned "the whole of that beautiful region from the character of a garden to a scene of drear and sickening desolation."[44]

Returning to the previous century, the force which John Mason commanded consisted of 500 Narragansetts, 70 Mohigans, and 180 Puritans. Native People made up 75% of John Mason's force, an example of Native peoples fighting Native peoples, the colonized Indigenes under the leadership of the colonizers. This was one of dozens upon dozens of examples of the "divide and conquer" strategy employed by the colonizing powers, France, England, and the U.S., during the first four centuries of Indigenous land theft. One of the groups that participated, the Algonquin, even considered themselves "killers of men."[45] So, when the whites decided on an aggressive policy against the Pequots, other native peoples either remained neutral or joined the white man against the Pequots in May 1637.

The Pequots, on the other hand, were an independent and sovereign people who distrusted the English, for good reason. After a number of incidents in the 1630s in which some whites were killed, the Connecticut General Court met and declared war on the Pequots on May 1, 1637. Or, as Ward Churchill writes, "the leadership of both Plymouth and Massachusetts collaborated with that of the unofficial colony of Connecticut to fabricate a pretext, and then set out on a war of extermination."[46]

The Pequots, under the leadership of Sassacus, retaliated, killing 30 whites and taking women and children captive, and then retreated to their palisaded town on the Mystic River.

Massachusetts sent Captain John Endicott to Block Island, off the coast of Rhode Island, where his task was "to kill every adult male residing there and capture as many women and children as possible, since "they would fetch a tidy sum in the West Indies slave markets."[47] The Pequots at Block Island did not engage the English and instead "simply melted away into the woods." The "frustrated English vented their racial fury and blood-lust by burning homes and fields."[48]

On the mainland, Captain John Mason , who had been appointed commander of the Connecticut troops, launched his attack on May 26, 1637 against the Pequots. The whites, with their native allies, attacked the town, setting fire to it, slaying men, women, and children as they fled the flames. The Narragansett People, one of the "native allies" who had long been at odds with the Pequots, accompanied Mason's troops. However, when the Narragansetts found out that Mason was planning nothing less than a wholesale massacre, they withdrew to the rear. Mason at the head of one of the attacking parties, and John Underhill leading the other, under cover of pre-dawn darkness, attacked the unsuspecting Pequots from two directions at once. The British swarmed into the Pequot town, slashing and shooting at anything that moved. Caught off guard, and with apparently few warriors in the community, some of the Pequots fled, "others crept under their beds," while still others fought back "most courageously." This only drove Mason and his men to greater fury. "We must burn them," Mason later recalled himself shouting,[49] whereupon he set fire to the mats and wigwams, and then wrote a description of the scene of the conflagration,

> And, indeed such a dreadful Terror did the Almighty let fall upon their Spirits, that they would fly from us and run into the very Flames, where many of them perished . . . [And] God was above them, who laughed his Enemies and the Enemies of his People to Scorn, making them as a fiery Oven: thus were the Stout Hearted spoiled, have slept their last Sleep, and none of their Men could find their Hands: Thus did the Lord judge among the Heathen, filling the Place with dead Bodies![50]

Cotton Mather, a prominent Puritan minister, later wrote that "in little more than one hour, five or six hundred of these barbarians were dismissed from a world that was burdened with them."[51]

Richard Drinnon writes this of the Pequot massacre: "The stench of frying flesh, the flames, and the heat drove the English outside the walls." Many of the Pequots "were burnt in the fort, both men, women, and children. Others who were forced out . . . our soldiers received and entertained with the point of the sword. Down fell men, women, and children."[52]

Here is historian Clifford Trafzer's summary of this same incident: "In an hour, pious Christian soldiers and their allies nearly exterminated one group of Pequot people. Some people survived and escaped, but when Puritans captured Pequot survivors, they sold them into slavery [a la the papal bull *Romanus Pontifex*] or trolled with them in Massachusetts Bay, feeding them to the sharks. Some of the Pequots, including Sassacus, fled and lived with Mohawks and other tribes, but in one morning, Puritans crushed one of the most hostile and populous tribes in New England."[53] These killers were well aware of and very knowledgeable about their God's Word.

Mason's description of the conflagration provides a wealth of references to Holy Writ. His reference to the "dreadful terror did the Almighty let fall upon their spirits" can be traced to several Old Testament passages in which the children of Israel, God's "chosen people," are fighting and killing their enemies (the Canaanites, the Hittites, et. al.) and stealing their lands. One such reference is found in Joshua 2:9, where we find Rahab saying to Joshua's two spies reconnoitering Jericho, ". . . I know that the lord hath given you the land, and that your terror is fallen upon us, and that all the inhabitants of the land faint because of you." (KJV) The Tanakh version of Exodus 15:15–16 reads, "Now are the clans of Edom dismayed; The tribes of Moab—trembling grips them . . . terror and dread descend upon them; Through the might of your arm they are still as stone . . . ." (One is reminded of the second of the four motives for Genocide cited by Chalk and Jonassohn, "to spread 'terror' among the enemies.")[54] Here in North America, John Mason thought that God, in helping the Christian English, caused terror to fall upon the Pequots.

"God . . . Laughed the Enemies of His People to Scorn"

The idea of "laughing" someone or many to "scorn" is found quite frequently in the Bible. There are a number of Biblical verses to which John Mason may have been referring. However, we'll briefly mention only three of the many verses to show that such verses exist in the Bible.

For example, one is Job 12:4, "I am as one mocked of his neighbour, and calleth upon God, and he answereth him: the just upright man is laughed to scorn." A second is Nehemiah 2:19, and a third is Ezekiel 23:32.

The theologians say nothing significant in their discussions of these three verses. Nehemiah 2:19 talks about Nehemiah's dream and desire to rebuild the walls of Jerusalem, and the opposition of others who are critical of Nehemiah and wish him to fail. The third verse, Ezekiel 23:32, refers to the idolatry of the Israelites when they worshiped other gods beside Yahweh. In spite of these facts, the Puritans, who viewed themselves as God's people, thought that their God was "laughing to scorn" the evil and wicked Pequots

"Making them as a Fiery Oven"

The phrase "fiery oven" uttered by John Mason, as he burned the dwellings of the Pequots, comes from verses such as:

> Thine hand shall find out all thine enemies: thy right hand shall find out those that hate thee. Thou shalt make them as a fiery oven in the time of thine anger: the Lord shall swallow them up in his wrath, and the fire shall devour them. (Psalms 21:8–9, KJV)

And . . .

For, behold, the day cometh that shall burn as an oven; and all the proud, yea, and all that do wickedly, shall be stubble; and the day that cometh shall burn them, saith the Lord of hosts . . . (Malachi 4:1, KJV)

Malachi 4:1 in the King James Version corresponds to Chapter 3:19 in the Tanakh: "For lo, That day is at hand, burning like an oven. All the arrogant and all the doers of evil shall be straw . . . shall burn them [the "arrogant"] to ashes . . ."

John Mason, et. al., considered themselves God's people and regarded the Pequots and other Indigenous Peoples as "enemies" and "sinners"—to not only the Western Europeans but also to the Jewish/Christian God. Thus, the English colonists believed that the Jewish/Christian God was helping them to fry the 900 Pequots, that the Jewish and Christian God was causing "terror" to fall upon the Pequots, and that the Lord was "making them to burn as a fiery oven," and, finally, that the Lord was judging the "enemies," by helping the colonizers perpetrate the Pequot Holocaust Readers can determine for themselves if the Christian colonists accurately applied the lessons of the Bible to their dealings with the Pequots.

"Judging the Heathen, Filling the Places with Dead Bodies"

He shall judge among the heathen, he shall fill the places with the dead bodies: he shall wound the heads ["break the leaders"] over many countries. (Psalm 110:6, KJV)

He [the Lord] works judgment upon the nations, heaping up bodies, crushing heads far and wide. (Tanakh)

Many times as I was researching the Bible verses quoted in relation to the holocaust and slaughter of the Pequots, I was amazed by the mass murderers' knowledge of Scripture. This one event, the Pequot Holocaust of 1637, plainly demonstrates how Bible verses were used to justify the mass murder of Indigenous Peoples. This genocidal event clearly illustrates the belief that these Christian English truly regarded themselves as the "chosen people," symbolic Israelites if you will; that they believed that Jewish/

Christian God of the Old Testament was helping them; and that they believed the "enemies" were the Indigenous Peoples (as had been the godless
Hittites and Canaanites). They further believed that the Pequot lands were
not only the "promised land," or the symbolic Canaan, "the land of milk
and honey," but also their "inheritance."

Basically, their God, the Old Testament God, had given them a license
to kill, and it was open season on Indigenous Peoples, particularly the Pequot. Stannard says something similar: "The colonists simply wanted to
kill Indians."[55] In another place, Stannard writes, "Hunting redskins became for the time being [17th and 18th centuries] a popular sport in New
England . . ."[56] As Vine Deloria, Jr. puts it, "The Country was founded in
violence. It worships violence, and it will continue to live violently."[57]

Sweet Sacrifices, Burnt Offerings, and Sweet Savour

William Bradford, the governor of Plymouth Colony, described the
British reaction to the Pequot conflagration:

> It was a fearful sight to see them thus frying in the fire and the streams of
> blood quenching the same, and horrible was the stink and scent thereof; but
> the victory seemed a sweet sacrifice, and they gave the praise thereof to God,
> who had wrought so wonderfully for them, thus, to enclose their enemies in
> their hand and give them so speedy a victory over so proud and insulting an
> enemy.[58]

Bradford's phrase, "the victory seemed a sweet sacrifice," is derived from
a number of Old Testament verses in which rams or lambs were offered up
to God for the sins of the people. One such verse, among dozens, is Leviticus 8:21, ". . . and Moses burnt the whole ram upon the altar: it was a burnt
sacrifice for a sweet savour, and an offering made by fire unto the Lord; as
the Lord commanded Moses." (KJV)

The Torah version reads, ". . . Moses turned all of the ram into smoke on
the altar: that was a burnt offering for a pleasing odor, an offering by fire
to the Lord . . ."

The meaning of this verse, in both versions, is very clear: the burning of
the ram was an act of worship to Yahweh. It is also apparent that the Christian English considered, in a similar grisly way, the burning by fire of the
Pequot was, literally, "a sweet sacrifice" and produced "a sweet-smelling
savour" (in spite of the fact that Bradford also wrote, "horrible was the
stink and scent thereof").

Thus, the Christian English "gave the praise thereof to God."

Another verse that refers to "a burnt offering," or "sacrifice" and "sweet savour" is Exodus 29:18, "And thou shalt burn the whole ram upon the altar: it is a burnt offering unto the Lord: it is a sweet savour, and offering made by fire unto the Lord." (KJV) The Torah reads, ". . . Moses turned all of the ram into smoke on the altar: that was a burnt offering for a pleasing odor, and offering by fire to the Lord—as the Lord had commanded Moses."

"An Holy Priesthood"

Protestants are taught that they, as Christians, are "an holy priesthood." Every Christian is a priest (in contrast to only ordained men being priests in Catholicism) according to I Peter 2:5: "Ye also, as lively stones, are built up a spiritual house, an holy priesthood, to offer up spiritual sacrifices, acceptable to God by Jesus Christ." (KJV)

Apparently, the Christian English, William Bradford, John Mason, John Underhill, et. al., were exercising their godly function as part of the holy priesthood to "offer up spiritual sacrifices," viz., the frying in the fire of the Pequots, "acceptable to God by Jesus Christ." The Christian Euro-Americans were merely obeying their Lord God and fulfilling His will as "holy priests."

" Praising God"

The idea of "praising God," to quote Bradford's clause, "and they gave the praise thereof to God," is found in numerous verses both in the Old and New testaments. For purposes of space, I will quote only two of them. One is found in II Chronicles 20:22, "And when they began to sing and to praise, the Lord set ambushments against the children of Ammon, Moab, and Mount Seir, which were come against Judah; and they were smitten." (KJV) Here the Israelites are praising God for his help and deliverance from their enemies.

Another verse is I Peter 2:9, "But ye are a chosen generation, a royal priesthood, a holy nation, a peculiar people; that ye should shew forth the praises of Him who hath called you out of darkness into his marvellous light:" (KJV).

The Christian English knew the Bible well and would have been familiar with these verses. They're illuminating because they give the reader insight into the Christian Euro-American mentality. By applying terms such as "chosen," "royal," and "a holy nation" to themselves, the Christian English elevated themselves to a position of superior morality and spirituality in contrast to the Pequots, and to all other Indigenous Peoples, who they considered uncivilized, pagans, barbaric, savage, and who needed to come from the "darkness" into the "marvelous light" of the gospel of Jesus Christ. They actually believed they were doing good and doing right in burning the Pequots alive, because they were offering a sacrifice unto God, an act of worship. Therefore, in this genocidal incident in 1637, the Pequot Holocaust, there was no sin, no crime against humanity.

Brandon writes of the wholesale massacres of non-combatants—women, children, "little ones, elders—that could scarcely be credited if not for the fact that it was the Puritans themselves [as we have seen above] who recorded them, often with relish."[59] For example, the shrieks of several hundred victims, mostly women and children, dying in the burning of a large Narraganset community in the winter of 1675 "greatly moved some of our soldiers. They were much in doubt and afterward inquired whether burning their enemies alive could be consistent with humanity and the benevolent principles of the gospel."[60] One suspects that this twinge of conscience by the Christian English was of little consolation to the Narragansett dead.

Bradford's phrase referring to God "who had wrought so wonderfully for them" can be found in I Samuel 6:6, "wherefore then do you harden your hearts, as the Egyptians and Pharaoh hardened their hearts? When he had wrought ["worked"][61] wonderfully among them, did they not let the people go, and they departed?" (KJV)

It appears that Bradford is comparing the English massacre of the Pequots and the burning of their town to the deliverance of the children of Israel out of bondage in Egypt. In both instances, God was helping the Israelites and the symbolic Israelites, the Euro-Americans, specifically, the Christian English.

Finally, Bradford's phrase referring to God's enclosing "their enemies [i.e., the Pequots] in their hands" can be found in the Old Testament:

And the Lord gave unto Israel all the land which he sware to give unto their fathers; and they possessed it, and dwelt therein. And the Lord gave them rest round about, according to all that he sware unto the fathers: and there stood not a man of all their enemies before them; the Lord delivered all their enemies into their hand. (Joshua 21 43–44, KJV)

Thus, did the Lord deliver the enemies, the Pequots, into the hands of the Christian English, the "chosen people" of God. Yea, the Christian English possessed the land and dwelt therein, in the land of the Pequots, at least, according to Bradford's interpretation of Holy Writ.

Let's conclude this chapter with a quotation from Philip Jenkins: "If Christians or Jews needed biblical texts to justify deeds of terrorism or ethnic slaughter, their main problem would be an embarrassment of riches."[62]

As you can see, the Pequot Holocaust provides an abundance of such "riches." The Pequot Holocaust of 1637, from the point of view of the colonizers and the murderers, was an instance of God helping His people, and an act of worship to God. The incineration of the Pequots was a "sweet sacrifice," a sweet-smelling "savour," unto the Lord.

Endnotes

1. *American Indian History: Five Centuries of Conflict and Coexistence*, by Robert Venables. Santa Fe, NM: Clear Light Publishers, 2004, p. 59.

2. Ibid.

3. *The Bethany Parallel Commentary On The New Testament*. Minneapolis: Bethany House Publishers, 1983, p. 1046.

4. Ibid.

5. Ibid.

6. *A Little Matter of Genocide: Holocaust and Denial in the America, 1492 to the Present*, by Ward Churchill. San Francisco, City Light Books, 1997, pp. 169–170.

7. Ibid., p. 169.

8. *The Last American: The Indian in American Culture*, by William Brandon. New York: McGraw-Hill, 1974, p. 202.

9. "Pensees," by Blaise Pascal, 1670, Section XIV, No. 894.

10. Brandon, op. cit., p. 177.

11. Ibid., 171.

12. Ibid.

13. Ibid.

14. Ibid., p. 202.

15. *Divinity of Doubt: The God Question*, by Vincent Bugliosi. Philadelphia: Vanguard Press, 2011, p. 145.

16) Ibid.

17. Ibid.

18. Churchill, op. cit., p. 172.

19. Merriam-Webster's Collegiate Dictionary Eleventh Edition, 2012, p. 593.

20. *Laying Down the Sword: Why We Can't Ignore the Bible's Violent Verses*, by Richard Jenkins. New York: Harper One, 2011, p. 6.

21. *American Holocaust: The Conquest of the New World*, by David Stannard. Oxford: Oxford University Press, 1992, pp. 111, 172.

22. Ibid., p. 111.

23. Ibid., p. 114.

24. Ibid.

25. "Trauma and Recovery: the Aftermath of Violence," by Judith Herman, MD, in *Domestic Abuse to Political Terror*. New York: Basic Books, 1997, p. 135.

26. The Torah. Jewish Publication Society of America, 1967, p. 328.

27. BPCOT, p. 337.

28. Ibid.

29. Ibid.

30. *The God Delusion,* by Richard Dawkins. London: Black Swan, 2016, p. 51.

31. BPCOT, p. 337.

32. "Red Lake Indian Reservation" http://en.wikipedia.org/wiki/Red_Lake_Indian_Reservation

33. Jenkins, op. cit., p. 33.

34. BPCOT, p. 416

35. Stannard, op. cit., p. 114.

36. Stannard, op. cit., p. 177.

37. Ibid.

38. Ibid.

39. Ibid., p. 112.

40. Ibid., p. 111. The phrase "smite our enemies in the hinder parts" is found in Psalms 78:66.

41. BPCOT, p. 1093.

42. Stannard, op. cit., p. 111.

43. Ibid., p. 120.

44. *Facing West: The Metaphysics of Indian-Hating & Empire-Building* by Richard Drinnon. Norman, OK: University of Oklahoma Press, 1997, p. 332.

45. *As Long As The Grass Shall Grow And Rivers Flow*, by Clifford Trafzer. New York: Harcourt College Publishers, 2000, p. 73.

46. Churchill, op. cit., p. 171.

47. Ibid.

48. Ibid.

49. Stannard, op. cit, p. 113.

50. Ibid., pp. 113–114.

51. Ibid., p. 114.

52. Drinnon, op. cit., p. 42.

53. Trafzer, op. cit., p. 74.

54. *The History And Sociology of Genocide*, by Frank Chalk and Kurt Jonassoh, New Haven, CT: Yale University Press, 1990, p. 29.

55. Stannard, op. cit., p. 112.

56. Ibid., p. 116.

57. *Custer Died For Your Sins*, by Vine Deloria, Jr. Norman, OK: University of Oklahoma Press, 1988, pp. 255–256.

58. Stannard, op. cit., p. 114.

59. *Indians*, by William Brandon. Boston, Houghton Mifflin, 1961 p. 176.

60. Brandon, *Last Americans*, op. cit., p. 207.

61. Stannard, op. cit., p. 114.

62. Jenkins, op. cit., p.6.

4

MANIFEST DESTINY
The Chosen People and the Promised Land

"For thou are an holy people unto the Lord thy God: the Lord thy God hath chosen thee to be a special people unto himself, above all people that are upon the face of the earth." (Deuteronomy 7:6, KJV)

And Abram passed through the land unto the place of Sichem, unto the plain of Moreh. And the Canaanite was then in the land. And the Lord appeared unto Abram and said, unto thy seed will I give this land . . .
(Genesis 12:6–7, KJV)

Manifest Destiny was devised in the 19th century and was the racist ideology which fueled invasion, mass killing, religious suppression, and the stealing of nearly an entire continent. It provided the rationale for the expansion of the United States, its empire-building, and the mass murder of its Indigenous peoples. (One could well argue that a similar ideology underlay all of the atrocities perpetrated by the Western European coloniz-ers from 1492 on.)

Historian David Stannard says, "[T]he Europeans of all eras considered themselves to be 'chosen people,' the inhabitants of the center and most civil domain of human life."[1] Under this belief system, Euro-Americans believed that "through divine ordination and the natural superiority of the white race, they had a right (and, indeed, an obligation) to seize and oc-cupy all of North America."[2]

After the colonial uprising of 1776 and the War of 1812, the U.S. had consolidated its power considerably, to the extent that many Indigenous nations were vulnerable to military invasion by U.S. forces, "pre-emptive strikes," if you will. The Indian Removal Act (an official policy of ethnic cleansing and land theft) was passed in 1830 by the U.S. Congress and was enthusiastically implemented by President Andrew Jackson ("the Devil," according to the Choctaws).[3] Thus, the removal, extermination, expropriation, exploitation, and subjugation of the Indigenous Peoples began in earnest in the eastern half of the United States.

The Indian Removal Act of 1830 led to what many white U.S. historians refer to as "the winning of the West" or "westward expansion," or what Richard Drinnon calls "the Metaphysics of Indian-Hating and Empire-Building"[4] in the mid and late 1800s. It was a time that Indigenous peoples remember as a time of resistance and a desperate struggle to defend and to protect the ancient homelands, the sacred sites, and burial sites, to defend the Indigenous ways of life, and to defend our freedom to live our lives as we wish.

The phrase "Manifest Destiny" was first used by John L. O'Sullivan, a lawyer, a journalist, and an ardent Jacksonian Democrat, in an article, "Annexation," in the *Democratic Review* in July 1845. O'Sullivan believed that the United States had an almost sacred duty to spread over all North America. He wrote that those who opposed the annexation of Texas were "limiting our greatness and checking the fulfillment of our manifest destiny to overspread the continent allotted by Providence for the free development of our yearly multiplying millions."[5] He capitalized the term "Providence," which means "God conceived as the power sustaining and guiding human destiny."[6]

Senator Thomas Hart Benton wrote in 1846, one year after O'Sullivan coined the term, "it would seem that the White race had alone received the divine command, to subdue and replenish the earth," and because "this land had been created for use . . . by the white races . . . according to the intentions of the Creator, for it is the only race that has obeyed it—the only race that hunts out new and distant lands, and even a New World, to subdue and replenish."[7] This is an excellent example of white supremacist ideology. The Indigenous Peoples were to be eradicated, removed, or to be drastically changed to make way for civilization. Benton's reference to "subdue the earth and replenish" is found in Genesis 1:28, "And God blessed them and God said unto them Be fruitful, and multiply and replenish the earth, and subdue it . . . ." (KJV) This connection between Scripture and massive land-theft is too obvious to further elaborate.

Another excellent example of "chosen people" and "promised land" notions, and white supremacy, can be found in the words of Senator Allen Beveridge in a speech to the U.S. Senate in 1900:

We will not renounce our part in the mission of our race, trustee, under God, of the civilization of the world. And we will move forward to our work . . . with gratitude for a task worthy of our strength, and thanksgiving to Almighty God that He has marked us as His chosen people, henceforth to lead in the regeneration of the world . . . Mr. President, this question is deeper than any question of party politics; deeper than any question of isolated policy of our country even; deeper even than any question of constitutional power. It is elemental. It is racial. God has not been preparing the English-speaking and Teutonic Peoples for a thousand years for nothing but vain and idle self-contemplation and self-admiration. No! He has made us the master organizers of the world to establish systems where chaos reigns. He has given us the spirit of progress to overwhelm the forces of reaction throughout the earth. He has made us adept in government that we may administer government among savage and senile peoples.

Were it not for such a force as this the world would relapse into barbarism and night. And of all our races, He has marked the American [read "white"] people to finally lead in the regeneration of the world. This is the divine mission of America, and it holds for us all the profit, all the glory, all the happiness possible for man . . .

At least Beveridge had the perhaps inadvertent honesty to place the term "profit" before "glory" and "happiness." Note that he says that God has "marked us," that is U.S. whites, as "His chosen people." His comments remind one of Rudyard Kipling's poem, "The White Man's Burden" (1898). Kipling wrote the poem "to remind" the United States of "her responsibilities toward Cuba and the Philippines consequent upon her victory over Spain in 1898." The poem's premise is that "the 'White Man' was carrying out a divine and completely altruistic mission in conquering and ruling the lands of those of darker skin."[9]

Today these racist, imperialist notions live on in the form of "American exceptionalism," which is expressed through military attacks upon and occupation of (invariably nonwhite) lands, plus the instigation of coups, support of brutally repressive governments, and the training of death squads and torturers. Iraq is but the worst recent example. In the 20th century, victim countries included Vietnam, Laos, Cambodia, Iran, Mexico, Nicaragua, Honduras, Guatemala, Chile, El Salvador, the Dominican Republic, Haiti, Cuba, China, Palestine, the Philippines, the Congo—the list goes on. The United States "has always been a militantly imperialistic world power eagerly grasping for economic control over weaker nations."[10] Amazingly,

all too many Euro-Americans still wonder why so many people throughout the world hate the United States of America.

The Chosen People and The Promised Land

The "chosen people" and "promised land" notions from the Old Testament were the basis for the concept and practices of Manifest Destiny: land
theft, violation of treaties, enslavement, extermination or removal of Indigenous Peoples from their ancient and ancestral homelands, suppression
of Indigenous religious ceremonies, and prohibition of Native languages.
There is a wealth of Old Testament verses from which this idea, Manifest
Destiny, is derived. We'll only discuss a few here. (See Appendix B for additional verses regarding the "Chosen People," Canaan, and the "Promised
Land" notions.)

Concerning the "chosen people" notion, consider this:

> For thou art an holy people unto the Lord thy God: The Lord thy God hath
> chosen thee to be a special [or chosen] people unto himself, above all people
> that are upon the face of the earth. (Deuteronomy 7:6, KJV)

Consider also:

> For thou are an holy people unto the Lord thy God, and the Lord hath chosen
> thee to be a peculiar people unto himself [or, "a people for His own posses-
> sion"], above all the nations that are upon the earth.
> (Deuteronomy 14:2, KJV).

The Torah renders Deuteronomy 7:6 as "For you are a people consecrated to the Lord your God: of all the people on earth the Lord your God
chose you to be his treasured people." And it renders Deuteronomy 14:2
as "For you are a people consecrated to the Lord your God: the Lord your
God chose you from among all other peoples on earth to be His treasured
people."

Note the terms and phrases applied to the Israelites by both the KJV
and the Torah: "holy people," "sacred," "chosen people," "special people," "consecrated," and "treasured people." As far as I can determine,
Yahweh, the Jewish God, applied these terms *only* to the Israelites. He did
not "choose" the Western Europeans or Euro-Americans as his "chosen
people" or his "treasured people"—or at least "He who sees all things," the
omnipotent, omniscient deity, failed to mention it when He had the opportunity.

However, in their arrogance and white supremacist attitudes, the Western Europeans and Euro-Americans applied these same adjectives to themselves. Even today, many Euro-Americans regard themselves and their nation state as "exceptional."

If this is the mentality of a people, then it is predictable that in their dealings with other peoples, whom they consider inferior, they will steal, kill, remove, occupy, exploit, suppress, and oppress—do anything they damn well please—and then think they are doing God's work. Indeed, that's exactly what happened in the Americas. What a God! What a chosen people! After all, according to the very popular song, "America," often proffered as a kinder, gentler alternative to the jingoistic "God Bless America," "God shed his grace on thee." And that God is, of course, the monster God of the Old Testament and Christianity.

The Promised Land

The "promised land" idea is found in a number of Old Testament books, notably Genesis, Leviticus, and Numbers. The following verses illustrate the idea:

> And Abram passed through the land unto the place of Sichem, unto the plain of Moreh. And the Canaanite was then in the land. And the Lord appeared unto Abram and said, Unto thy seed will I give this land.
> (Genesis 12:6–7, KJV)

Note that the Canaanite was "then in the land." That is, they were already living there. Apparently, this made no difference to Yahweh.

> Abram dwelled in the land of Canaan . . . For all the land which thou seest, to thee will I give it, and to thy seed for ever. (Genesis 13:12, 15, KJV)

> But I have said unto you, Ye shall inherit their land, and I will give it unto you to possess it, a land that floweth with milk and honey . . .
> (Leviticus 20:24, KJV)

> If the Lord delight in us, then He will bring us into this land, and give it to us: a land which flows with milk and honey. (Numbers 14:8, NKJV)

The Torah renders Genesis 12:6–7 this way: "The Canaanites were then in the land." And it renders Genesis 13:12 and 15 as, "Abram remained in the land of Canaan . . . 'for I give all the land that you see to you and your offspring forever.'" It renders Leviticus 20:24 as, ". . . You shall possess their land, for I will give it to you to possess, a land flowing with milk and honey." And lastly, Numbers 14:8 reads, "If the Lord is pleased with us, He will bring us into that land, a land that flows with milk and honey, and give it to us;"

Euro-American Christians, and Euro-Americans in general, took and applied the above-quoted verses, believing they were God's "chosen people." The lands of the Indigenous Peoples were the "promised land." And, the Native Peoples were the equivalent of the godless and pagan Canaanites and Hittites who needed to be exterminated or driven out of the "promised land." It made as little difference to the Euro-Americans that the Native Peoples had been living in these lands for thousands upon thousands of years, as had the Canaanites, Hittites, et. al., in the Old Testament "promised land." And, of course, as with the Israelite royalty the U.S. government saw no need to pay for stolen lands.

The Indigenous Peoples of the United States, like the Canaanites and Hittites of the Old Testament before the Israelites, had no rights that the white man or the Israelites needed to respect. Thus, if God's invading "chosen people" killed the "Indians"/Canaanites, who resisted the theft of their lands, the Euro-Americans/Israelites were merely fulfilling God's purpose and were following God's will.

They were merely doing what is commanded in Deuteronomy, that is, to kill and steal. Another passage reads:

> When the Lord thy God shall bring thee into the land whither thou goest to possess it, and hath cast out many nations before thee, the Hittites, and the Girgashites, and the Amorites, and Canaanites, and the Perizzites, and the Hivites, and the Jebusites, seven nations great and mightier than thou; And when the Lord thy God shall deliver them before thee; thou shalt smite them and utterly destroy them . . . (Deuteronomy 7:1–2)

This is the God, who, supposedly, is all-good, just, and plenteous in mercy.

Let's compare these Old Testament genocidal sentiments with the statements and actions of some American "heroes," starting with Andrew Jackson. On March 27, 1814, during the Creek War (1813–1814), Jackson and his men massacred approximately 800 Muskogee (or "Creek," the colonizer name), and then mutilated the corpses of the bodies of the men, women, and children they had massacred. Jackson said that he preserved "the scalps of my killed." Jackson also cut off the noses to count, and sliced "long strips of flesh from their bodies to tan and turn into bridle 'reins.'" This same U.S. hero, Andrew Jackson, in the 1830s, recommended that U.S. troops "specifically seek out and systematically kill Indian women and children who were in hiding, in order to complete their extermination."[11]

Many Euro-Americans still revere and honor this "hero." Their ancestors elected this murderer as U.S. president in 1828, and later put a picture of Jackson on their twenty-dollar bill. One hopes the reader can understand why the Muskogee People, the Choctaw People, and other Indigenous Peoples do not regard Andrew Jackson so highly.

(Speaking of the twenty-dollar bill, Harriet Tubman, a genuine American hero, a former slave, abolitionist, and women's rights activist, will eventually replace slave holder and mass murderer Andrew Jackson on the twenty-dillar bill, though the Trump Administration has temporarily blocked this long-overdue change.[12] There is a delicious irony and symbolism, and karmic justice involved in a black woman replacing a monstrous white man, and a former slave replacing a slave owner on U.S. currency.)

As another example, the Rev. Colonel John Chivington, of Sand Creek Massacre infamy, said in a speech that his policy was to "kill and scalp all, little and big." He also said that "nits make lice, since Indians were lice, their children were nits—and the only to get rid of lice was to kill the nits as well."[13]

General Philip Sheridan provides a third example. He believed in "total war," and said, "If a village is attacked, and women and children killed, the responsibility is not with the soldier, but with the people whose crimes necessitated the attack."[14] Brandon writes of this statement, "The frontier, with the usual frontier tendency toward a policy of extermination, generally approved."[15] Sheridan also said, "The only good Indians I ever saw were dead."[16] Brandon says that this statement of Sheridan was "the extermination philosophy in a nutshell."[17]

These types of statements are but the most prominent ones which illustrate the concept known by the rather pretentious name, Manifest Destiny. Note the expression of this mind-set at the highest levels of U.S. government, in the United States Congress (Congressional Record 2462):

> Congress must apprise the Indian that he can no longer stand as a breakwater against the constant tide of civilization . . . An idle and thriftless race of savages cannot be permitted to stand guard at the treasure vaults of the nation which hold our gold and silver . . . the prospector and miner may enter and by enriching himself enrich the nation and bless the world by the result of his toil.[18]

Note the terminology—"idle," "thriftless," "savages"—which is applied to the Native Peoples. Also, note the phrase "the treasure vaults of the nation which hold *our* gold and silver." (italics added) To sum this all up, Native Peoples had, and have, no rights to their own lands on which they had lived for thousands of years, no rights to the resources, the gold, the silver, the lakes, the forests, farmlands, etc. Those are for the "chosen people."

The genocidal destruction of First Nations Peoples was part and parcel of Manifest Destiny.

In fact, "By the mid-19th century, U.S. policymakers and military commanders were stating—openly, frequently, and in plain English—that their objective was no less than "the complete extermination of any native people who resisted being dispossessed of their lands, subordinated to federal authority, and assimilated into the colonizing culture."[19] By the end of the 19th century, all the lands, approximately three billion acres, had been stolen by the United States government and its Euro-American citizenry; at the same time, the Native population had been reduced to approximately 237,000 in 1900, according the U.S. Bureau of Census; this was down from an estimated 16,000,000 circa 1500,[20] and a conservative estimate is that 110,000,000 Indigenous Peoples had been killed in the Americas over the previous four centuries, in "the most massive act of genocide in the history of the world."[21] This monstrous genocide was not perpetrated by the dark-skinned, long-haired, non-Christian, non-English-speaking "savages," nor by the Nazis, nor by the Russian or Chinese Communists, nor by Muslims, nor by Al Qaeda or ISIS. It was perpetrated, primarily, by white allegedly civilized Christians.

Manifest Destiny in Action

In the 18th and 19th centuries, U.S. military and paramilitary troops, as well as settlers and farmers, perpetrated hundreds of genocidal massacres or cruel removals all over the U.S., starting in the East, with many of the worst atrocities occurring in the West. Yet even today the extent of these crimes is not widely known. David Bolin comments that "the best interests of the American philosophy of education would not be served if third-graders were taught that during the 19th century" the Euro-American "farmer was perhaps the most ruthless and relentless exterminator of the Indians, or that American frontiersmen, cowboys, and soldiers often excelled in the use of barbaric torture, brutality, and slaughter in their encounters with Indians."[22]

Minnesota

Then you shall drive out all the inhabitants of the land from before you . . .
(Numbers 33:52, NKJV)

In the early 1860s, in the state of Minnesota, there was talk that the war with the Dakota, in 1862, was deliberately provoked by the Euro-Minnesotans as an excuse for exterminating the Dakota, or at least driving them out of the state and opening their lands to settlement ("to possess it"). Roy Meyer, a white historian, says that there is not enough evidence to support this contention,[23] although I suspect that could very well have been the case. I say this because there definitely is a difference in the way Indigenous Peoples look at history than the way the Euro-Americans (in this case, Euro-Minnesotans) look at the same history. People who had their lands stolen will definitely look at history differently than the people whose ancestors stole the lands. In any event, there was land-lust as well as blood-lust. Even though Meyer says there isn't enough evidence to support the contention that the war was deliberately provoked by the whites, Meyer does raises the question of white land-lust, "What better way was there to mask this greed than to wave the bloody shirt and call righteously for the extermination of the 'inhuman fiends' who had heretofore stood in the way of Manifest Destiny, Minnesota brand?"[24]

The Bible passage quoted above, Numbers 33:52–53, contains phrases such as "You shall drive out," and "dispossess the inhabitants of the land." In Minnesota, Governor Alexander Ramsey, the military, and the Euro-Minnesotan citizenry, self-styled "chosen people," actually did "drive out" and "dispossess" the Dakota People, the first Minnesotans, of their lands, Mini Sota Makoce, "Land Where the Waters Reflect the Skies, or Heavens."

The Minnesota State Legislature passed a law titled "An Act for the Removal of the Sisseton, Wahpaton, Mdewakanton, and Wahpakoota Bands of Sioux or Dakota Indians and for the disposition of their lands in Minnesota and Dakota,"[25] and on May 4, 1863, the Dakota People were forcibly removed, or ethnically cleansed, from their ancient homelands in Mini Sota Makoce. Even though, as far as I know, there is no documented case of a Christian Euro-Minnesotan citing Numbers 32:52–53, nor any similar Old Testament verses, the white Minnesotans most certainly did "drive out" and did "dispossess" the Dakota People.

South Dakota

And the Lord our God delivered him [Sihon] over to us: . . . And we . . . utterly destroyed the men, women, and little ones . . .
(Deuteronomy 2:33–34, NKJV)

The Wounded Knee Massacre took place on December 29, 1890 in South Dakota. Dr. Russell Thornton characterizes it as "perhaps the best-known genocide of North American Indians."[26]

The U.S. Seventh Cavalry slaughtered more than 300 Lakota People—men, women, children, babies, toddlers, and elders; the massacre was reminiscent of the Old Testament mass killings ordered by Yahweh, "kill all that hath breath," "leave no survivors."

Ward Churchill, in *A Little Matter of Genocide*, describes the bloodlust-frenzy. "On the morning of the 29th, the troops proceeded to massacre their unarmed prisoners, using both rifles and Hotchkiss [Gatling] guns carefully placed on the surrounding hills for the purpose." Then he goes on to quote Ralph Andrist's *Long Death*.[27]

[All] witnesses agree that from the moment it opened fire, [the Seventh] ceased to be a military unit and became a mass of infuriated men intent on butchery. Women and children attempted to escape by running up a dry ravine, but were pursued and slaughtered—there is no other word—by hundreds of maddened soldiers, while shells from the Hotchkiss [machine] guns, which had been moved to allow them to sweep the ravine, continued to burst among them. The line of bodies afterward was found to extend more than two miles from the camp—and they were all women and children.

A few survivors eventually found shelter in brushy gullies here and there, and their pursuers had scouts call out that women and children could come out of hiding because they had nothing to fear . . . Some small boys crept out and were surrounded by soldiers who then butchered them. Nothing Indian that lived was safe.[28]

Note the statement—"and they were all women and children." This hearkens back to the Pequot Holocaust of 1637 in which John Underhill said, "sometimes the Scripture declareth women and children must perish with their parents."[29] Clifford Trafzer quotes Black Elk's description of the Wounded Knee Massacre:

Dead and wounded women and children and little babies were scattered all along there where they had been trying to run away. . . . [S]oldiers had followed along the gulch, as they ran, and murdered them in there. Sometimes they were in heaps because they had huddled together, and some were scattered all along. Black Elk saw people who had been "torn to pieces where the wagon guns [machine guns] hit them. I saw a little baby trying to suck its mother, but she was bloody and dead." When he saw many dead Lakota, Black Elk said, "I wished that I had died too, but I was not sorry for the women and children. It was better for them to be happy in the other world, and I wanted to be there, too."[30]

Such descriptions are heart-rending, almost too much to bear. It is important for the reader to remember that the Old Testament God commanded the mass killing of innocents—women, children, and elders. Thus, if God and his "chosen people," the Euro-Americans, considered their victims (i.e., the Lakota, Dakota, and other Indigenous Peoples) to be wicked, idolaters, inferior, uncivilized, children of Satan, animals, subhuman, then, it was an act of righteousness to slaughter these savages.

L. Frank Baum, editor of South Dakota's *Aberdeen Saturday Pioneer and* the author of *The Wonderful Wizard of Oz* and other children's books, urged the "wholesale extermination" of all U.S. Native Peoples. Baum wrote:

[T]he nobility of the Redskin [referring in particular to the Lakota] is extinguished, and what few are left are a pack of whining curs who lick the hand that smites them. The Whites, by law of conquest, by justice of civilization, are masters of the American continent, and the best safety of the frontier settlements will be secured by the total annihilation of the few remaining Indians. Why not annihilation? Their glory has fled, their spirit broken, their manhood effaced; better that they should die than live the miserable wretches that they are.[31]

Four days after the Wounded Knee Massacre, Baum wrote in the *Saturday Pioneer*, "we had better, in order to protect our civilization, follow it up . . . and wipe these untamed and untamable creatures from the face of the earth."[32]

Here we see the other side of this beloved children's author: a hateful, blood-lusting zealot who would have fit right in with Yahweh's mass-murdering barbarians. As would the Seventh Cavalry, the ones who coldly and brutally carried out the Wounded Knee Massacre.

Colorado

Now go and smite Amalek, and utterly destroy all they have; do not spare
them but kill both man and woman, infant and suckling, . . .
(I Samuel 15:3, NOAB)

The Amalekites were nomadic descendants of Esau (Genesis 36:12) who
fought against Israel at Rephidim (Exodus 17:8–13) and were placed under divine judgment (Deuteronomy 25:19). The New International Version translates God's commands in I Samuel 15:3 as, ". . . totally destroy
everything that belongs to them. Do not spare them; put to death men and
women, children and infants . . ."

According to a a footnote, the phrase "totally destroy" refers to a ban
which "involved devoting cities, persons, animals, and possessions to the
Lord for destruction in accordance with Deuteronomy 7:2–6; 12:2–3; and
20:16–18."[33] The footnote goes on to say, "Although this practice was se-
vere, it was a just punishment."[34]

The U.S. Army, along with civilian Euro-Coloradoans "did not spare
them; put to death men and women, children and infants" on November
29, 1864 at the Sand Creek Massacre. The commander of the troops was
Colonel John Chivington, who was also a Methodist minister. (A side note:
Reportedly, Chivington, a six-feet-four, 260 pound man, when he would
preach, would place his two pistols on either side of the Bible on the lectern
of the Denver Methodist Church, and "then proceed to dispense with either
hot hell or hot lead.")[35] The Reverend Chivington and his troops butchered
approximately 500 Cheyenne, mostly old men, women, children, infants,
and toddlers.

> A white witness later testified, "They were scalped, their brains were knocked
> out; the [white] men used their knives, ripped open women, clubbed little
> children, knocked them in the head with their guns, beat their brains out,
> mutilated their bodies in every sense of the word . . . worse mutilated than
> any I ever saw before . . . children two or three months old; all lying there,
> from sucking infants to warriors.[36]

Patrick Mendoza's book, *Song of Sorrow* (1993), states, "The orders by
Colonel Chivington and Colonel Shoup were simple: there were to be no
prisoners!"[37]

Regarding George Bent, a mixed-race (white/Cheyenne) ex-Confeder-
ate soldier, Mendoza says:

What he and his Cheyenne companions witnessed on their run [from the massacre] was horrible—old men, women and children, "lying thickly scattered on the sand, some dead, and the rest too badly wounded to move."[38]

As the wounded Bent took cover in the hole, Chivington's troops surrounded their position. Worked into a killing frenzy, the soldiers poured murderous fire into the besieged Cheyenne shelter . . . Under night's cover, this band of half-naked survivors escaped and fled north.[39]

When the morning first exploded into gunfire, White Antelope emerged from his lodge with his arms raised and shouted in English, "Stop. Stop!" But the carnage continued. When he realized it was hopeless, he stood tall and folded this arms and began to sing the Cheyenne Death Song . . . Although unarmed, seventy-five years old White Antelope was shot down and killed.

A soldier dismounted from his horse and took out his knife. He then scalped the old chief. He also cut off White Antelope's nose, ears and private parts and bragged he was going to make a new tobacco pouch from the freshly severed genitalia.[40]

[One woman was lying] whose leg had been broken by a shell. A soldier came up to her with drawn saber. She raised her arm to protect herself when he struck, breaking her arm; she rolled over and raised her other arm when he struck breaking it, then he left without killing her.[41]

Robert [Bent] also witnessed a group of about forty women run to a gully for protection. When the soldiers approached, the women sent a young six-year-old girl out with a white flag. He remembered the sight of this child as she was shot in the head by a soldier. The others were also killed. He watched in silent rage as soldiers raped, scalped, and mutilated the women—one young mother was found with her unborn child cut out and lying beside her.[42]

Historian Stannard records another eyewitness:

There was one little child, probably three years old, just big enough to walk through the sand . . . The little fellow was perfectly naked, traveling on the sand. I saw one man get off his horse, at a distance of about seventy-five yards, and draw up his rifle and fire—he missed the child. Another man came up and said, "Let me try the son of a bitch; I can hit him." He got down off his horse, kneeled down and fired at the little child, but he missed him. A third man came up and made a similar remark, and fired, and the little fellow dropped.[43]

It's hard to interpret these events in any other way than that these atrocities, these heinous acts, these crimes against humanity, were perpetrated by devils directly from the pits of the Christian hell.

The Methodist minister, Rev. Colonel John Chivington, himself provided this revelation into his character and his "morality":

> Damn any man who sympathizes with Indians! . . . I have come to kill Indians, and believe it is right and honorable to use any means under God's heaven to kill Indians . . . Kill and scalp all, big and little; nits make lice.[44]

One presumes the Lord God was well pleased with his servant, John Chivington.

President Theodore Roosevelt said that the Sand Creek Massacre was "as righteous and beneficial a deed as ever took place on the frontier."[45] Yet, this racist, who praised this genocidal act, is revered by most of white America, and his visage desecrates a sacred place to not only the Dakota/Lakota/Nakota, but also to other Native Peoples, at Mt. Rushmore.

Ward Churchill has this to say about the Sand Creek Massacre:

> [W]ith the active encouragement of their officers [the soldiers] not only scalped the dead, but performed an altogether astonishing array of other mutilations, including the severing of male genitalia to be turned into tobacco pouches. When the "Bloody third" returned to parade triumphantly down the streets of Denver a short while later, the white Coloradoan citizenry turned out to cheer them as they rode by, waving scalps and with other such "trophies"—female genitals stretched over hats and saddle pommels, for example—plainly in view.[46]

The military unit that carried out the atrocity, the Third Colorado Volunteer Cavalry Regiment, had been formed "exclusively for the purpose of killing Cheyennes, Arapahos, and any other native peoples they might encounter over a 100-day period," according to a poster created on August 13, 1864 under the auspices of Colorado Governor John Evans.[47] This call for volunteers to pursue and kill Native Peoples "was done in a climate which was exterminationist in the extreme."[48] As Trafzer puts it, Governor Evans "proclaimed open season" on Native Peoples.[49]

William N. Byers, the founder and editor of Denver's *Rocky Mountain News*, like his counterparts Frank Baum in South Dakota and Jane Swisshelm in Minnesota, was an advocate of genocide. Byers wrote, "Eastern humanitarians who believe in the superiority of the Indian race will raise a terrible howl over this policy [of extermination], but it is no time to split hairs nor stand upon delicate compunctions of conscience. Self preservation demands decisive action, and the only way to secure it is through a few months of active extermination against the red devils."[50]

On the same day Byers wrote this statement, Governor John Evans declared, "any man who kills a hostile Indian is a patriot."[51] Governor Evans is also quoted as saying, in the Annual Report of the U.S. Commissioner of Indian Affairs, 1863, that if there were a war against the Cheyennes, "it would be a war of extermination to them."[51]

These statements illustrate how horrific this event, the Sand Creek Massacre, was, and continues to be today. It displays the barbarity, cruelty, and savagery of the white soldiers, of Governor Evans and the white citizenry. It displays the racial hatred for not only the Cheyenne and Arapaho, but also for all the Indigenous Peoples of the Americas.

Even though the Euro-Coloradoans may or may not have been quoting the scriptures—the primary author of the massacre, Methodist minister John Chivington, was well aware of the relevant genocidal commands of the Old Testament God—they certainly were doing, in spirit, what the Lord wanted: to kill every man, woman, infant, "little ones," and elders of the hated target groups. As the Rev. Colonel Chivington said, he would "use any means under God's heaven to kill Indians."[52]

Stannard makes a comment relevant to the Sand Creek Massacre and other atrocities:

> [M]assacres of this sort were so numerous and routine that recounting them eventually becomes numbing, and, of course, far more carnage of this sort occurred than ever was recorded. So, no matter how numbed—or even, shamefully, bored—we might become at hearing story after story of the mass murder, pillage, rape, and torture of America's Native Peoples, we can be assured that however much we hear, we have heard only a small fragment of what there was to tell.[53]

Kansas

> . . . And ye shall dispossess the inhabitants of the land, and dwell therein: for I have given you the land to possess it. (Numbers 33:53)

Here, I'll be quoting liberally from Dr. Clifford Trafzer's *As Long as The Grass Shall Grow and Rivers Flow*:

During the 1870s, white citizens wanted to purge Kansas of Native Peoples. One newspaper editor characterized Indians in Kansas as "a set of miserable, dirty, lousy, blanketed, thieving, lying, sneaking, murdering, graceless, faithless, gut-eating skunks who should be 'exterminated.'"[54]

(This nearly exactly parallels newspaper editor Jane Swisshelm, of St. Cloud, Minnesota, who in 1862 compared the Dakota People of Minnesota to animals, and wrote, "Exterminate the wild beasts.")[55] Dr. Trafzer continues:

> Instead of killing them immediately, the United States moved the Kansas [Kaws] to the northwestern portion of Indian Territory and Osages east, onto lands known as the Cherokee Outlet . . . but within a short time the Euro-Kansan Christians attacked them, murdering, burning, and driving them out of their homes.[56]

Even though the Euro-Kansans may not have been quoting Numbers 33:52, "and ye shall drive out all the inhabitants of the land from before you," they were, indeed, following this command of the Lord with "holy" exuberance. And the racial epithets Trafzer quotes are typical.

California

> And the Lord hearkened to the voice of Israel, and delivered up the Canaanites; and they utterly destroyed them and their cities; and he called the name of the place Hormah ["utter destruction" or "ban"].
> (Numbers 21:3, KJV)

In California, the genocidal campaign—advocated by the governor and other high officials, as in Minnesota, Colorado, and Kansas—resulted in extermination of 95% to 98% of California's Native People. California governor Peter Burnett's 1851 message to the legislature called for the "total eradication of the natives."[57] Burnett, like Governor Alexander Ramsey of Minnesota and Governor John Evans of Colorado, advocated extermination "until the Indian becomes extinct."[58] Another California state official said that the state would "make war upon the Indian which must of necessity be one of extermination to many of the tribes."[59]

Stannard writes, "This straightforward advocacy of genocide by the highest American officials in the land emerged in a cultural milieu that habitually described the Indigenous Peoples of California as 'ugly, filthy, beasts, swine, dogs, wolves, snakes, pigs, baboons, gorillas, and orang-utans,' to cite only a few of the press' more commonly published characterizations."[60]

This dehumanization process, comparing Indigenous People to animals, was similar to the newspapers' characterizations of Native People in Kansas (not to mention the characterization of Jews by Nazis in the 1930s). As Stannard writes, "the eradication of such abominable creatures could cause little trouble to most consciences of the" Christian Euro-Californian "citizenry."[61]

Vine Deloria, Jr., in his book *God Is Red*, discusses the "systematic genocide" against the Indigenous Peoples of California.[62] Deloria refers to the "Sunday Shoots"[63] in which bands of whites would attack Native villages, indiscriminately killing as many unsuspecting, helpless, and unresisting Native People, women, children, elders, and "little ones" as they could. It's all too easy to picture the fine Christian white folk of California worshiping and praising the Lord, and thanking merciful Jesus, on a Sunday morning, and then massacring "Indians" that afternoon. (This is not unlike pious Christian Euro-Minnesotans celebrating the birth of their Lord and Savior on December 25, 1862, and then celebrating and cheering, the next day, the hanging of 38 Dakota men on December 26, 1862, in Mankato, the largest mass execution by hanging in the history of the United States.)

Ward Churchill describes many other genocidal incidents, among "several hundred such comparable atrocities," involving the Native Peoples of California. One occurred in May 1852 when a peaceful rancheria of 148 Indians, including women and children, was attacked, and nearly the whole number was destroyed by a mob of whites led by the sheriff of Weaverville, California.[64]

There was also "a horrible massacre" of 200 First Nations People in Humboldt County in January 1860. A writer describes what happened: The attack was made at night, when the Natives were in their little settlements or villages at some sort of merry making. The men were known to be absent . . . Under these circumstances, bands of white men, armed with hatchets— small bands, but sufficiently numerous for the purpose—fell on the women and children, and deliberately slaughtered them, one and all.

Simultaneous attacks were made on different rancherias or encampments . . . Regularly organized bodies of armed men attacked the settlements of friendly Indians and murdered them in like manner.[65]

All this was completely in line with Numbers 21:3, "and they utterly destroyed them."

Russell Thornton describes another incident which occurred in the mid-1860s, which involved a Yahi Yana group who were killed, probably in retaliation for their having killed a steer. In this event, four whites, led by a man named Norman Kingsley, murdered and scalped 33 Yahi at a cave north of Mill Creek. Kingsley, "as he explained afterwards, changed guns during the slaughter, exchanging his .56-caliber Spencer rifle for a .38-caliber Smith and Wesson revolver, because the rifle 'tore them up so bad,' particularly the babies."[66] Such compassion!

How do we know about such genocidal atrocities? The killers either wrote or told someone about what they did, often with relish.

There were several hundred such genocidal incidents in the period of slaughter (1840s through the 1860s, approximately) of Indigenous Peoples in California.[67] Like a lot of other states, the "'vigilantes' who carried out the butchery of Native Peoples" were paid bounties by the state government "for the scalps of their victims."[68]

Russell Thornton, in his book *American Indian Holocaust and Survival*, says that the genocide of the Native Peoples of the United States was "probably most blatant in northern California and southern Oregon around the middle of the nineteenth century."[69] Thornton goes on to say that much of the killing in California and Oregon resulted, directly and indirectly, from the discovery of gold in 1849, accompanied by the subsequent influx of miners and settlers. One statement by Thornton is chilling: "It was not uncommon for small groups or villages of Indians to be attacked by the immigrants, sometimes in the name of a particular war, and be virtually wiped out overnight."[70] As in Minnesota and other states, newspapers not only documented the atrocities but also the genocidal comments of governors, soldiers, and settlers, which comments, then, further inflamed the racial hatred and incited the killing of more Native People by the state of California and by its Christian Euro-Californian citizenry.

Oklahoma

But I have said unto you, Ye shall inherit their land, and I [the Lord] will give it unto you to possess it, a land that floweth with milk and honey. (Leviticus 20:24)

In 1830, the U.S. Congress passed the Indian Removal Act. This act authorized the removal of Native Peoples east of the Mississippi River to west of the Mississippi, to Indian Territory, which is now known as Oklahoma. Probably the most famous of the forcible removals (or "ethnic cleansings"), was the Trail of Tears in the 1838 removal of the Tsalagi (or Cherokee). Almost half of the people, 8,000 out of approximately 17,000, were murdered on the death march from Georgia to Oklahoma. This Trail of Tears "was almost as destructive as the Bataan Death March of 1942, the most notorious Japanese atrocity in all of World War II."[71]

Several comments could be made here.

First, the force-marched distance was far greater in the Tsalagi Death March than in the Bataan Death March, since the Cherokee were force-marched almost all the way across the South.

Second, in the Bataan Death March in 1942, it was Japanese soldiers who were force-marching U.S. soldiers, whereas in the Cherokee Death March, in the 19th century, it was U.S. soldiers who were force-marching the Tsalagi People, Tsalagi civilians.

Third, one of these atrocities, the Bataan Death March, involved soldiers committing war crimes during time of war. In the Removal atrocity, U.S. soldiers committed the atrocity during what passed for peacetime. Both the Cherokee People in 1838, and the U.S. soldiers in 1942, experienced hunger, exposure, fear, disease, cruelty, murder, and death. In addition, the Tsalagi women experienced rape, and, sometimes murder, as so many Native women experienced in other forced marches perpetrated by U.S. soldiers, as in the forced removal of the Dakota People of Minnesota from their ancient homelands. What made the Tsalagi experience so tragic, so heart rending, and so different from the Bataan Death March, is that women, children, infants, and elders (the most vulnerable groups in any society) comprised most of the victims.

Fourth, these forced marches and forcible removals fulfill criterion (c) of the 1948 UN Genocide Convention, "Deliberately inflicting on the group conditions of life calculated to bring about its physical destruction in whole or in part."[72] These death marches would also fulfill Frank Chalk's and Kurt Jonassohn's "Four Common Motives of Genocide," particularly, the first motive, "to eliminate groups of people who the perpetrators imagine are threats."[73]

✱ ✱ ✱

The Indian Removal Act, which was passed by Congress on May 28, 1830, as noted above, instituted forcible removal of Native Peoples from east of the Mississippi River to west of the Mississippi. This act set in motion the "ethnic cleansing" of the Muskogee (or Creek), Tsalagi (Cherokee), Choctaw, Chickasaw, Seminole, and scores of other Indigenous Peoples east of the Mississippi. This was an act of massive state-sponsored land theft, for it opened up millions upon millions of acres "for the exclusive use and occupancy of Euro-American settlers and occupiers, along with their Black slaves."[74] It was also an act of state-sponsored genocide, for tens of thousands of Indigenous People were calculatingly and "legally" murdered in these mass removals.

And of course the massive lend theft didn't end once the Natives were driven into "Indian Country."

The Oklahoma Land Rush of 1889 (a euphemism for "Land Theft of 1889") involved the stealing of two million acres of Native lands. The land rush started on noon of April 22, 1889, with an estimated 50,000 land-thieves lined up for their slice of the "land-pie."[75]

However, some white land-stealers did not play fair. There was no honor among these thieves. A number of people who participated in the land rush entered what they called the "unoccupied" land early ("unoccupied," another inaccuracy, for the original Native Peoples were there, plus the recently and forcibly removed "immigrants"), "and hid there until the legal time of entry to lay quick claims to some of the most choice of homesteads." These people came to be known as "Sooners." The University of Oklahoma football team still uses this nickname: the Oklahoma Sooners. Oklahoma, and its Euro-Oklahoman citizenry, have glorified the name "Sooners" to gloss over a criminal act and massive land theft. Perhaps, Oklahoma ought to change the U of O's sports team name to the "Oklahoma Land-Thieves."

Illinois

> . . . And the Lord . . . delivered up the Canaanites and they [the Israelites] utterly destroyed them and their cities; and he called the name of the place Hormah ["utter destruction"]. (Numbers 21:2–3, KJV)

The Bad Axe Massacre happened in the late summer of 1833 at the junction of the Bad Axe and Mississippi Rivers. Trafzer states, "Of the 1,000 Sac and Fox people who had entered Illinois, only 150 lived to tell their side of the Bad Axe tragedy."[77] William Brandon adds, "It was a horrid sight to witness little children, wounded and suffering the most excruciating pain, although they were of the 'savage enemy.'"[78]

Note the phrase "a horrid sight to witness little children, wounded and suffering . . ." As John Underhill declared some 200 years before, after the Pequot Holocaust of 1637, "sometimes the Scripture declareth women and children must perish with their parents."[79] Note the euphemistic phrase, "must perish," instead of saying that the women and children "must be murdered." Ward Churchill says, "The Indians who had remained on the east bank of the Mississippi attempted to surrender, but the troops, frustrated by weeks of fruitless pursuit . . . stormed their position in an eight-hour frenzy of clubbing, stabbing, shooting and scalping."[80]

Black Hawk, the leader of the Sac and Fox People, "was imprisoned for a year, then shipped about as a traveling exhibit 'to 'humble' and 'humiliate' even the most arrogant of savages . . .'" Churchill further writes that Black Hawk's bones were disinterred and displayed as trophies in a museum in Iowaville, Iowa.[81] This is similar to what happened in Minnesota where the Minnesota Historical Society displayed the remains and scalp of Little Crow, and kept his scalp and remains for 108 years, from 1863 to 1971, even though relatives at the turn of the century (1900) were asking for the return of Little Crow's remains.

What kind of people do these types of things?

Texas

And they utterly destroyed all that was in the city, both man and woman, young and old, and ox, and sheep, and ass, with the edge of the sword. (Joshua 6:21, KJV)

In 1835, Texas declared its independence from Mexico, and the Mexican Army responded by moving troops into the rebellious region. After winning important victories at the Alamo and Goliad, Mexican troops led by General Santa Anna lost the Battle of San Jacinto. Soon, Texas became an independent nation with Samuel Houston as president.

The establishment of a bounty system on Indigenous scalps was "one of the very first acts of the legislature, initially of the republic, then, of the state after Texas was admitted to the Union."[82] The Texas government after Houston followed a Native policy comparable to that of the United States, but from the outset Texas refused to recognize Native title to any land. (96) Texas Indigenous policy centered around forced removal or extermination, not unlike the policies of Colorado and California, or the policy of Governor Alexander Ramsey of Minnesota, who frequently uttered "extermination or removal."[83]

The Texas Rangers executed this policy. They were "organized to kill Indigenous People and hang horse thieves, cattle rustlers, and the more general varieties of outlaws."[84] They were assiduous in their "duty" toward First Nations Peoples. Some of these Indigenous People "served as scouts for the Texas Rangers, particularly when the rangers operated against Kiowas and Comanches, people who once disliked most eastern tribes almost as much as they did the rangers."[85] Yet in spite of Native loyalty to Texas, demonstrated by the service of some as scouts, the white citizenry and government turned against them just as they did against the other Indigenous groups.

"The hatred" for the Aboriginal Peoples, "that had characterized white-Native relations in the East and in Mexico, had moved into Texas."[86] Texans "used racial hatred to justify the annihilation or forcible removal of most of the" First Nations Peoples in the state. Texas Rangers attacked and killed Native men, women and children, forcing most survivors to flee into "Indian" Territory or Mexico, where most of them live to this day.[86]

Trafzer notes that "the United States was not impartial, because the army protected the "citizens' of the nation and state [of Texas, prior to annexation], not the Native nations. Besides, federal troops and Texas Rangers reflected racial views of the country, which did not protect Native lives, liberties, or rights."[87] In addition, Churchill quotes W.W. Newcomb, Jr., who wrote, "The facts of history are plain: Most Texas Indians were exterminated or brought to the brink of oblivion by Spaniards, Mexicans, Texans," and the Euro-Americans "who often had no more regard for the life of an Indian than they had for that of a dog, sometimes less."[88]

The first two papal bulls, *Romanus Pontifex* and *InterCaetera*, laid the foundation for the Church Doctrine of Discovery and for Conquest. The third bull, *Sublimus Dei*, called for spreading the gospel of Jesus Christ and proselytizing the Indigenous Peoples of the Americas. These bulls became United States government policy. The Supreme Court ruling in one of the Marshall Trilogies court cases, Johnson v. M'Intosh, in the 1830s, used these bulls as part of the argument determining the dependent sovereignty status of today's modern Indigenous Peoples as "wards" of the U.S. government.[89] The Supreme Court Ruling in Johnson v. M'Intosh adopted the same principle of subjugation expressed in the *Inter Caetera* bull.[90]

When the "Great Commission" of Christ" ("Go therefore, and make disciples of all the nations,") and the genocidal commands of the Old Testament ("Kill everything that hath breath") were added to the papal bulls, the consequences were disastrous, and continue to be so to this day.

Vine Deloria, Jr. sums up the situation this way:

Christianity thus endorsed and advocated the rape of the North American continent, and her representatives have done their utmost to contribute to this process ever since.

Deloria could quite appropriately have included both Central America and South America in this statement.

Endnotes

1. *American Holocaust,* by David Stannard. Oxford: Oxford University Press, 1992, p.167.

2. "International Law and Politics," by Glenn T. Morris in State of Native America, M. Annette Jaimes, ed. Boston: South End Press, 1992, p. 67.

3. *As Long As The Grass Shall Grow and Rivers Flow*, by Clifford Trafzer. New York: Harcourt College Publishers, 2000, pp. viii, & 153.

4. *Facing West: The Metaphysics of Indian Hating & Empire Building*, by Richard Drinnon. Norman, OK: University of Oklahoma Press, 1997, title page. Norman and Oklahoma,

5. "Annexation," by John O'Sullivan, July 1845,

6. Merriam-Webster's Collegiate Dictionary, Eleventh Edition. Springfield, MA: Merriam-Webster, 2012, p.1001.

7. Senator Thomas Hart Benton, U.S. Senate, Congressional Globe, Appendix, 74, 27th Cong., 2nd Sess., U. S. Government Printing Office, Washington, D.C., 1846.

8. Senator Albert Jeremiah Beveridge, "In Support of an American Empire" 345(1900), U.S. Senate, Congressional Record, 56 Cong, I Sess., pp. 704–712.

9. "The White Man's Burden," in *British Literature: Blake to the Present Day*, Hazelton Spencer et al. eds., Boston: D.C. Heath, 1952, p. 876.

10. *Custer Died For Your Sins:: An Indian Manifesto*, by Vine Deloria , Jr. Norman, OK: University of Oklahoma, 1988, p. 51.

11. Stannard, op. cit., p. 121.

12. "Tubman's replacement of Jackson on the $20 a deeply symbolic move: Indians remember deadly marches president forced," *Minneapolis Star Tribune*, April 22, 2016, Section A, p. 1.

13. Stannard, op. cit., p. 131.

14. *The Last Americans*, by William Brandon. New York: McGraw-Hill, 1974., p. 386–387.

15. Ibid.

16. *Indians*, by William Brandon. Boston: Houghton-Mifflin, 1987, p. 366.

17. Ibid., p. 366.

18. Morris, op. cit., p. 67.

19. "The Demography of Native North America: A Question of American Indian Survival," by Lenore A. Stiffarm, with Phil Lane, Jr. in *The State of Native America*, p.34.

20. Ibid., pp. 36–37.

21. Stannard, op. cit., p. x.

22. "North America: the Blind Spot in History," by David C. Bolin. *Random Magazine*, November 1969, p. 27.

23. *History of the Santee Sioux: United States Indian Policy on Trial*, by Roy Meyer. Lincoln, NE: University of Nebraska Press, 1983, p. 125.

24. Ibid., p. 125.

25. *What Does Justice Look Like? The Struggle for Liberation in Dakota Homeland*, by Waziyatawin. St. Paul: Living Justice Press, 2008, p. 55.

26. *American Indian Holocaust and Survival: A population History Since 1492*, by Russell Thornton. Norman, OK: University of Oklahoma Press, 1987, p. 107.

27. *A Little Matter of Genocide: Holocaust and Denial in the America, 1492 to the Present*, by Ward Churchill. San Francisco, City Light Books, 1997, pp. 351–352.

28. Ibid., p. 244.

29. Stannard, op. cit., p. 114.

30. Trafzer, op. cit., pp. 320-321.

31. Stannard, op. cit., p. 126.

32. Ibid., p. 127.

33. *The Ryrie Study Bible, New International Version*, by Charles Caldwell Ryrie. Chicago: Moody Press, 1986, p. 384.

34. Ibid.

35. *Song of Sorrow: Massacre at Sand Creek*, by Patrick M Mendoza. Denver: Willow Wind Publishing Company, 1993, pp. 35 & 44.

36. Churchill, op. cit., p. 234.

37. Mendoza, op. cit., p. 93.

38. Ibid., p. 95.

39. Ibid., p. 96.

40. Ibid., p. 97.

41. Ibid.

42. Ibid., p. 98.

43. Stannard, op. cit., p. xi.

44. "A Mass Murder That Happened One Hundred and Fifty Years Ago Today in Eastern Colorado," by Dartagnan. Daily Kos, November 29, 2014,

45. Stannard, op. cit., p. 134,

46. Churchill, op. cit., p. 186.

47. Ibid., p. 228.

48. Ibid.

49. Trafzer, op. cit., p. 211.

50. Churchill, op. cit., pp. 228–229.

51. Ibid., p. 229.

52. Ibid., p. 281f.

53. Stannard, op. cit., p. 126.

54. Trafzer, op. cit., p. 233.

55. "A woman of contradiction" by Tim Post, Minnesota Public Radio, September 26, 2002

56. Trafzer, op. cit., p. 233.

57. Stannard, op. cit., p. 144.

58. Ibid.

59. Ibid., pp. 144–145.

60. Ibid., p. 145.

61 Ibid.

62. *God is Red A Native View of Religion*, by Vine Deloria, Jr. Golden, CO: North American Press, 1972, p. 5.

63. Ibid.

64. Churchill, op. cit., p. 220.

65. Ibid.

66. Thornton, op. cit., p. 110.

67. Churchill, op. cit., pp. 107–109.

68. Ibid., p. 220.

69. Thornton, op. cit., p. 107.

70. Ibid.

71. Stannard, op. cit., p.123.

72. Ibid, p. 280.

73. *The History and Sociology of Genocide*, by Frank Chalk and Kurt Jonassohn. New Haven, CT: Yale University Press, 1990, p. 29.

74. "Key Indian Laws and Cases," by Churchill and Morris in *The State of Native America*, op. cit., p. 14.

75. "Land Rush of 1889," Wikipedia.

76. Trafzer, op. cit., p. 142

77. Brandon, The Last Americans, op. cit., p. 299.

78. Stannard, op. cit., p. 114.

79. Churchill, op. cit., p. 218.

80. Ibid.

81. Ibid., p. 187.

82. Trafzer, op. cit., p. 188.

83. Ibid., p. 189.

84. Ibid.

85. Trafzer, op. cit., p. 189.

86. Ibid.

87. *The Indians of Texas*, by W.W. Newcomb, 1961, p. 344, quoted by Churchill, op. cit., p. 187f.

88. Ibid.

89. Thornton, op. cit., p. 107.

90. Stannard, op. cit., p.123.

5

DESTROY THEIR ALTARS

The Bible, Religious Suppresion
and Native Ceremonies

"But you shall destroy their altars, break their sacred pillars,
and cut down their wooden images."
(Exodus 34:13, NKJV)

Why is a chapter on religious suppression of Indigenous spirituality, ceremonies, and religious traditions included in this book, which is on the Bible and genocide of the Indigenous Peoples of what is now the United States? The main reason is the parallel between the religious suppression of the Canaanites by the Israelites and the religious suppression of Indigenous ceremonies and worship by the U.S. government and its Euro-American citizens. Both the ancient Hebrews and the more contemporary Christians wanted to eliminate competition to their respective beliefs, values, and gods. Just as religious suppression was closely linked to the genocide and land theft of the Canaanites by the Israelites, so was religious suppression closely connected to the genocide and land-theft of Indigenous lands by the Euro-American Christians.

Another relevant factor is the fourth common motive of genocide identified by Chalk and Jonassohn: "to impose an ideology or a belief upon the victim group."[1]

As is obvious, Christianity is a religious ideology that was imposed upon the Indigenous Peoples of the Americas, beginning with Columbus and the Catholic missionaries on the islands of the Caribbean. Hence, the following discussion on parallels and links between the two situations—genocide, land theft, and religious suppression—involving Israelites and Canaanites on the one hand, and the United States and Indigenous Peoples on the other.

One of the ironies of U.S. history is the entrenched myth that the United States of America was built on religious freedom and freedom from religious persecution. The Constitution, Article 1, states, "Congress shall make no law respecting an establishment of religion, or prohibiting the free exercise thereof; or abridging the freedom of speech, or of the press, or the right of the people peaceably to assemble, and to petition the Government for a redress of grievances."

However, it appears, over the well over two centuries the United States has been in existence, that Christianity is, indeed, the established religion of the USA. Evidence of this includes the following: the motto on a U.S. one dollar bill, "In God We Trust" (presumably, Yahweh, the Judeo and Christian God); the prayer to the Judeo-Christian God that starts U.S. Congressional sessions; prayers in school, generally Christian prayers; the pledge of Allegiance with the phrase, "One Nation Under God (no guesses as to which one); president after president swearing on the Christian Bible at their inaugurations; the Christian holidays of Christmas and Easter, which are imposed on both Christians and non-Christians alike; etc., etc. etc.

The notion that the United States was built on the principle of religious freedom is an outright lie. The Western Europeans, who eventually became Euro-Americans, wanted the freedom to not only practice their own brands of Christianity, but also the freedom to persecute others with different beliefs, including other Christians..

Despite the fact that the Constitution supposedly guarantees religious freedom—to Euro-American Christians, for sure; and, probably, to Jews and, possibly, Muslims—in practice, Native Peoples have had the "freedom" to choose between Catholicism, Protestantism, Mormonism, the Assemblies of God, the Baptists, Episcopalians, Presbyterians, Lutherans, Methodists, and other Christian sects.

But until quite recently, Native Peoples did not have the freedom to follow their ancestors' beliefs, traditions and ceremonies, the freedom to practice their Creator-given spirituality.

Since citizenship was not imposed on the Native Peoples until 1924, 148 years after the Declaration of Independence, the First Amendment guarantee of religious freedom did not apply to the Aboriginal Peoples until then, and even since then it's often been ignored: there was criminalization of Indigenous spirituality and religious ceremonies of the First Nations Peoples on U.S. reservations from 1883 to 1934. Lobo and Talbot write that "in 1902 Indian Commissioner W.A. Jones issued his 'short-hair' order, which banned . . . long hair . . . the wearing of Indian clothing, religious dances, and 'give-away ceremonies'" (for the Dakota, the "Ituhan"—our Gift-Giving Ceremony).² Lobo and Talbot further write, "These policies [of religious Suppression] were not reversed until 1934, under John Collier, Commissioner of Indian Affairs, in the Roosevelt New Deal administration. Nevertheless, some important Indian religious ceremonies and other customs have continued to be banned or subtly discouraged by non-Indian individuals and institutions up to the present."³

But the United States Congress must have felt a twinge of conscience about stifling the religious ceremonies of the Indigenous Peoples (at least, I would like to believe this). Perhaps that is why in 1978 Congress enacted The American Indian Religious Freedom Act, almost exactly two hundred two years after the United States was founded.

Lobo and Talbot also mention the "Courts of Indian Offenses" set up by the Indian Office, and that these courts deemed Indigenous ceremonies and other religious traditions as "offensive."⁴ These ceremonies included the sacred Canduhupa ("Pipe"); the Wiwanyag Wacipi (or the Sun Dance); the Inipi ("Make-Alive Ceremony," a purification ceremony); the Hanbde Ceyapi (the Vision Quest); and the gift-giving ceremonies ("Ituhan," mentioned above).

Church and State worked hand in hand in this process of suppression, especially in the establishment of residential boarding schools (both State and Christian denominational). Another aspect of this religious suppression was that the military took Native children and forced them into the foreign, strange, and hostile environment of those boarding schools. There, the Native children were to be civilized, educated, Christianized, and assimilated. (Residential boarding schools fulfill criterion (e) of the 1948 UN Genocide Convention, "forcibly transferring children of the group to another group.")

Numbers 33:52, "Then you shall drive out all the inhabitants of the land from before you, destroy all their engraved stones, destroy all their molded images, and demolish all their high places," (NKJV) is a key verse regarding religious suppression. (Numbers 33:52 in the Tanakh reads this way, " . . . you shall destroy all their figured objects; you shall destroy all their molten images, and you shall demolish all the cult places.")

Regarding this verse, theologian Matthew Henry writes, "They ["the children of Israel"] are here strictly charged utterly to destroy all the remnants of idolatry."⁵ Jamiesson, Fausset, and Brown and Adam Clarke, basically reiterate Henry's comment.

Note that the first of the ten commandments that Yahweh gave to Moses is "thou shalt have no other gods before me." (Exodus 20:3, KJV) The Old Testament God did not want his "chosen people," the Israelites, to "bow down," nor "worship," nor "serve" any other god, "for I the Lord thy God am a jealous God, visiting the iniquity of the fathers upon the children unto the third and fourth generation that hate me." (Exodus 20:5) We see here that God will not only punish the sinner for worshiping another god, but will also punish his children and grandchildren. Please also note that Christians habitually refer to their god, Yahweh, as "just."

Further, Yahweh, by commanding the destruction of the sacramental objects of the Canaanites, was demonstrating his approval of the suppression of the religions of the Native Peoples of the promised land (e.g., the Hittites, Jebusites, et. al.). It is very easy to understand why many of the adherents of Christianity appreciate the Old Testament God: He, Yahweh, gives them permission to steal, kill, destroy, and suppress. Today, ISIS kills people who refuse to bow to its religious ideology. This is not unlike the attitude and actions of the Israelites in the Old Testament, under Yahweh, against the Indigenous Peoples of Canaan. And it is not unlike the genocidal actions of the U.S. government and its Euro-American citizenry against the First Nations Peoples of what is now the U.S.A.

Deuteronomy 7:5 deals with religious suppression. In it, Yahweh commands the Israelites, ". . . you shall destroy their altars, and break down their sacred pillars, and cut down their wooden images, and burn their carved images with fire." (NKJV) The Torah renders the verse this way, ". . . you shall tear down their altars, smash their pillars, cut down their sacred posts, and consign their images to the fire."[6] The Old Testament God, when he says "them" or "their," in this verse, is referring to the Hittites, the Canaanites, et. al.

Regarding Deuteronomy 7:5, Matthew Henry, our Presbyterian theologian, writes the following, ". . . let not us then make covenants with them ['the people of these abominations'], nor show them any mercy, but mortify and crucify them, and utterly destroy them."[7]

This is chilling. As the old R&B song goes, "Where is the Love?" Or, where is "the loving kindness"? In Jeremiah 9:24, we read, ". . . I am the Lord, exercising loving kindness, judgment, and righteousness in the earth. For in these I delight . . ." (NKJV). Apparently, Yahweh exercises "loving-kindness" to only His "chosen people," those in whom he "delights," the Israelites, not the Indigenous Peoples of Canaan, the Canaanites, Hittites, et. al.

Along with the genocidal passages in other Old Testament books, there are about two dozen verses in the Psalms which refer to the "loving kindness" of the Lord. This makes sense if you realize that Yahweh reserves his "loving kindness" for his chosen people.

Regarding Deuteronomy 7:5, Jamiesson, Fausset, and Brown say, "The removal of the temples, altars, and everything that had been enlisted in the service, or might tend to perpetuate the remembrance, of Canaanite idolatry, was likewise highly expedient for preserving the Israelites from all risk of contamination."[8]

They also make a comment similar to Matthew Henry, "This relentless doom of extermination which God denounced against those tribes of Canaan cannot be reconciled with the attributes of the divine character, except on the assumption that their gross idolatry and enormous wickedness left no reasonable hope of their repentance and amendment."[9] The "relentless doom of extermination" refers to Deuteronomy 7:2 in which "the Lord thy God" commands the Israelites to "utterly destroy them." The theologians are thoroughly in agreement with the genocidal commands of Yahweh. Again, this type of religious thinking, this religious extremism, has led directly to atrocities. It appears, according to Jamieson, Fausset, and Brown, that there are some things which are unforgiveable such as "gross idolatry and enormous wickedness," which deserve the "relentless doom of extermination." And mass murder, child rape, and land theft, do *not* merit such "relentless doom, and indeed are meritorious, "if carried out by God's chosen people.

Another example of what the theologians agree with reads:

You shall utterly destroy all the places, where the nations which you shall dispossess served their gods, on the high mountains and on the hills, and under every green tree . . . And you shall destroy their altars, break their sacred pillars, and burn their wooden images with fire; you shall cut down the carved images of their gods and destroy their names from that place. (Deuteronomy 12:3, NKJV)

The Torah renders this verse as:

You must destroy all the sites at which the nations you are to dispossess worshiped their gods, whether on lofty mountains and on hills or under any luxuriant tree. Tear down their altars, smash their pillars, put their sacred posts to the fire, and cut down the images of their gods, obliterating their name from that site.

Religious Suppression: Historical & Personal Events

During the six months (November of 1862 through April of 1863) of the concentration/death camp experience for our Dakota women, children, and elders, Bishop Henry Benjamin Whipple conducted a ceremony of religious suppression. Whipple had the Dakota prisoners bring in their sacramental objects, their sacred pipes, their medicine bundles, their sacred dolls, their tobacco, sage, and sweet grass, their eagle feathers, etc. These sacramental objects were placed in a large pile and then burned in a huge bonfire.[10] This hearkens back to the Old Testament God's commands to "burn," "break," "cut down," "tear down," and "smash," those things which were sacred to the Indigenous Canaanites, Hittites, et. al.

In the the 1860s, Episcopal Bishop Whipple, too, was obeying the destructive and suppressive commands of the Lord to "destroy" the objects of "idolatry." Vine Deloria, Jr., a fellow Dakota, an academic, and an attorney, also attended a seminary in which he earned a degree in theology, and had enough credits for another degree in Christian Theology. Deloria says this about missionaries, the primary individuals responsible for suppressing and supplanting Native religions and ceremonies:

> One of the major problems of the Indian People is the missionary. It has been said of missionaries that when they arrived they had only the Book and we had the land; now we have the Book and they have the land. An old Indian once told me that when the missionaries arrived, they fell on their knees and prayed. Then, they got up, fell on the Indians, and preyed.[11]

Deloria goes on to say that "Columbus managed to combine religion and real estate in his proclamation of discovery, claiming the new world for Catholicism and Spain." Since that time, Deloria says, "Missionaries have been unable to distinguish between their religious mission and their hunger for land,"[12] and that "land acquisition and missionary work always went hand in hand in American history."[13]

Another significant point that Deloria makes is that the Christian missionaries prohibited the practice of Native spirituality and ceremonies, that "Indian religious life was forbidden."[14] Finally, Deloria comments on the purpose of missionaries: "Their primary message sought to invalidate the totality of Indian life and replace it with Christian values,"[15] basically to eradicate and to supplant Indigenous values and spirituality.

Who, then, was this Bishop Henry Benjamin Whipple? Euro-Minnesotans, and white Christian people, specifically, honor and revere Whipple and describe him as a friend of the Dakota People. Let us look at what two Indigenous scholars, Dr. George E. Tinker, an Osage man, and Dr. Waziyatawin ("Woman of the North"), a Dakota woman, have to say about this supposedly holy white man. Dr. Tinker states, "The story of Henry Benjamin Whipple and Indian People is an example of cultural genocide with clear political and religious aspects." He adds, "[M]odern Indian oppression and dysfunctionality are as much the heritage of Whipple's involvement in the Indian context as of the U.S. cavalry or the federal policies he worked so hard to reform."[16]

One of the more disturbing facts which Dr. Tinker points out is that Bishop Whipple believed that the Dakota and other Native children had to be separated from their parents in order to Christianize and civilize them. Professor Tinker says this "meant . . . separating children from parents, even from Christian parents, in order to remove the more promising children from the tribal environment entirely."[17] Thomas Williamson, a Presbyterian missionary to the Dakota People of Minnesota, also believed it necessary to separate the "promising children" from their parents at as early an age as possible.[18] This is genocide, according to the 1948 UN Genocide Convention, in which criterion (e) is "forcibly transferring children of the group to another group." It doesn't make any difference how godly or well intentioned Bishop Whipple or any of the other missionaries were or are, because removing children from their parents is still genocide.

Dr. Waziyatawin quotes Bishop Whipple as saying, "As a Christian I take issue with anyone who claims that God has created any human being who is incapable of civilization or who cannot receive the gospel of Jesus Christ."[19] This statement is reminiscent of one made by Pope Paul III in the *Sublimus Dei* bull of 1537. In that bull, Pope Paul III said, "Hence Christ, who is the Truth itself, that has never failed and can never fail, said to the preachers of the faith whom He chose for that office 'Go ye and teach all nations.' He said 'all,' without exception, for all are capable of receiving the doctrines of the faith."[20]

Pope Paul III also said, "the Indians are truly men and that they are not only capable of understanding the Catholic Faith but, according to our information, they desire exceedingly to receive it."[21]

Of course, these statements by Bishop Whipple, in 1862, and by Pope Paul III, in 1537, are both echoing the religious imperialism of Jesus Christ, who dictated to his followers in Matthew 28:19, "go forth therefore, and make all nations my disciples." (NEB) Dr. Waziyatawin says this about the proselytizing aspect of Christianity, and about Bishop Whipple who believed mass extermination of the Dakota was unjust, that Bishop Whipple "wanted the rest of the population alive so that he could pursue his own imperialistic path by converting heathen souls to Christianity."[22] It is fair to say that what Bishop Whipple, and the missionaries, wanted for the Dakota People was, in general, aligned with the U.S. government, its generals, its agents, and its white citizenry. Those who didn't want the complete extermination of the Dakota people wanted those Dakota who were "left remaining" and still "breathing" (see Joshua 10:28–40) to be civilized, Christianized, educated, and assimilated.

The traditional Dakota might ask, "Why do we need to abandon our beliefs and ceremonies that we have received from Tunkansida Wakan Tanka ("Grandfather Great Mystery") and that we have been following for centuries, long before white Christians came to the Americas, long before the lost Columbus stumbled on the islands in the Caribbean, since time began? We are not asking you to accept our ancient ways, nor are we saying that you must accept our way of believing. Can you not respect, also, our ceremonies and ways?"

Through both their words and actions the white Christians answered with an emphatic "No!"

The Sun Dance of the Oyate

Cut down the Sacred Poles. (Deuteronomy 7:5, NAB)

One of the most sacred of the ceremonies that members of the Oyate (Dakota, Lakota, and Nakota), which means the "People," is the Wiwanyag Wacipi, literally, "Watching the Sun While Dancing," or the Sun Dance. In this holy ceremony, the dancers dance, pray for the People, and go four days and nights without food and water. The Dancers sacrifice themselves as they pray for the People. One of the sayings that arise from this Wiwanyag Wacipi is "heced Oyate nipi kte," or "That the People May Live."

On one of the chosen days, the dancer is pierced. There is a rope, one end of the rope is attached to the tree, "the sacred pole," in the center of the sacred circle, while the other end of the rope is attached to the skewers which are attached to the chest of the dancer. During the time the Sun Dancers are in the sacred circle, there is a drum group and the singers are singing. And, at a certain time during the ceremony, the spiritual leader will signal when it is time to break, and the dancer will dance backward from the sacred tree, and then break free of the skewers attached to his chest. There is physical pain involved. The dancer endures not only pain, but also hunger, thirst, heat, exhaustion, rain, cold, etc., and sacrifices of himself, his flesh and blood, "that the People may live!" These are some basic details of the ceremony that I observed in the Sun Dance for four straight years on a reservation in north-eastern South Dakota.

In this ceremony, one of the four days is devoted to healing. People are allowed to come into the sacred circle to pray, and individuals are escorted by a Sun Dancer into the circle to the sacred tree in the middle of the circle, where s/he prays. Sometimes, wonderful things happen. Perhaps a person has cancer, and comes in to pray, and later, the cancer goes into remission. Or a person comes in with crutches and prays, and afterward, the person does not need the crutches anymore. Wakan Tanka, the "Great Mystery," or God (not the Jewish God), has honored the sacrifice of the dancers by healing the people, "that they might live."

Yet, this beautiful and sacred ceremony was criminalized by the Courts of Indian Offenses in the early 1880s[23]; it was banned and suppressed. The Sun Dance Pole, or our "sacred tree," was figuratively "cut down" by the United States government, with the approval of the churches, seminaries, missionaries, educators, and the white Christian citizenry.

I do not know if the U.S. Government or the missionaries were aware they were obeying the religious-suppression commands given millennia ago by the jealous, vindictive Old Testament God, but they certainly did what the Old Testament God told the Israelites to do: to suppress and then supplant what they considered heathen and idolatrous ceremonies.

As a result, the Dakota People of Minnesota, and our Lakota and Nakota traditional people, took the ceremonies underground and conducted them in secret in remote locations. As a Dakota elder from the Cansaypi Otunwe, "Redwood Community," a small Dakota community in southwestern Minnesota, put it, "Nahma Wacipi." That is, "they," the traditional Dakota People, "danced in secret."[24]

(Before continuing, a few personal notes: First, I have withdrawn from the church and Christianity, and have returned to the ancient and traditional religious ceremonies and practices of my ancestors. This ceremony, the Wiwanyag Wacipi ["Watching the Sun While Dancing," or Sun Dance], was, and is, one of the greatest spiritual experiences of my life. Second, I made a four-year commitment to the Sun Dance, that is, I had to participate in the annual ceremony for four years. Third, as I indicated earlier, the

Sun Dancers dance for four days and nights without food and water. I, also, had, and still have, diabetes. At the end of each day, a nurse would check my blood sugar. My readings were good. Even at the end of the ceremony, after four days with no food or water, my last test was good, within the normal range for a diabetic. There is no doubt in my mind that I had spiritual and physical help from the unseen world, from Tunkansida Wakan Tanka, "Grandfather Great Mystery," during this most sacred of ceremonies.)

Another religious tradition or custom that was suppressed and criminalized was the Ituhan—the Gift-Giving Ceremony, also called the "Give-Away."[25] At important events in an individual's life, a gift-giving ceremony was held, along with a feast of thanksgiving. Such events could include the Wokiksuye Wotapi, the "Remembrance Feast," held one year after a loved one dies; a name-giving ceremony; the making of relatives; a Wopida Wotapi, a "Feast of Thanksgiving".

Today such events, viz., the Ituhan, etc., could include a graduation from high school, or earning a Baccalaureate, or a Masters, or a J.D., or a Ph.D., or for someone who has been honorably discharged from military service and/or has come home from combat. My mother, Elsie (Two Bear) Cavender and family, put on a Feast of Thanksgiving ("Wopida Wotapi") and gift-giving ceremony ("Ituhan") for me when I received my Ph.D. from the University of Minnesota in June 1974.

At the end of my fourth year of Sun-Dancing, I sponsored an Ituhan, a Gift-Giving Ceremony, in which I presented gifts to my fellow dancers, the fire-keepers, et. al. The purpose was to give thanks to all who made the Wiwanyag Wacipi possible. Each Sun-Dancer would do this, i.e., the Ituhan, after they completed their four-year commitment to the Sun Dance.

Earlier in the book, I mentioned the two Dakota women who attended the Pezihuta Zizi Presbyterian Church, in my home community, and their saying that "Ituhan kin he Wakan Sica etanhan."

That is, "The gift-giving ceremony is from the devil." These two Dakota women might not have known that Jesus said, "It is more blessed to give than to receive." (Acts 20:35). Their attitude was a divisive and destructive result of Christian teaching. Their judgmental attitude, along with their negative public statements, matched the self-righteous attitude of the white missionaries. The comment by the two Dakota women regarding the Ituhan, the gift-giving ceremony, is an excellent example of religious suppression and of the negative, divisive, and destructive impact of Christianity upon the Dakota People, their ceremonies, their religious customs and traditions, and upon their society.

To further illustrate this divisive, self-righteous, and judgmental attitude, I heard about the following incident that occurred sometime during the 1950s.[26] Some of the young Dakota people who drank alcohol and partied heavily were kicked out of the Yellow Medicine Presbyterian Church for their drunken behavior. The good, pious, Dakota Presbyterian Christians apparently, didn't know that Jesus came to save sinners, not kick them out of the church. For example, Jesus said , " . . . He will save His people from their sins" (Matthew 1:21, NKJV). In another verse, Jesus says, ". . . the Son of Man [Jesus] has power on earth to forgive sins." (Matthew 9:6, NKJV) The Dakota Christians apparently didn't know that the sinners couldn't be "forgiven" or "saved" by Jesus if they weren't allowed in the church and weren't provided the opportunity to come to Jesus. Their Dakota Hymnal (Dakota Odowan) even has a hymn titled "Jesus Ed U," which means "Come To Jesus." This is somewhat ironic.

The Hazelwood Republic

A group formed in my community, Pezihuta Zizi Otunwe, "Yellow Medicine Community," in southwestern Minnesota, in 1856. They called themselves the Hazelwood Republic. This group emerged from the local church, the Pezihuta Zizi Presbyterian Church, and formed with the encouragement of a white missionary, Rev. Stephen R. Riggs. It was "a voluntary organization whose members agreed to abandon their Dakota manners and dress and begin farming on individual allotments of land."[27]

They were going to cut their hair like the white man. They were going to speak English like the white man, they were going to dress like the white man, and live in houses just like the white man. They were going to be dark-skinned white people. Little did these Christianized and colonized Dakota People know that they would never be accepted by the white man, whom they desperately attempted to please.

The Hazelwood Republic didn't last long. There was growing hostility between the traditional Dakota and the Christian Dakota, between those "who wished to adopt the manners of the whites, and those who violently opposed any such move toward civilization."[28] At first, the hostility manifested in the burning of haystacks and stables. Then in the killing of cattle. Later, the hostility advanced to the stage where there were open threats against the lives of those who wished to live like the white man. Finally, because of a "succession of murders and retaliations" in the spring of 1860, there was "a break-up of the Hazelwood Republic."[29]

Christianity, with its missionaries and biblical teachings, created division among the Dakota People of Minnesota. Christianity and Christ were not "uniters" but "dividers." This division among the Dakota reminds me of a statement by Jesus Christ, "Do not think that I came to bring peace on earth. I did not come to bring peace but a sword." He continues, "For I have come to set a man against his father, a daughter against her mother, and a daughter-in-law against her mother-in-law.'" (Matthew 10:34–35, NKJV)[30] Jesus Christ came to divide, and his missionaries did in fact split families and communities; in this particular situation, Christian missionaries split the Dakota People of Pezihuta Zizi K'api Makoce.

As for the theologians, in regard to Matthew 10:34–35, none of the theologians say a word about it.[31]

Now let's consoider the "Prince of Peace" phrase, and idea, which comes from Isaiah 9:6: "[F]or unto us a child is born, unto us a son is given: and the government shall be upon his shoulder: and his name shall be called Wonderful, Counsellor, The Mighty God, the Everlasting Father, The Prince of Peace." (Isaiah 9:6, KJV). This verse supposedly refers to the birth of Jesus Christ. The New Oxford Annotated Bible makes the comment that the "Prince of Peace, [is] the king who brings peace and prosperity."[33] This is hard to square with that same "Prince" bringing not peace but a sword.

All of the translations of Matthew 10:34–35 state clearly that Jesus did not come to bring peace but came to bring either a "sword," or "division," or "set at variance" ("in conflict")[32] among families because some will choose to believe in Him and others will not. In other groups and nations there will be separation, division, and probably discord, controversy, and worse, eventual armed conflicts (e.g., Protestants v. Catholics, etc.) up to and including religious wars (the Crusades, the 40 Years War, etc.). Is this a good thing? One suspects that most Christians realize that it isn't, so they (but for some extreme fundamentalists) tend not to mention it. It's part of what I refer to as the "hidden Bible," that is, one of those verses/issues which are not discussed by most Christians.

We can see how this divine separation and division played out in the Hazelwood Republic, which provided an excellent example of the destructive impact of Christianity and its teachings upon the religious beliefs and ceremonies of the Dakota People of Minnesota and upon the Indigenous Peoples of the Americas. These teachings were proclaimed and implemented by the missionaries. Christianity was, most certainly, an instrument (i.e., an ideology) of colonialism, i.e., "the behaviors, ideologies, and economies which enforce the exploitation"[34] and continued oppression of the colonized people, in this case, the Dakota People. Christianity, like many of the other institutions of the colonizers divided the Dakota People between those traditional people who wished to retain the ancient ways, ceremonies, and traditions and those who embraced Christianity. This division was fostered by the Christian denominations, churches, seminaries, and their missionaries, with the approval and support of the U.S. government.

This division, and sometimes hostility, still exists among the Dakota People of not only Minnesota but also among the Dakota of other states and several provinces of Canada. Now, in the 21st century, some Dakota, both traditional and Christian, are attempting to bridge the gap. They are engaged in the work of decolonizing Christianity (e.g., curbing, or ignoring, the proselytizing command of Jesus Christ and moderating the judgmental attitudes of Dakota Christians, among other things), and reconciling Dakota with Dakota, because we, the Oyate (the "People"—the Dakota, Lakota, and Nakota) are all one People.

Endnotes

1. *The History and Sociology of Genocide*, by Frank Chalk and Kurt Johassohn. New Haven, CT: Yale University Press, 1990, p. 29.

2. *Native American Voices*, by Susan Lobo and Steve Talbot. Upper Saddle River, NJ: Prentice Hall, 2001, p. 188.

3. Ibid.

4. Ibid.

5. The Torah. Philadelphi: Jewish Publication Society of America, Philadelphia, 1967, p. 338.

6. *Bethany Parallel Commentary on the Old Testament*, p. 345.

7. Ibid.

8. The Holy Bible, New King James Version, Nashville: The Gideons International, 1985, p. 310.

9. My wife showed to me a picture from the Minnesota Historical Society (MHS) of the burning of Dakota sacred objects. When she checked again at the MHS, the picture was not to be found.

10. *Custer Died For Your Sins: An Indian Manifesto*, by Vine Deloria, Jr. Norman, OK: University of Oklahoma Press, 1988, p. 101.

11. Ibid.

12. Ibid., p. 102.

13. Ibid., p. 106.

14. Ibid., p. 105.

15. Ibid.

16. *Missionary Conquest: The Gospel And Native American Cultural Genocide*, by George E. Tinker. Minneapolis: Fortress Press, 1993, p. 95.

17. Ibid., p. 102.

18. *History of the Santee Sioux*, by Roy Meyer. Lincoln, NE: University of Nebraska Press, 1993, p. 66. Meyer said this of the missionary, Thomas Williamson: "He believed that the children should be separated from their parents as early as possible."

19. "Colonial Calibrations: The Expendability of Minnesota's Original People," by Waziyatawin. *William Mitchell Law Review*, Vol. 39.2, p. 458.

20. *Sublimus Dei*, by Pope Paul III.

21. Waziyatawin, op. cit., p. 458.

22. Ibid.

23. Lobo and Talbot, op. cit., p. 188.

24. David Larsen, Sr., oral history, obtained in personal conversation with his son, David Larsen, Jr.

25. Lobo & Talbot, op. cit., p. 188.

26. Personal anecdote, from Harry Running Walker, an older half-brother, who was one of those asked to leave because of their alcohol-drinking behavior.

27. Meyer, op. cit., p. 102.

28. Ibid., p. 107.

29. Ibid.

30. The Holy Bible, Containing the Old and New Testaments (New King James Version). Nashville, TN, 1985, p. 941.

31. BPCOT, p. 92.

32. The New Oxford Annotated Bible With the Apocrypha: An Ecumenical Study Bible, Revised Standard Version, 1977, p. 833.

33. The Holy Bible: Giant Print Reference, King James Version, 1976, p. 1413.

34. *From a Native Daughter: Colonialism and Sovereignty in Hawai'i*, by Haunani-Kay Trask. Honolulu: University of Hawaii Press, 1999, p. 251.

6

THE PROMISED LAND

Genocide of the Dakota People of Minnesota

"And God blessed them, and God said unto them, Be fruitful, and multiply, and replenish the earth, and subdue it: and have dominion over the fish of the sea, and over the fowl of the air, and over every living thing that moveth upon the earth." (Genesis 1:28, KJV)

In this writer's home state of Minnesota, the Wasicu (a Dakota term), i.e., the Western Europeans, came to Dakota homelands in the mid-seventeenth century.[1] The white men, who would eventually become the Euro-Minnesotans, came with "a total system of foreign power,"[2] a system of alien values, strange languages, a different religion, and a diametrically opposed world view to that of the Dakota. When these strange people came, they had no land. Today, they have virtually all the land, and we, the Dakota People, have only insignificant remnants of the vast lands we once had. Dr. Waziyatawin writes, "Now, the Dakota people occupy about .006 percent of our original land base."[3] Most of the white farmers surrounding our communities, individually, have more land than our four little Dakota communities combined. They came, they, stole, they conquered.

Because of the coming of the Wasicu, the Dakota People experienced the most traumatic and tragic event in their history, the Dakota-U.S. War of 1862–1863 and its aftermath.[4]

In the early 1860s, the Dakota Oyate ("People" or "Nation") were subjected to military attack, forced marches, scalp bounties, forcible removal, concentration camps, and mass executions. (Because this writer is a Dakota person, I'm devoting more space to the Dakota People than to other equally important First Nations Peoples.)

Here, we'll look at the Bible verses (e.g., "subdue the earth," etc.), scriptural injunctions, and biblical allusions (e.g., Canaan, land of milk and honey, etc.) which the State of Minnesota, its governor (Alexander Ramsey), and its Euro-Minnesotan citizenry used to justify the land theft, the religious suppression, and the genocide of the Dakota People. The evils suffered by the Dakota continue to the present day in the form of racial discrimination, racial hatred, racist acts, and continued dispossession.

One of the most grievous acts during the Dakota-U.S. War was the forced march on November 7–13, 1862, when 1,700 Dakota, primarily women, children, and elders, were force marched 150 miles from the Lower Sioux Community, near the towns of Morton and Redwood Falls in southwestern Minnesota, to the concentration camp at Ft. Snelling near Minneapolis. (The writer's mother, Elsie [Two Bear] Cavender, an oral historian, referred to this forced march as "a death march.") Following the forced march, the Dakota were forced into two concentration camps, one at Mankato, in south-central Minnesota, for the men, and the other at Ft. Snelling, near the present-day Twin Cities for the women, children, and elders.

The Dakota People were still suffering from the cruelty and barbarity of the brutal six-month concentration camp imprisonment (November 1862–April 1863) at Ft. Snelling when, in July 1863, the Minnesota government authorized bounties on Dakota scalps. Initially, the amount of the bounty was $25, then it was raised to $75, and, finally, to $200.[5] Also, on May 4, 1863, the Dakota were forcibly removed by boat from their traditional homelands in Minnesota, an ethnic cleansing, if you will.[6] This was one of many such ethnic cleansings perpetrated by the U.S., its military, and its Euro-American citizenry from 1830 on, when the U.S. Congress passed the Indian Removal Act (which could more suitably be called the Ethnic Cleansing Act or the Land-Theft Act).[7]

Exterminate the Wild Beasts

In Mini Sota Makoce, "Land Where the Waters Reflect the Skies, or Heavens,"[8] or Minnesota, the three most outstanding examples, among many, of the rhetoric of extermination are as follows. The first example is from Governor Alexander Ramsey, who publicly called for "extermination or removal" of the Dakota People, not once but many times. Governor Ramsey, on September 9, 1862 declared before the Minnesota State Legislature, "The Sioux Indians of Minnesota must be exterminated or driven forever beyond the borders of the State."[9] Dr. Waziyatawin writes, "This was an unambiguous directive in 1862 and it remains a clearly and concisely stated genocidal decree today. Ramsey's statement provides the first element required in defining genocide, and that is the aspect of intent."[10] Ramsey vigorously proceeded to perpetrate crimes against humanity on the Dakota People of Minnesota.

The second example of the rhetoric of extermination is from newspaper editor Jane Swisshelm, who wrote the words "Exterminate the wild beasts" in the pages of the *St. Cloud Democrat*.[11] She was an abolitionist, an early feminist, and a genocidal racist. In her mind, there was no cognitive dissonance between advocating for equality and freedom for slaves and women, and at the same time arguing against equality, freedom, and life itself, for the Dakota People.[12]

Swisshelm also said, "Kill the Lazy Vermin."[13] Her comparison of the Dakota to "vermin" foreshadowed Hitler and the Nazis' stigmatization of their victims as "vermin" prior to their genocide of the Jews, Romanis, physically and mentally handicapped, et. al.

In much the same vein, in 1864 another Euro American, the Reverend Colonel John Chivington, a Methodist minister referred to the Cheyenne and Arapaho as vermin, as lice, when he said, "kill and scalp all, little and big," "nits make lice."[14] and that the only way to get rid of lice was to "kill the nits as well."[15] David Stannard puts it this way, "It would be more than half a century . . . before Heinrich Himmler would think to describe the extermination of another people as 'the same thing as delousing.'"[16]

A third example of extermination rhetoric was provided by Major General John Pope, the Commander of the Military Department of the Northwest, headquartered in St. Paul. General Pope encouraged Henry Sibley, the leader of the punitive military expedition against the Dakota in the mid-1860s, to exterminate the Dakota. Pope wrote, in a letter dated September 17, 1862, "it is my purpose utterly to exterminate the Sioux if I have the power to do so even if it requires a campaign lasting the whole of next year . . . They are to be treated as maniacs or wild beasts, and by no means as people with whom treaties or compromises can be made."[17]

Note the term "utterly," which was used in many of the genocidal commands of the Old Testament God to the Israelites, e.g., to "destroy utterly" the Canaanites, the Hittites, et. al., who occupied Canaan, the "Promised Land." Example: Deuteronomy 7:2, "And when the LORD thy God shall deliver them before thee; thou shalt smite them, and utterly destroy them; thou shalt make no covenant with them, nor shew mercy unto them."[18]

Note also the parallel between the command in Deuteronomy, "make no covenenant with them," and General Pope's comment that the Dakota were "by no means as people with whom treaties or compromises can be made." As well, note Pope's use of the phrase, "wild beasts," a phrase which Jane Swisshelm also used to characterize the Dakota People. Such words dehumanized the Dakota People and so made it easier for the Euro-Minnesotans to murder the Dakota by reducing the guilt of and easing the consciences of the murderers and their confederates.

The Forced March

On November 7–13, 1862 1,700 Dakota women, children, and elders were force marched by the U.S. military, by soldiers with guns and bayonets from Southwest Minnesota to Ft. Snelling near Minneapolis. Colonel William Rainey Marshall, commander of the troops, later became governor of the State of Minnesota. (The forced march fulfills criterion (c) of the 1948 UN Genocide Convention, "Deliberately inflicting on the group conditions of life calculated to bring about its physical destruction in whole or in part.")

My grandmother was bayoneted in the stomach by a white soldier on horseback during the march. Her wrongdoing was not understanding an order given in a foreign language, English. She didn't speak English and so did not understand the order to keep moving; and so the white soldier became angry and bayoneted her, murdering her. A koda ("friend"), who is now deceased, had a grandmother who was also on this forced march and she needed to relieve herself. So, she headed for the trees which were along the route of the march. A white soldier motioned with his arm for her to get back in line. My friend's kunsi (grandmother) marched until she could no longer contain herself and, so, again, she headed for the trees. This time the white soldier shot and killed her. Her wrongdoing was trying to relieve herself and to do so in the trees for modesty's sake.

We do not know how many of our grandmothers were similarly murdered. Other Dakota, who grew up in a home with the oral tradition, will have to come forward and recount their stories, their memories, of murder and atrocities perpetrated against their grandmothers. These types of atrocities and crimes against humanity also occurred on other forced marches, especially during the 19th century, after the Indian Removal Act was passed in 1830 by the U.S. Congress.

We do not know how many of our grandmothers, mothers, children, and elders were murdered along the 150-mile march. We do not know how many died of gunshots or stabbings, or were killed by starvation or thirst, of sickness, or of exposure to the cold Minnesota winter. We do not know how many of our women were raped, as were so many other Indigenous women on other forced marches, e.g., those of the Choctaws, Seminoles, Tsalagi (Cherokees), and Dineh (Navajo).

As for whether these marches were genocidal events, the size, scale, or the number murdered are not the determining factors in whether or not genocide was perpetrated. A forced march is a genocidal act. Ramsey, Swisshelm, General Pope, et. al., certainly had the intent to exterminate the Dakota People of Minnesota. Even though we do not know specifically, how many Dakota were murdered along the march—in all probability at least dozens—we do know that about 1,700 Dakota, mostly women and children survived, and were still alive to be counted at the concentration camp at Ft. Snelling, during the winter of 1862–1863. Hundreds more were murdered there. Why do we use the terms "killed" or "murdered" if some of the Dakota children, women, and elders were victims of hunger, thirst, exposure, sickness, despair, or terror? Their deaths were forced upon them.

It's relevant to mention here how a Jewish psychologist, Yael Danieli, would respond to her Jewish clients who were survivors of the Holocaust. When a survivor would say that their relatives "died" at Auschwitz, Dr. Danieli would say, "No, they were murdered."[19] Dr. Robert Venables says something similar to this: "Does it matter that millions of the Indians who perished died of diseases and malnutrition rather than by the sword? Are we not to count the Jews who died of disease and starvation, and only those gassed or shot?"[20]

To amplify this, historian David Stannard says:

Although at times operating independently, for most of the long centuries of devastation that followed 1492, disease and genocide were interdependent forces acting dynamically—whipsawing their victims between plague and violence, each one feeding upon the other, and together driving countless numbers of entire ancient societies to the brink—and often over the brink— of total extermination.[21]

Thus, we, the Dakota, can, also, say that our relatives who "died" on the 150-mile forced march were murdered. The march was deliberately inflicted upon the Dakota women and children with the intent of causing their extermination in whole or in part. (This forced march, then, fulfills criterion (c) of the 1948 UN Genocide Convention, "deliberately inflicting on the group conditions of life calculated to bring about its physical destruction in whole or in part.")

The Concentration Camps

After our women, children, and elders were force-marched 150 miles, and after watching some of their family members, relatives, and friends murdered by white soldiers or murdered through exposure, hunger, terror, and disease, our grandmothers had to suffer another genocidal atrocity. They had to spend six months in a concentration camp during the cold Minnesota winter of 1862 and 1863. It is almost too much to bear to imagine what these experiences were like for them.

There were two concentration camps in Minnesota. One was at Ft. Snelling, in the area where the Minnesota River joins the Mississippi River, and where the Twin Cities now stand. This camp was for the women, children and elders.

The other was located at Maka To, or Mankato, in south-central Minnesota, where the Dakota men were imprisoned. There was gender separation so as to prevent the begetting of children. (This fulfills criterion (d) of the 1948 UN Genocide Convention, "preventing live births within the group.")

Jack Weatherford provides an excellent definition of a concentration camp in his book, *Native Roots*. He was viewing some photographs of Ft. Snelling and realized that the pictures offer "a strange glimpse of a form that was to haunt the twentieth century. These pictures show us the birth of an institution, the beginning of a whole new social practice of concentrating innocent civilians into an area and imprisoning them for protracted periods without charging them with any crime."[22]

Using Weatherford's definition, we can say that the Dakota women, children, infants, and elders ("innocent civilians"), were "concentrated into an area," i.e., Ft. Snelling, and "imprisoned" there for a "protracted period of time," for six months from November 1862 to May 1863, "without charging them with any crime." Their only "crime" was that they had Dakota blood flowing in their veins.

According to various oral historical accounts, there were burials from sun-up to sundown.[23] The People used sticks, stones, their hands, and whatever was available, to dig shallow graves and bury the dead, because they had no digging tools. In the mornings, dogs ran around the camp with human bones and flesh in their jaws, carrying the remains of babies, grandmothers, and grandfathers who had been buried the day before.

The Dakota were murdered by sickness, by hunger and what was quite probably terrible food, by exposure (to the freezing cold), by terror, and by despair. The women, children and the elders were further traumatized and some reduced to despair when they learned that 38 of their relatives—husbands, fathers, brothers, cousins, uncles, grandfathers—had been hung at Mankato on December 26, 1862.

(The concentration camps correspond to several of Chalk & Jonassohn's "Four Common Motives for Genocide," The first is "to eliminate groups of people whom the perpetrators imagine are threats." The removal, imprisonment, and murder of these women, children, infants, and elders at Ft. Snelling, fulfills another of the "four common motives": "to acquire economic wealth," in this case,the rich farming lands of southern Minnesota, around 24–35 million acres, which were part of the homelands of the Dakota.[24] The six-month imprisonment at the concentration camp also, fulfills criterion (c) of the 1948 UN Genocide Convention, "Deliberately inflicting on the group conditions of life calculated to bring about its physical destruction in whole or in part." Hundreds of the Dakota People were murdered. The conditions in the concentration camps and the news of the mass hanging of their relatives also produced "serious mental harm" as described in criterion (b) of the 1948 UN Genocide Convention, "Causing serious bodily or mental harm to members of the group.")

Talk about suffering, sorrow and calamity! This was genocide. This is The Great Evil.

Mass Executions

On December 26, 1862, the largest mass execution by hanging in the history of the United States occurred in Mankato when the State of Minnesota and the United States of America hanged simultaneously 38 Dakota men on a single gallows. Euro-Minnesotans made reservations for places to stay in Mankato weeks in advance. It was an event not to be missed.

The hanging took place on December 26, the day after Christmas. The good Christian white folk on the day before were reading their Holy Bible and celebrating the birth of their merciful Lord and Savior, Jesus Christ, and on the next day were celebrating and cheering the mass hanging. The sin, or crime, of the Dakota men was defending their homelands and attempting to drive the invaders and land-stealers out of the Minnesota River Valley. One Euro-Minnesotan writer said that when the trap-door was sprung, and the 38 were hanging, "one, loud, drawn-out cheer" rose up from the throats of the thousands of white people (4,000, by some estimates) who were present.[25]

The blood lust of the Euro-Minnesotans was satisfied, temporarily, by this horrible injustice. The Dakota men should have been treated as prisoners of war. Instead, they were treated as war criminals. This act was a crime against humanity—it was "legalized murder."[26] These Dakota men were the first patriots of Minnesota. They actually did fight for their homelands. They fought for their people, they fought for their freedom, they fought for their way of life, and they fought for their burial and sacred sites on the lands on which the Dakota had lived from time immemorial. The Dakota People didn't defend their lands or fight for their freedom across the oceans in some far-away lands, as the U.S. military claims to be doing. Instead, our ancestors fought, here in Minnesota, against dangerous, criminal immigrants, the land stealers, and against the U.S. military and the State of Minnesota which were enabling the land stealers. The mass killing was fulfilling what Governor Ramsey wanted and publicly expressed many times, "extermination or removal" of the Dakota People. Thus the killers, had a reason to celebrate. The land thieves could now continue to safely steal Dakota lands.

To the Dakota who watched the mass "legalized murder"[27] and "military injustice,"[28] to the Dakota (e.g., the Dakota women and children at the Ft. Snelling concentration camp) who later learned of the mass execution, and to the Dakota relatives of today, this was a gut-wrenching, spirit-killing, demoralizing event. For some of us, this genocidal action instilled, and continues to instill, feelings of anger, hatred, bitterness, resentment, and a desire for vengeance. These emotions are very "appropriate responses" to horrific and enduring historical injustices.[29]

For many Dakota, today (including this writer), this Evil, which was perpetrated against our relatives in the 1860s, feels like it happened yesterday. The emotional wounds are still fresh. This murderous and genocidal act of mass hanging is unforgivable.

(This mass murder and execution of 38 Dakota men fulfills criterion (a) of the UN Genocide Convention of 1948, "Killing Members of the Group." And many individual Dakota women, children, and elders, as individuals, were murdered in the various genocidal experiences to which the Dakota were subjected. These events would fulfill criterion (a) of the 1948 UN Genocide Convention "Killing Members of the Group.")

Forcible Removal

On May 4, 1863, the much-reduced population of 1,300 at the Ft. Snelling concentration camp (down from 1,700) was forcibly removed from their homelands. At a landing on the Minnesota River, the Dakota were loaded onto two cattleboats, or steamboats, with horses and other animals. They were moved down the Mississippi River and up the Missouri river. Some were left at Santee, Nebraska. The remainder were taken to Crow Creek, South Dakota. Here, hundreds more of the Dakota grandmothers, mothers, their children, and elders died, or ,more accurately, were murdered. (This act of forcible removal, of ethnic cleansing, fulfills criterion (c) of the 1948 UN Genocide Convention, "Deliberately inflicting upon the group conditions of life calculated to bring about its physical destruction in whole or in part.")

Of the loading of the Dakota on the cattle boats on the Minnesota River, the missionary John P. Williamson wrote this on May 4, 1863 about the forced exile and the subsequent deaths:

> When 1300 Indians [Dakota—the actual name, *not* "Indians"] were crowded like slaves on the boiler and hurricane decks of a single boat, and fed on musty hardtack and briny pork, which they had not half a chance to cook, diseases were bred which made fearful havoc during the hot months, and the 1300 souls that were landed at Crow Creek June 1, 1863, decreased to one thousand . . . So were the hills soon covered with graves.[30]

Dr. Waziyatawin writes of this imprisonment of the Dakota grandmothers, mothers, children, and elders at the concentration camp at Crow Creek: "Imprisonment was no accident. It was a callous and inhumane government and citizenry that continued to subject Dakota People to long-term confinement while our people were dying. Yet, they continued to deny our Dakota ancestors their freedom."[31] It is good to reiterate that this forcible removal, this "ethnic cleansing," of the Dakota People from their ancient homelands of thousands upon thousands of years, is part of The Great Evil.

(The U.S. government, its military, and its Euro-American and Euro-Minnesotan citizens need to be held accountable. A good first step toward accountability is to acknowledge the truth of what was done to the Dakota People of Minnesota and who did it. Then, this truth needs not only to be acknowledged, but also to be taught in the schools, both public and private, and to be published in U.S. History textbooks.) This act of forcible removal could, also, be considered a crime against humanity. Crimes against humanity involve what the Rome Statute of the International Criminal Court Explanatory Memorandum refers to as "odious offenses" which constitute a serious attack on human dignity or grave humiliation or a degradation of human beings," in this case the "degradation" of Dakota women, children, infants, and elders.[32]

These offenses were part of a "wide practice of atrocities tolerated or condoned by a government."[33] in this case two governments: those of the State of Minnesota and the United States. Crimes against humanity can include any of the following as part of a widespread or systematic attack against any civilian population: murder; deportation, or forcible transfer of the population; imprisonment; rape, or any form of sexual violence,[34] all of which were perpetrated against our women, children, infants, and elders by this supposedly "civilized," "just," Christian, and "superior" Euro-American and Euro-Minnesotans.)

Imprisonment of Dakota Men at Davenport, Iowa

The U.S. government imprisoned over 400 Dakota men at Camp Mc-Clellan, at Davenport, Iowa, for a period of three years, during which time a third of the men died (more accurately, were murdered).

According to one oral account,[35] the windows of the cells of the Dakota men did not face the river, but faced in the opposite direction away to the side of a hill, a deliberately cruel act. So, our men couldn't even see the water, which is considered wakan ("sacred") and pezihuta ("medicine"). Our people say "mini wiconi," or "water is life" ("Mini Wiconi" was the slogan used by the Water Protectors at the Standing Rock Reservation, in their 2016 resistance to the Dakota Access Pipe Liine.).

I had a relative on my father's side, by the name of Wicanhpi Nunpa, or "Two Stars," who was imprisoned, murdered, and buried at some unknown place at Camp McClellan, if he was buried at all.

(This three-years imprisonment fulfills criterion (c) of the 1948 UN Genocide Convention, "Deliberately inflicting conditions of life calculated to bring about its physical destruction in whole or in part." This was also an inhumane act which intentionally caused serious mental, emotional, and spiritual harm to our Dakota men. This fulfills criterion (b) of the 1948 UN Genocide Convention, "Causing serious bodily or mental harm to members of the group." The forced marches, the mass executions, the forcible removals, the concentration camps, etc. all caused, in addition to the physical deaths, much bodily and mental harm to the Dakota People.

Approximately one-third of Dakota men at Fort McClellan were murdered there because of the brutal physical conditions. This act by the U.S. government of forcibly removing the Dakota men from their ancient homelands and then imprisoning them at Davenport also constitutes crimes against humanity in addition to the genocide.

Again, the Dakota men didn't simply "die." They were murdered either through physical violence or through means of disease, hunger, horrible living conditions, and despair.

The Punitive Military Campaigns of 1863

The blood lust and atrocities continued in 1863 with the punitive military campaigns waged by Henry Sibley and Alfred Sully in the areas now known as South and North Dakota. In these campaigns, Sibley and Sully indiscriminately slaughtered Dakota women, "little ones," and elders, and destroyed, wholesale, Dakota villages. Then these killers had the gall to call these massacres battles, e.g., at Whitestone Hill in North Dakota.[36] Like the Rev. Colonel John Chivington at the Sand Creek Massacre in Colorado in 1864, Sibley and Sully wished "to be wading in gore"[37] and "to kill all Indians" (Dakota, in this case).[38]

Hundreds upon hundreds of Dakota women, children, elders, and men were murdered in these wanton slaughters. The winter stores of food and supplies were burned and destroyed. So, if the white man's bullets and bayonets didn't kill the Dakotas, then hunger, starvation, sickness, and exposure in the brutal winters of the north-central plains helped finish the job, thus fulfilling the savage "extermination or removal" cry of Governor Ramsey and other Euro-Minnesotans.

The men like Chivington who "desired to take Native scalps" seemed to relish the killing.[39] Sully, for example, wanted more than just scalps and mutilations. Sully wanted and had the skulls of Dakota people mounted on poles to adorn the entry to his headquarters.[40] Further, Sully admitted he was in the business of "extermination."[41] When I hear white academics, especially, U.S. historians, say, "There was no genocidal "intent," I think how ludicrous this statement is when there is an abundance of genocidal rhetoric, an "embarrassment of riches." I suspect these historians are either ignorant of what was done to the Indigenous peoples, and who did it, or are willfully suppressing this knowledge.

(These punitive military campaigns against the Dakota People cannot be called anything other than genocide. The campaigns most definitely fulfill criterion (a) of the 1948 UN Genocide Convention, "Killing Members of the Group.")

Bounties on Dakota Scalps

One of the most heinous, barbaric, and savage acts that can be perpetrated by one group upon another group is the placing of bounties on human scalps. This genocidal practice was not uncommon. The colonists, the U.S. government, the states, and their Euro-American citizens hunted down First Nations people like animals, for their scalps, and many thousands were slain. Vine Deloria, Jr. writes, "Bounties were set and an Indian scalp became more valuable than beaver, otter, marten, and other animal pelts."[42] Ward Churchill writes that the practice of placing bounties on Native scalps was used, "at one time or another by every state and territory in the Lower Forty-Eight."[43]

The State of Minnesota joined its fellow scalpers in 1863 when it authorized bounties on the scalps of Dakota people.[44] In addition, authorization of scalp bounties on Dakota People by the state legislature clearly indicates genocidal intent as well as action. When Governor Alexander Ramsey advocated on a number of occasions, "extermination or removal," he was clearly indicating his intent to murder all of the Dakota People of Minnesota. How do we know this? We know this because Ramsey said this publicly, and advocated it before the Minnesota State legislature.[45] Because of Ramsey's position as governor of the state and because of the influence and power integral to that position, as Dr. Waziyatawin writes, "Ramsey may be viewed as the architect of Minnesota's official genocidal policies that would follow."[46]

Hitler said, on many occasions to his inner circle that he "admired" the "efficiency" of the U.S. genocidal programs against the Indigenous Peoples of the U.S., and "viewed them as forerunners for his own programs."[47] Hitler's victims, his hated target groups, did not fit into his imagined-superior Aryans. And, of course, Ramsey and his Euro-Minnesotan citizenry thought that the hated Dakota did not fit in with their superior group, the "chosen people," the Euro-Minnesotans. Hitler admired the "concentration camp" that the United States used against Indigenous Peoples.[48] We know this because Hitler wrote and spoke publicly of those things he "admired" about the U.S.[49] Since Ramsey, too, in the 1860s, wrote down and stated publicly his genocidal intent regarding the Dakota People of Minnesota., and since Hitler was a student of U.S. history, it would not be surprising if it turned out that Minnesota was one of the states, and that Ramsey was one of the men, that he he admired for their murderous "efficiency."

The terrible things that happened to the Dakota People of Minnesota —the land theft, the broken treaties, the religious suppression, the prohibition and suppression of Native languages, the extermination, the forcible removal, the bounties, and the concentration camps—happened dozens upon dozens of times to scores of other Indigenous Nations and to millions of the Aboriginal Peoples of what's now the eastern United States in the the 1500s, 1600s, and 1700s.

The people who committed these unforgiveable genocidal atrocities were evil. These acts are beyond the "ambit of reconciliation."[50]

Dominion Over Earth Vs. Mother Earth

Then God blessed them, and God said to them, Be fruitful, and multiply; and fill the earth, and subdue it; have dominion over the fish of the sea, over the birds of the air, and over every living thing that moves on the earth. (Genesis 1:28, NKJV)

(To reiterate, because the writer is Dakota, he will spend more time on what happened to the Dakota People of Minnesota than on other Indigenous genocides.)

Concerning the concept of "dominion" over creation from Genesis 1:28, another Bible verse comes to mind, from Psalms:

When I consider the heavens, the work of thy fingers, the moon and the stars, which thou has ordained; . . . What is man, that thou are mindful of him? And the son of man, that thou visitest him? . . . For thou hast made him a little lower than the angels, and hast crowned him with glory and honour . . . Thou madest him to have dominion over the works of thy hands; thou hast put all things under his feet. (Psalms 8:3–6, KJV).

This verse expands on the idea of "dominion" found in Genesis 1:28, and indicates what man's relationship should be to the natural world and to creation. This idea is vastly different from that of the Indigenous Peoples of the Americas toward the earth, the animals, toward all of life. These verses, Genesis 1:28 and Psalm 8:3–6, make it quite clear that man has dominion over all creation. In other words, "he" (always "he") has license to do whatever he damn well pleases to the earth and the animals that inhabit it.

The worldview of the Dakota People could hardly be more different. The earth is regarded as Ina Maka, "Mother Earth," and as Unci Maka, "Grandmother Earth." This Dakota/Indigenous belief is diametrically opposite to that of the Judeo-Christian belief expounded in the Bible, Genesis 1:28 and Psalms 8:6, and to the belief of the western European and Euro-American Christians who adhere to the Old Testament.

The ideas "subdue the earth," have "dominion" over the earth, and "cursed ground"[51] are repugnant ideas to traditional Indigenous Peoples. One religious perspective shows superiority over and a negative perception (e.g., the "cursed earth" notion) toward the Earth, and the other worldview, the earth as "Mother" or "Grandmother," illustrates caring, love, respect, and kinship, to the Earth. When I was in the classroom, in my "Indigenous Spirituality and Worldview" course, I would ask which perspective toward the Earth, the creation, and the animals is better? Which is more civilized?"

Blood Crieth Unto Me — A Call to Vengeance

And He (GOD) said, "What hast thou done? The voice of thy brother's blood crieth unto me from the ground." (Genesis 4:10, KJV)

Then He said, "What have you done? Hark, your brother's blood cries out to Me from the ground." (Torah)

Genesis 4:10, a reference to Cain and Abel, was used to justify the killing of Dakota People. Governor Alexander Ramsey used this phrase before the Minnesota State Legislature on September 9, 1862: "The blood of the murdered cries out to heaven for vengeance . . ."[52] Apparently, Governor Ramsey was referring ("the blood of the murdered") to the Euro-Minnesotans who were killed by the Dakota because they were stealing Dakota lands. The Dakota resisted this theft, as any other group of human beings would. However, to Ramsey, the Dakota had no rights to their own land, land that they had been living on for thousands of years.

Further, Ramsey and other Euro-Minnesotans (the Swedes, Norwegians, the Germans, et. al.) who thought they were God's chosen people, believed they had a right to the "promised land." They believed that the Dakota had no right to their own land, and thus their killing of white land stealers was murder. So, Ramsey said to the Minnesota State Legislature that the blood of the Euro-Minnesotans, the "innocents," was calling out to God in heaven to wreak "vengeance" upon the "wild beasts," the savage

Dakota.[53] And Governor Ramsey and the Euro-Minnesotans were going to be the Lord's instruments of vengeance.

Another person who referred to the same verse which contained "blood crieth out," that Ramsey used in addressing the State Legislature, was newspaper editor Jane Swisshelm of St. Cloud, Minnesota, who despite being an abolitionist, and an early feminist, thought that the Dakota People should not fight back.[54] Swisshelm, like Ramsey, thought that the Euro-Minnesotan land stealers were "innocent," and that their blood was now calling for "vengeance." She wrote, "Exterminate the wild beasts, and make peace with the devil and all his hosts sooner than these red-jawed tigers, whose fangs are dripping with the blood of the innocents."[55] "Get ready, and as soon as these convicted murderers are turned loose, shoot them and be sure they are shot dead, dead, dead, dead! If they have any souls, the Lord can have mercy on them if he pleases! But that is His business. Ours is to kill the lazy vermin and make sure of killing them."[56]

"The Lord was Opening the Way"

A letter written by the Reverend Stephen Return Riggs, a Presbyterian missionary among the Dakota People, in the first half of the 19th century, including in this writer's home community, provides a good example of how the Euro-Minnesota Christians thought the Lord was helping them. In his letter to S.B. Treat on April 21, 1863, Riggs wrote the following:

> On Sabbath afternoon I preached to a mass meeting in the camp—the largest I ever preached to on the benefits to be derived from suffering. I told them that we had been for several years thinking of how we could get the Gospel to the Yankton Dakota. Now the Lord was opening the way in a manner none of us had thought of.[57]

The setting of this letter was the concentration camp site at Ft. Snelling, and Riggs was extolling the "benefits" of having a captive audience. The Dakota women, children, and elders had spent the past six months in this concentration camp, and hundreds had been murdered. There had been burials from sun up to sundown each day. The Dakota had suffered hunger, cold, disease, fear, terror, and despair. Our Dakota women had been raped, and some had been violently murdered by white soldiers. I would not be surprised if the Dakota women and elders were skeptical about the possible benefits of "suffering," from rape, murder, freezing cold, hunger, disease, forced marches, and imprisonment in concentration camps.

Concerning the rape, sexual abuse, and murder of Dakota women at the Ft. Snelling concentration camp, Dr. Waziyatawin writes:

On November 27, 1862, a girl from Red Wing, for example, reported about Fort Snelling, 'There are a few squaws killed up at the fort every week . . . always cut their throats by running against a knife. The Third (Regiment) buries them in a hole, face downwards.' White soldiers could routinely perpetrate sexual violence against Dakota women and girls and then simply disposed of their bodies. Moreover, they could do so without fear of retributive violence from male Dakota relatives who were helpless to defend their women and children because they were imprisoned elsewhere."[58]

Back to Rev. Riggs and his grossly insensitive remarks about the Dakota women, children, and elders in the concentration camp, the "The Benefits To Be Derived from Suffering." One wonders how much suffering Rev. Riggs endured in his life. Likely comparatively little, let alone the horrors of being force-marched, deported, imprisoned, sexually abused, and murdered. Thus it was easy for Riggs to see the benefits in the suffering of *others*. However, Riggs was not alone in his ignorance and obliviousness, even today most Euro-Minnesotans are equally ignorant of and insensitive to what was really done to the Dakota People, and to who did it.

It was in this setting, when the spirits of our Dakota people were broken, and their bodies weak, and they were feeling helpless and hopeless, that Christianity may have begun to have an effect upon them. Charles Eastman, a fellow Wahpetunwan ("Dwellers In the Leaves") Dakota, seems to suggest this when he wrote, ". . . and it was not until his spirit was broken and his moral and physical constitutions undermined by trade, conquest, and strong drink, that Christian missionaries obtained any real hold upon him."[59]

* * *

The notion of the Lord helping and "showing the way" to the Euro-Americans and Euro-Minnesotans hearkens back to an epidemic during the years 1616–1619. Thousands of Native People were killed in the epidemic, probably by smallpox. And the Christian colonists were jubilant over the deaths of so many Indigenous People. As Brandon states, "the church colonists exulted, with reverence, over the frightful epidemic of 1616–1619 that had cleared so many heathen from the path of the Chosen People."[60] One colonist wrote of "The Wonderful Preparation the Lord

Christ by His Providence Wrought for His People's Abode in this Western World." This same writer further wrote with particular satisfaction that "the plague had swept away 'chiefly young men and children, the very seeds of increase.'"[61]

Another writer, a Thomas Morton of Merry Mount, observed that in "this, the wondrous wisedome and love of God, is shewne, by sending to the place his Minister, to sweepe away . . . the Salvages . . . ."[62] Of course, as we've seen in previous chapters, the Old Testament God was perfectly willing and able to do this sort of thing, as He, the Lord, sent all sorts of plagues upon the enemies of the Israelites, particularly, upon the innocent Egyptian common people when the Israelites were in bondage in Egypt. So, is it any wonder that the Christian colonists thought that God would do the same thing for them?

Subdue the Earth

And God blessed them, and God said unto them Be fruitful, and multiply, and replenish the earth, and subdue it: and have dominion over the fish of the sea, and over the fowl of the air, and over every living thing that moveth upon the earth. (Genesis 1:28, KJV)

The "subdue the earth" notion helped provide the rationale for stealing Dakota lands, for removing Dakota People from their ancient homelands. This idea was expounded by white supremacist Charles A. Bryant, who said of the Dakota-U.S. War of 1862 that it was "a conflict of knowledge with ignorance, of right with wrong," since the Dakota did not obey the divine injunction to subdue, they were "in the wrongful possession of a continent required by the superior right of the white man."[63] Roy W. Meyer aptly notes that the "insufferable smugness and complacency of the white man finds its ultimate expression in the words of Charles Bryant."[64]

In a similar vein to that of Bryant, Senator Thomas Hart Benton said in 1846: "It would seem that the white race had alone received the divine command, to subdue and replenish the earth," and indigenous people had no right to the land of the Americas because this land had been "created for use . . . by the white races . . . according to the intentions of the Creator, for it is the only race that has obeyed it . . . to subdue and replenish."[65]

People like Charles Bryant and Senator Benton seemed to forget, or were just plain ignorant, of the fact that the Indigenous Peoples of the Americas, including North America, had been farming for centuries before the white man ever came to our Indigenous homelands, and that the Native Peoples of the Americas had domesticated hundreds of different crops[66] as well as medicinal plants.[67] They were also ignorant of, or forgot, that the early towns and colonies would not have survived if they had not received agricultural technical assistance from the Native Peoples living along the East Coast.

* * *

What do the theologians have to say about dominion and subduing the earth? Matthew Henry, says regarding both Genesis 1:28 and Psalms 8:6, "Though man is a worm [Job 30:6], yet man is above all the creatures in this lower world."[68] Henry also uses the phrase, "lives of the inferior creatures . . ."[69] As we can see, Henry agrees with the Jewish God's idea of man's "dominion" over the "lower creatures."

(This view is diametrically opposite to the traditional Dakota worldview in which the animals, birds, fish, etc. are peoples and are our relatives. In our ceremonies, we talk of the Wambdi Oyate, the "Eagle People," the "Sunktanka Oyate, the Horse People," the Wakinyan Oyate, the "Thunder People," and the Tunkan Oyate, the "Stone People," among others.)

Jamieson, Fausset, and Brown comment on Psalms 8:6, "Thou madest him to have dominion over the works of thy hands; thou hast put all things under his feet," (KJV) "The position assigned man is that described (Genesis 1:26-28) that 'man is still invested with some remains of this original dominion.'"[70]

What does Adam Clarke, our Methodist theologian, have to say about these verses? Concerning Genesis 1:28, Clarke refers to man as "this lord of creation."[71] And as the "lord of creation," man has the right to "subdue the earth" and "have dominion" over the "inferior." No surprise here!

The Promised Land

Probably the most powerful and influential Bible verses and teachings, for both Euro-Americans and Euro-Minnesotans, were and are those regarding the "promised land," "Canaan," and "chosen people." These notions, along with the genocidal commands of the Old Testament God, justify not only the massive land theft from Native peoples, but also the mass murdering of them.

The "promised land" notion is found in a number of Old Testament books. One such reference is in Genesis:

And Abram passed through the land unto the place of Sichem, unto the plain of Moreh. And the Canaanite was then in the land. And the Lord appeared unto Abram and said, "Unto thy seed will I give this land." (Genesis 12:6–7, KJV)

The New American Bible also says that "The Canaanites were then in the land." Even the Torah, the Jewish Scriptures, acknowledges that "The Canaanites were then in the land." Again, note that all three versions/translation say that the Old Testament God was giving the land to Abram and the Israelites while the Canaanites and the other Indigenous Peoples were still living in the land and had been there first; that did not stop Yahweh from giving the Canaanite homelands to the Israelites. This is the parallel with their God "giving" Native lands to the new "chosen people," the Euro-Americans and Euro-Minnesotans. (One might note that these same biblical injunctions, millennia after they were written, are still causing suffering and ongoing, brutal conflict in Palestine/Israel.)

What do the theologians say about Genesis 12:6–7? Matthew Henry acknowledges that the promised land was already "peopled and possessed by Canaanites,"[73] though he doesn't say anything remotely negative about God giving land to Abram while the Canaanites still "peopled and possessed" it. Jamieson, Fausset, and Brown, and Adam Clarke also say nothing specific about God giving away land to one people while other peoples were still living in that land and had been for who knows how long.

Apparently, to the theologians, it's fine for God to do this—to arbitrarily give away somebody else's land to another people, because the land was "to serve as the cradle of a divine revelation designed for the whole world."[73]

Adam Clarke writes that the promised land would serve as the place for "the dispensation of the mercy of God to all the families of the earth through the promised Messiah."[74]

Thus, theft from and mass murder of the Canaanites, Hittites, et. al., was justified, as they were idolators, were full of iniquity, and were "pagans in the promised land,"[75] obstacles to God's "dispensation of mercy." Thus, these pagans were expendable and had no rights that the Israelites needed to respect. All of the theologians agree on this.

Concerning the question, "With whom do Indigenous Peoples identify? With the Israelites? Or, with the Canaanites?" let me quote Robert Allen Warrior, an Osage man, and an academic:

The obvious characters in the story for Native Americans to identify with are the Canaanites, the people who already lived in the promised land. As a member of the Osage Nation of American Indians who stands in solidarity with other tribal peoples around the world, I read the Exodus stories with Canaanite eyes. And, it is the Canaanite side of the story that has been overlooked by those seeking to articulate theologies of liberation. Especially ignored are those parts of the story that describe Yahweh's command to mercilessly annihilate the Indigenous populations.[76]

Now, let's look at how the notion of "Canaan, land of milk and honey" played out in Minnesota and other states in the north central U.S.

To start, let's consider a paper written by George M. Stephenson, from the University of Minnesota, which was titled "When America was the Land of Canaan."[77] It was read at the first Hutchinson session of the eighth state historical convention on June 14, 1929. At its beginning, there's a statement which says that the author "will study the documents that betray the spirit, hopes, and aspirations of the humble folk who tilled the soil, felled the forest and tended the loom—in short, who followed the occupations that fall to the lot of the less favored majority in every land."[78]

Moving right along, Stephenson talks of the thousands of letters that found their way from the USA back "to the small red cottages hidden among the pine-clad, rocky hills of Sweden."[79] These letters talked about a new and ideal land and that these "America letters" "fell like leaves from the land of Canaan," "the wonderful country across the Atlantic—a land of milk and honey."[80]

One letter written in May 1846 talks about a "beggar girl from Kisa, who has gone up into the more level country to ply her trade, is said to have painted America in far more attractive colors than Joshua's returned spies portrayed the promised land to the children of Israel."[81] A letter from Iowa in November 1849 says, "No one need worry about my circumstances in America, because I am living on God's noble and free soil, neither am I a slave under others . . . I sincerely hope that nobody in Sweden will foolishly dissuade anyone from coming to this land of Canaan."[82]

Then there's a letter written on October 9, 1849 by Steffan Steffanson, taken from the Swedish Historical Society of America 1926 Yearbook: "My words are inadequate to describe with what joy we are permitted daily to draw water from the well of life and how we have come to the land of Canaan flowing with milk and honey, . . . which the Scriptures tell us the Lord has prepared for his people."[83] Note the clause, "which the Scriptures tell us the Lord has prepared for his people."

These Swedish immigrants truly believed that the Jewish God of the Bible promised and prepared Minnesota for them. They really believed that they were the "chosen People," that they were symbolic Israelites, as did the Germans, the Norwegians, and the other Western European immigrants, who were to become Euro-Minnesotans.

Stephenson writes about equality in dress and speech:

> In the promised land they were all, men and women, classified as "Mrs." and "Mr." In Sweden the maid slept in the kitchen, shined shoes, and worked long hours; in America she had her own room, limited working hours, regular times for meals, and time to take a buggy ride with Ole Olson, who hailed from the same parish.[84]

In a letter written before 1850, we read, "Not until this year have I fully realized how grateful we ought to be to God who by His grace has brought us away from both spiritual and material misery."[85] Stephenson goes on, "In some parts of Sweden the 'America letters' from near relatives brought Chicago closer to them than Stockholm. They knew more about the doings of their relatives in Center City, Minnesota, than about Uncle John in Jonkoping."[86] "If many letters were stained with tears in the little red cottages in Sweden, there were not a few written by trembling hands in the log cabins of Minnesota and later in the sod houses of Nebraska."[87]

A final quote from Stephenson:

> Miraculous things happened in the land of Canaan; it could transform a conservative Swedish bonde [a farmer, a peasant] into a 'hundred per cent American' in spirit, but it could not so easily sever the ties of blood. Neither could the storm-tossed Atlantic prevent sisters, cousins, uncles, and aunts from accepting invitations embalmed in "America Letters" to attend family reunions in the land of Canaan.[88]

In Conclusion

It's easy to see how powerful and pervasive the biblical notions of the "promised land," "Canaan," and the "land of milk and honey" were upon not only the Swedish immigrants but also upon other western European immigrants—the Norwegians, the Germans, the Belgians, the Dutch, the Irish, et. al. They all came here to stay. They were not going to let some human beings whom they considered savages, nonChristians, uncivilized, pagan, such as the Dakota People, stand in their way. Like the Israelites of old, who exterminated, removed, and stole from the Canaanites, the Hittites, et. al., these Swedish immigrants, as well as the other Euro-Minnesotans, were also going to exterminate, remove, and steal the lands from the Dakota People, with help from Yahweh, the same killer God of the Old Testament.

Hopefully, the reader can see that Genesis 1:28, along with Psalms 8, with its subdue-the-earth and dominion-over-the-animals teachings, in addition to the verses dealing with Canaan, the promised land, and land of milk and honey (Genesis 12:6-7; Genesis 13:12, 14-15; Leviticus 20:24; plus Genesis 4:10 (Cain killing Abel), in addition to the verses recording Yahweh's genocidal commands, were powerful influences in justifying the stealing of the lands, the physical removal, the religious suppression, and the killing of the Dakota People. These verses, with their emphasis on "dominion," contributed to the "chosen people" and white supremacy notions, and also served as the basis of Manifest Destiny, Minnesota-style. The writer would like to think that the reader can now see, if not before, how significant the Bible and some of its teachings were so instrumental in what was done to the Dakota People of Minnesota, and other Indigenous peoples, and who did it.

Endnotes

1. *History of the Santee Sioux: United States Indian Policy On Trial,* by Roy Meyer. Lincoln, NE: University of Nebraska Press, 1993, p. 1.

2. *From a Native Daughter: Colonialism and Sovereignty in Hawai'i,* by Hannah-Kay Trask, 1993, p. 251.

3. *What Does Justice Look Like,* by Waiyatawin. St. Paul: Living Justice Press, 2008, p. 61.

4. Meyer, op. cit., p. 132.

5. Ibid., p. 135.

6. Waziyatawin, op. cit., p. 55.

7. "Key Indian Laws and Cases," by Ward Churchill and Glenn T. Morris, in *The State of Native America: Genocide, Colonization, and Resistance,* edited by M. Annette Jaimes. Boston: South End Press, 1992, pp. 13–14.

8. Author's translation. Another Wahpetunwan Dakota writer, Dr. Charles Eastman translates Mini Sota Makoce as "Land of Sky-Blue Waters." Both translations refer to the thousands upon thousands of lakes in Dakota Homelands in North Central United States, and in southern Ontario, Canada. "Minnesota comes from the Dakota "Mini Sota."

9. Waziyatawin, op. cit., p. 39.

10. Ibid.

11. "A Woman of Contradiction," by Tim Post, Minnesota Public Radio, September 26, 2002.

12. Sam Grey, e-mail, March 20, 2014.

13. Post, op. cit.

14. *American Holocaust,* by David Stannard. Oxford: Oxford University Press, 1992, p. 131.

15. Ibid.

16. Ibid.

17. Waziyatawin, op. cit., pp. 459–460.

18. The Holy Bible, Nashville: Thomas Nelson Publishers, 1976, p. 301.

19. *Trauma and Recovery,* by Judith Herman, M.D. New York: Basic Books, 1997, p. 135.

20. "The Cost of Columbus: Was There a Holocaust?" by Robert Venables, Ph.D., in *Northeast Indian Quarterly,* Fall 1990, p. 31.

21. Stannard, op. cit., p. xii.

22. *Native Roots,* by Jack Weatherford. New York: Crown, 1991, p. 178.

23. Dr. Barbara Feezor-Buttes, Video, "Wacipi,"

24. Waziyatawin, op. cit., p. 34.

25. *North Country: The Making of Minnesota*, by Mary Lethert. Minneapolis: University of Minnesota Press, 2010, p. 327.

26. Meyer, op. cit., p. 138.

27. Ibid.

28. "The United States-Dakota War Trials: A Study in Military Injustice," by Carol Chomsky, p. 1.

29. "The Ambit of Reconciliation," by Sam Grey, pp. 1–19, an unpublished paper.

30. Waziyatawin, op. cit., p. 56.

31. Ibid.

32. Rome Statute of the International Criminal Court Explanatory memorandum, "Crimes Against Humanity," July 17, 1998, p. 1.

33. Ibid.

34. Ibid.

35. From a conversation with Reuben Kitto.

36. "Forgotten Clash Still Divides," by Patrick Springer. *Fargo Forum*, August 4, 2013.

37. Stannard, op. cit., p. 131

38. *Song of Sorrow: Massacre at Sand Creek,* by Patrick M Mendoza. Denver: Willow Wind Publishing Company, 1993, p. 79.

39. Stannard, op. cit., p. 131

40. Churchill, op. cit., p. 180.

41. Springer, op. cit.

42. *Custer Died For Your Sins: An Indian Manifesto,* by Vine Deloria, Jr. Norman, OK: University of Oklahoma Press, 1988, p. 7.

43. *On the Justice of Roosting Chickens,* by Ward Churchill. Oakland: AK Press, 2003, pp. 7, 12, 13.

44. Waziyatawin, op. cit., pp. 47–49.

45. Ibid. pp. 10, 17, 39.

46. Ibid., p. 39.

47. Stannard, op. cit., p. 153.

48. *Hitler,* by John Toland. New York: Anchor Books, 1976, p. 702.

49. Ibid., p. 702. Also, in Stannard's *American Holocaust,* p. 153.

50. "The Ambit of Reconciliation," by Sam Grey. Unpublished paper, pp. 1, 158.

51. The Holy Bible, King James Version, Giant Print Reference Edition Nashville: Thomas Nelson Publishers, 1976, on Genesis 1:28 and Genesis 3:17.

52. "Colonial Calibrations: The Expendability of Minnesota's Original People," by Waziyatawin, *William Mitchell Law Review,* Vol. 39:2, p. 459.

53. Ibid.

54. Post, op. cit.

55. Ibid.

56. Ibid..

57. Waziyatawin, "Colonial Calibrations," op. cit., footnote #118, p. 482.

58 Ibid., p. 475.

59. *The Soul of the Indian,* by Charles Eastman. Lincoln, NE: University of Nebraska Press, 1911, 1980, p. 20.

60. *The Last Americans,* by William Brandon. New York: McGraw-Hill, 1974., p. 202.

61. Ibid.

62. Ibid.

63. Meyer, op. cit., p. 116.

64. Ibid.

65. *Ecocide of Native America: Environmental Destruction of Indian Lands and Peoples,* by Donald A. Grinde, Bruce E. Johansen. Santa Fe, NM: Clear Light Publishers, 1995, pp. 9,10.

66. *Indian Givers: How the Indians of the Americas Transformed the World*, by Jack Weatherford. New York: Fawcett, 1988, (1988), Fawcett Columbine, New York, New York, pp. 59–78. "The American Indians cultivated over three hundred food crops, and many of them had dozens of variations. . . . The Indians gave the world three- fifths of the crops now in cultivation" (p. 71).

67. *American Indian Medicine*, by Virgil Vogel. Norman, OK: University of Oklahoma Press, 1970. "The most important evidence of Indian influence on American medicine is seen in the fact that more than two hundred indigenous drugs which were used by one or more Indigenous Peoples (Vogel used "Indian tribes") have been official in the The Pharmacopeia of the United States of America . . ."

68. BPCOT, p. 976.

69. Ibid.

70. Ibid.

71. Ibid., p. 6.

72. Ibid., p. 42

73. Ibid.

74. Ibid.

75. *Pagans In The Promised Land*, by Steven T. Newcomb. Golden, CO: Fulcrum Publishing, 2008, title page.

76. "A Native American Perspective: Canaanites, Cowboys, and Indians," by Robert Allen Warrior, in *Christianity and Crisis 49*, #12, 1989, P. 279.

77. "When America Was The Land of Canaan," by George M. Stephenson, a paper read on June 14, 1929 at the first Hutchinson session of the eighth state historical convention, p. 237.

78 Ibid.

79. Ibid., p. 238.

80. Ibid.

81. Ibid., p. 239.

82. Ibid., p. 247.

83. Ibid., p. 251.

84. Ibid., p. 257.

85. Ibid., p. 246.

86. Ibid., p. 259.

87. Ibid., p. 260.

88. Ibid., p. 260.

7

No Justice, No Peace

"And you shall know the truth, and the truth shall make you free."

(John 8:32, NKJV)

The Bible and Murder

It is clear that Western Europeans and the Euro-Americans, since 1492, have used Bible verses as one of the major rationales for stealing from, killing, suppressing, and enslaving, the Indigenous Peoples of the Americas. Just as the Israelites were the "chosen people" of the Old Testament God, so, too, did the Euro-Americans believe they were a "chosen people" of the same Old Testament God. Just as the Israelites believed the godless Hittites and Canaanites needed to be exterminated and removed, so too did U.S. whites believe that the Indigenous Peoples of the United States needed to be exterminated or removed, as exemplified by Minnesota Governor Alexander Ramsey's cry of "extermination or removal."

Further, just as the Israelites considered the lands of the Canaanites and Hittites to be the "promised land" and "the land of milk and honey," so, too, did U.S. Euro-Americans consider the three billion acres of Indigenous homelands, in what is now known as the United States of America, as their "promised land," or, as Canaan, as the "land of milk and honey." In addition, just as Yahweh, the Old Testament God helped the Israelites to steal the lands of the Canaanites, the Hittites, the Amorites, et. al., and had commanded the "chosen people" to kill the Jebusites, the Girgashites, the Hivites, the Perizzites, et. al. ("leave none standing," etc.), so, too, did the Western Europeans, and Euro-Americans think that God was helping them to steal the homelands of and to kill the Indigenous Peoples of the United States (the Pequot People, the Tsalagi People, the Dakota People, the Cheyenne and Arapaho, et. al.). These notions of "chosen people," "promised land," "Canaan, land of milk and honey," and the genocidal commands of the Old Testament God, and God's leading, commanding, helping, and protecting His "chosen people," were the basis of what the U.S. government, its Euro-American citizenry, and Euro-centric U.S. historians called Manifest Destiny.

Hidden Genocide and Hidden History

In March 2011, Rutgers University and Bergen Community College, in Newark, New Jersey, held a conference titled "Hidden Genocides." I was asked and honored to present a paper there concerning the hidden genocide of the Indigenous Peoples of the United States. One of the reasons that there is a "hidden genocide" and a "hidden history" of Indigenous Peoples of the U.S. is the fact that if what was really done to the Native Peoples of the U.S. (and who did it) was acknowledged, confronted, and taught, it would reflect very negatively on the U.S., its military, its colonial institutions, and its Euro-American citizenry.

Around 1500, modern demographics indicate that there were approximately 16 million Native Peoples living in what's now the continental United States.[1] Some demographers place this figure higher than that. By 1900, there were only about 237,000 First Nations People alive according to the U.S. Bureau of Census.[2]

What happened? The answer, according to Native scholars and academics, as well as some non-Native academics and scholars,[3] is genocide, extermination. For the United States to proclaim itself as moral, exceptional, and a champion of freedom and human rights is ludicrous, and is belied by the facts of genocide and the "hidden history" of the Indigenous Peoples of the U.S., which repudiate the moral claims of the U.S. and its defenders.

Thus, the history of Indigenous genocide is rarely taught in the schools, colleges, and universities, or in textbooks. If the Republicans, conservatives, jingoists, racists, and white supremacists have their way, the history of the Indigenous Holocaust will never be taught.

David Stannard, in his book *American Holocaust*, says that in the islands of the Caribbean, Columbus and his soldiers killed eight million Native People in 21 years, by "violence, disease, and despair,"[4] significantly exceeding the number of Jews killed by Hitler and the Nazis.

Further, the Indigenous Holocaust, begun with Columbus, had not yet reached the U.S. mainland, where another 16 million First Nations Peoples would be murdered by violence, disease, and despair, in the 1500s, 1600s, 1700s, and 1800s.[5] If one adds the eight million to the 16 million, we end up with 24 million Indigenous People killed by genocide, four times the number of Jews murdered by Hitler and the Nazis. The magnitude of this Indigenous Holocaust is summarized by Stannard as "The worst human holocaust the world had ever witnessed, roaring across two continents non-stop for four centuries and consuming the lives of countless tens of million of people, [before it] finally had leveled off. There was, at last, almost no one left to kill."[6] This, too, is part of the "hidden history."

Many Indigenous academics, elders, traditional Native Peoples, and some white academics and allies think that an Indigenous Holocaust Museum ought to be erected in Washington, D.C., similar to the Jewish Holocaust Museum. This hasn't been done—or even widely considered— even though the genocide occurred right here in the United States, and the numbers of Indigenes killed dwarfs the numbers killed in the Nazi genocide. It is obvious that racism is one of several major factors in this. U.S. Indigenous Peoples are considered "unworthy" victims while Jews are regarded as "worthy victims."[7] As we've seen in the preceding chapters, we have been called many derogatory and demeaning names including "wild," "savage," "uncivilized," "redskins," "vermin," "children of the Devil," and "subhuman." Because these names have dehumanized us, we are considered "unworthy" victims. The fact that millions upon millions of First Nations Peoples were mass murdered is considered insignificant (or ignored). In reply, we, Native Peoples, say to the U.S. government, to the Euro-American academic powers that be, and to the Euro-American citizenry, "Indigenous Lives Matter!"

It is time, after more than 500 years, to acknowledge the genocide of the Indigenous Peoples of the U.S. and of the Americas. It is time for truth telling!

The hidden history includes, in addition to the genocide, the massive land theft perpetrated by the U.S. government and its Euro-American citizenry, the 400+ treaties made and broken by the U.S., the suppression and prohibition of Native languages, religious ceremonies and practices, and the destruction of sacred sites and burial sites

The land theft involved the stealing of approximately three billion acres of land which now comprises the continental United States, land which, basically, has not been paid for.[8] When the first Western Europeans, Columbus, his soldiers, and missionaries, came to the islands of the Americas, they had no land. Yet, by the end of four centuries—the 1500s, the

1600s, the 1700s, and the 1800s—the western Europeans and, eventually, the Euro-Americans had stolen *all* of the Indigenous homelands, from the Atlantic coast to the Pacific coast, in addition to the islands in the Caribbean.

When the first Western Europeans (Pierre Radisson and Sieur des Groseillers), came to the homelands of the Dakota People around 1660, they had no land.[9] After a little over two centuries, the Euro-Minnesotans had stolen all of the lands which comprise the present-day State of Minnesota, around 54 million acres.[10] Most of these lands have either not been paid for or were sold (under duress) for a pittance. This is simply wrong, a part of the Great Evil.

The "hidden history" of the United States also includes the making and breaking of several hundred treaties by the U.S. government and its Euro-American citizenry. Vine Deloria, Jr., a fellow Dakota (now deceased), an attorney, scholar, and prolific author, says that approximately 400 treaties and agreements were violated by the United States.[11] Deloria also said back in the 20th century that "it would take Russia another century to make and break as many treaties as the United States has already violated."[12]

In 2017, Bill O'Reilly was interviewing President Trump regarding Vladimir Putin. Trump was defending Putin, and said that he respected Putin. O'Reilly replied, "But he's a killer."[13] Trump replied, "there are a lot of killers. You think our country's so innocent?" This is one of the very few times I've agreed with Trump, that the United States is no better morally than Russia. When you consider the mass murder, broken treaties, land theft, forced marches, and massacres perpetrated against Native Peoples, it becomes obvious that Euro-Americans ought not to make any moral claims, nor assert that the U.S. is more moral than Russia, China, or North Korea.[14]

Another relevant observation by Deloria is, "In looking back at the centuries of broken treaties, it is clear that the United States never intended to keep any of its promises."[15]

Yet another aspect of the "hidden history" is the suppression of Indigenous spirituality and ceremonies, as well as cultural traditions and customs. It's good to remember that the Courts of Indian Offenses was a mechanism used to stamp out Indigenous cultures and their social and religious institutions. The practicing of our cultural traditions was criminalized, and missionaries deemed many of our religious traditions and customs as "offensive."[16] To reiterate, this was religious suppression, and all of it was totally contrary to onr of the colonizers' sacred documents, the U.S. Constitution's First Amendment, which holds sacrosanct religious freedom.

One might also mention the American Indian Religious Freedom Act of 1978.[17] In my classes, I used to ask, "is there a Norwegian-American Religious Freedom Act? Is there a German-American Religious Freedom Act or a Swedish-American Religious Freedom Act (AIRFA)?" (In the state of Minnesota, there are many descendants of Norwegians and Germans.) These were rhetorical questions—and, of course, the answer is "no." Then, I would ask, "Why, then, is there congressional legislation titled the American Indian Religious Freedom Act?" This act helped to counter, at least on paper, such suppressive mechanisms as the Courts of Indian Offenses, U.S. government policies, and church and missionary practices and actions, which suppressed First Nations' religious freedom.

AIRFA included beautiful rhetoric but had no teeth, no enforcement provisions. Thus, the Native person who is a follower of the traditional spiritual ways, rituals, and customs, still lacks full religious freedom, especially access to sacred sites, a great many of which are located on federal, state, county, municipal, or private lands. However, AIRFA made congresspeople feel good. Not so much the Native Peoples. At the time of this writing, the sacred sites and burial sites of the Standing Rock Reservation have been, and are being, desecrated and destroyed, because of the capitalists and big oil greedily building the Dakota Access Pipe Line (DAPL).

Another part of the "hidden history" of the United States and what happened to the Indigenous Peoples is the prohibition and suppression of Indigenous languages. In any given language, there are many inherent concepts, beliefs, values, and a worldview. An example, as I understand it, is that almost every Indigenous language in the Americas has the concept of "Mother Earth" (with the Dakota, it is Ina Maka; also Unci Maka, "Grandmother Earth"). It is part of the worldview, values, and belief systems, which are an integral part of a traditional Native person's identity. Settlers, missionaries, churches, educators, schools, government agents, and residential boarding schools all contributed to cultural suppression through language suppression. If the perpetrators of genocide suppress the spirituality/ceremonies and also, suppress Native languages, then the Native Peoples will lose their identity, and the killers don't have to kill anyone physically anymore. They'll have killed them spiritually. However, that certainly didn't stop them from physical killing.

Finally, I would like to briefly mention one more aspect of the "hidden history" of the United States in which Church and State worked hand in hand. This was the residential boarding school system, which was comprised of schools run by both the State (the U.S. government) and the

Church (the denominations, missionaries, educators, both Catholic and Protestant). There were three residential boarding schools close to my home community, the Upper Sioux Community, near Granite Falls in southwestern Minnesota. One was at Pipestone, Minnesota, which is 75 miles away; another was at Flandreau, South Dakota, about 15 miles from Pipestone, and the third was at Wahpeton, North Dakota. One of the ways in which the State collaborated with the Church was to provide congressional funding for the Native children education endeavors, and, then, these funds were given to the church-run boarding schools, since the churches had the infrastructure in place.[18] There was no separation of church and state when it came to Indigenous education. The purpose of these residential boarding schools was to "Kill the Indian but save the man."[19] Their job was to educate, Christianize, civilize, and assimilate Indigenous children.

(One extremely important point is that such schools, i.e., church-run boarding schools, in this case, as well as the state-run schools, fulfilled criterion (e) of the 1948 UN Genocide Convention, "Forcibly transferring children of the group to another group." These residential boarding schools were flatly and unequivocally genocide of the Dakota People, as well as of other First Nations Peoples. These schools were a major part of the Wosice Tanka Kin, "The Great Evil.")

Also, there is a Bible verse which I quoted earlier: "Train up a child in the way he should go, and when he is old, he will not depart from it." (Proverbs 22:6) Of course, the U.S. government and the churches wished to "train up" the Native "child in the way he should go," which was, and is, the Euro-American Christian "way."

When one considers the genocide of Indigenous Peoples of the United States, the massive land theft, the broken treaties, the suppression of both the First Nations' religious ceremonies/practices, and of Native languages, the residential boarding schools, etc., it is not difficult to understand why Professor Roger Buffalohead said,

> As skilled teachers of American Indian Studies will agree, it is difficult to tell the truth about Indian experiences in America without leaving the impression that the United States is a wicked, dishonest, immoral, hypocritical, racist, and self-serving nation.[20]

(Professor Buffalohead served on my Ph.D. Oral Examination Committee and my Ph.D. Final Oral Examination Committee at the University of Minnesota, Twin Cities Campus. My basic knowledge of Indigenous Nations Studies was gleaned from his classes at the U of M, and this knowledge has contributed to the writing of this book. Thus, I owe Professor Buffalohead a debt of gratitude.)

A fellow Dakota, Vine Deloria, Jr., used similar terms, including treaty-breakers, treacherous, betrayers, militantly imperialistic, perfidious, and violent.[21]

I, too, have a description of the USA, based upon my own studies: The United States of America is "a greedy, arrogant, hypocritical, racist, white supremacist, evil, and war-mongering nation." I suspect that most Indigenous academics have similar perceptions.

The Hidden Bible

One of the things that I have noticed about Bible readings in some Protestant church services—Episcopal, Lutheran, and others—is that they do not include, generally, passages which feature the genocidal commands of Yahweh, the Old Testament God (e.g., Leviticus 20), nor are there many readings from the books of Joshua or Esther, or the inclusion of other "controversial" verses which deal with killing, religious suppression, enslavement, and land theft.

One of the genocidal commands is from Deuteronomy 7:2, "And when the Lord thy God shall deliver them before thee; thou shalt smite them and utterly destroy them; thou shalt make no covenant with them, nor shew mercy unto them." Another is found in Joshua 10:40, "So Joshua smote all the country of the hills, and of the south, and of the vale, and of the springs, and all their kings: he left none remaining, but utterly destroyed all that breathed, as the Lord God of Israel commanded." There are more than four dozen such passages (see Appendix A, which is not definitive) which call for the total destruction or extermination of nations and peoples.

As Philip Jenkins notes, "The Bible overflows with texts of terror."[22] Also, "If the Qur'an urges believers to fight, as it undoubtedly does, it also commands that enemies be shown mercy if they surrender."[23] Some frightful portions of the Bible, in contrast, "order the total extermination of enemies, of whole families and races—of men, women, and children, elders, and even their livestock, with no quarter granted."[24] (See for example Deuteronomy 7:2 and Joshua 10:40.) Finally, Jenkins says, "If Christians or Jews needed biblical texts to justify deeds of terrorism or ethnic slaughter, their main problem would be an embarrassment of riches."[25] The Old Testament God not only commands killing and genocide, but facilitates it.

So, saintly killers can feel righteous and holy because they've fulfilled the commands of God.

Two "controversial" Bible verses which are rarely if ever read in Sunday morning church services deal with Yahweh's commands to kill children. The first is found in Deuteronomy.

> And the Lord our God delivered him; and we smote him, and his sons, and all his people And we took all his cities at that time, and utterly destroyed the men, and the women, and the little ones, of every city, we left none to remain.[26] (Deuteronomy 2:34, KJV)

The second verse is found in Numbers.

> Now therefore kill every male among the little ones, and kill every woman who has known a man intimately. (Numbers 31:7, NKJV)

These two verses are especially troubling. I cannot help asking, "What kind of God is this?"

If the United States is a "Christian nation," and if the Christians believe in this vindictive, mass-murdering, killer God of the Old Testament, then it's understandable why the United States seems to be so addicted to war, with its 1,000-plus military bases and installations around the world.[27]

The values of Indigenous poples tend to be quite different. My tahan-si (Dakota for "cousin," male to male) Floyd Red Crow Westerman once stated this about Dakota beliefs and values, especially for the Dakota men: "1) Honor and Protect our Children; 2) Honor and Protect our Women; 3) Honor and protect our elders; and, 4) Honor and protect Mother Earth."[28] In our stories, songs, prayers, ceremonies, and in talks that I have heard given by our spiritual leaders and elders, I have found no commands by Wakan Tanka ("The Great Mystery") to kill "little ones."

I can see why there is a "hidden Bible." Who can be edified by a God that orders the extermination of a nation or a people, or who is commanding the killing of babies and children? What kind of spiritual nourishment can people get from such verses? It is understandable why such books, chapters, and verses are not read in the churches. These verses reveal a darker side, a damning side, of the Jewish and Christian God. It ought not to puzzle anyone why some call Yahweh "the vindictive, genocidally racist jealous monster God of the Old Testament."[29] Nor should it be puzzling why his most fervent followers engage in so much evil.

Jesus Christ, Son of the Old Testament God

We have seen what a monster God, a killer God, the Old Testament God, Yahweh, is. Even though this God commanded, "Thou shalt not kill," He violated his own commandment many thousands of times, even to the point of wiping out the whole known earth, except for Noah and his family and some animal relatives.[31] Still, many people, including Christians, always contrast the violence and the genocide of the Old Testament with what they say is the love, faith, hope, and peace of the New Testament and Jesus Christ. Let's check out this supposed contrast.

First, in Matthew 5:18 Christ specifically endorses everything in the Old Testament, including the murderous verses: "For verily I say unto you, Till heaven and earth pass, one jot or tittle shall in no wise pass from the law [Old Testament], till all be fulfilled." (KJV) So, the supposed contrast doesn't stand: Christ himself said in essence, "It's a package deal."

We've already talked about the "Great Commission," found in Matthew 28:19, "Go therefore and make disciples of all the nations, baptizing them in the name of the Father, and of the Son, and of the Holy Spirit." (NKJV).

The other verse regarding the "Great Commission" is Mark 16:15, ". . . Go ye into all the world, and preach the gospel to every creature." Jesus Christ in these two verses is advocating religious imperialism.

Also, Jesus' command to "make all nations my disciples" fulfills one of Chalk's and Jonassohn's "Four Common Motives of Genocide," "to impose an ideology or a belief upon the victim group."[32] Jesus' command to impose a religious ideology, viz., Christianity, upon "the victim group," is a component of genocide.

Let's look at the afterlife. John 3:18 reads, "He who believes in Him is not condemned; but he who does not believe is condemned already because he has not believed in the name of the only begotten Son of God." (NKJV)

Mark 16:16 is also relevant: "He who believes and is baptized will be saved; but he who does not believe will be condemned." (NKJV). We see Jesus here saying either directly, or by implication, that those who do not accept him as God's son and their savior are "condemned" and will suffer eternal damnation.

Where will these unbelievers be sent? Apparently, they will be cast into a lake of fire. Revelation 20:15 says, "And anyone not found written in the Book of Life was cast into the lake of fire." Revelation 21:8 adds, "But the cowardly, unbelieving, abominable, murderers, sexually immoral, sorcerers, idolaters, and all liars shall have their part in the lake which burns with fire and brimstone . . ." (NKJV). Still another New Testament verse, Matthew 13:41-42, says, "The Son of Man (Jesus Christ) will send out His angels, and they will gather out of His kingdom all things that offend, and those who practice lawlessness, And will cast them into the furnace of fire. There will be wailing and gnashing of teeth." (See also John 25:46.and Revelation 14:10-11.)

In one sense, Jesus Christ, in sending a person to eternal torment if s/he does not believe in Jesus Christ, makes Yahweh, the monster God of the Old Testament, look lenient.[33] As Vincent Bugliosi writes, "Jesus wasn't any cup of tea either."[34] Bugliosi makes the point that if God is love (John 3:16) and that "Jesus loves us with an infinite love," "how infinite can this love be if for those who reject him as being their savior, he consigns them to an everlasting hell?"[35] Bugliosi quotes Robert Ingersoll, who said, "In the New Testament, death is not the end, but the beginning of punishment that has no end. In the Old Testament, when God had a man dead, he let him alone."[36] We can see that Jesus Christ appears to be just as cruel and brutal as his father. One could say that the apple does not fall far from the tree.

In another part of the "Hidden Bible," Jesus says:

> Think not that I am come to send [bring] peace on earth: I came not to send peace, but a sword. For I am come to set a man at variance ["in conflict"] against his father, and the daughter against her mother, and the daughter in law against her mother in law. And a man's foes (enemy) shall be they of his own household.[37] (Matthew 10:34–36, KJV)

This does not sound like a unifier, instead, it sounds like a divider. This does not sound like a man of peace but a man advocating family disunity, dissension, and conflict. I would think that anyone who believes in the importance of family would be horrified by this statement.

However, true believers, religious zealots, will say, "My God, right or wrong," or "My Jesus, right or wrong." Others will ponder the question of what kind of man is Jesus Christ, the son of the killer God of the Old Testament, who wishes to make all nations his disciples, to divide households, and consign nonbelievers to eternal torment? What kind of man is this who commands his disciples to impose his beliefs upon others?

Epilogue

The Irrelevance of Reconciliation and Forgiveness

Why am I speaking of "Reconciliation" and "Forgiveness" in a book about genocide, the Bible, and the Indigenous Peoples of the United States? In my experience, each and every time our Dakota People interacted with Euro-Minnesotans regarding the Dakota-U.S. War of 1862—they, the good Christian white folk—immediately began talking about "reconciliation," "forgiveness," "healing," and "apologies." Let's look at three separate times when this kind of interaction occurred.

The year 1987 was the 125th anniversary of the Dakota-U.S. War of 1862. In fact, Minnesota's governor at the time, Rudy Perpich, declared 1987 "The Year of Reconciliation." Many white people, particularly Christians, came forth and wanted to have events in which there would be reconciliation, forgiveness, healing, and apologies. Some of these white people wanted forgiveness from the Dakota People and offered apologies to the Dakota People. Some of them were willing to put on feasts to which Dakota People would be invited. We, supposedly would eat together, laugh together, say nice things to and about each other, and the whites would allow their feathered friends to dress up in their regalia and dance for their entertainment.

Then we would all go home with warm fuzzy feelings and be "reconciled." In fairness, and in the interest of full disclosure, I need to make known the following since it is obvious that at present I really do not like the term, "reconciliation," which raises the question, "Why, then, did I recommend the term back in 1987?"

When my group, the Dakota Studies Committee, was discussing what name we should apply to the 125th anniversary of the Dakota-U.S. War of 1862, I suggested the title "The Year of Reconciliation." I had just come out of Seabury-Western Theological Seminary in Evanston, Illinois, and in the year-and-a-half that I spent studying there, I learned that white people, and in particular, white Christians, really liked the term "reconciliation."

This term meant to them, I think, that they wouldn't have to do anything unpleasant or inconvenient like paying for stolen lands, acknowledging their ancestors perpetrated the genocide of the Dakota People of Minnesota, or making reparations for genocide. It also meant that they would not have to worry about honoring the dozen or so treaties made between the U.S. and the Dakota People of Minnesota, and keeping the financial obligations therein, i.e., paying for the stolen lands, etc. Despite this, our group, the Dakota Studies Committee, recommended this name. Then, because the white people liked the term "reconciliation," with their help and with the help of some white institutions, the Minnesota governor declared 1987 "The Year of Reconciliation."

The Dakota Studies Committee (DSC) was a group of both Dakota and non-Dakota people. The purpose of the DSC was to present the beauty, richness, and truth of the history and culture of the Dakota People of Minnesota. There were representatives of the four Dakota communities in the state, of colleges and universities, of various organizations (e.g., The Science Museum and Minnesota Historical Society), and of interested individuals. I was the organizer and chairperson of the Committee. We planned, organized, and implemented the programs and activities of the Year of Reconciliation.

The second call for "reconciliation" came in 2008, which was the 150th anniversary of Minnesota as a state, and the Minnesota Historical Society wished to celebrate the 150th birthday of Minnesota. Some of our young Dakota women and men approached the Sesquicentennial Commission and told them that the Dakota People of Minnesota had nothing to celebrate. They said that Minnesota was built on Dakota blood and lives, and on Dakota lands and resources. They further said that it was the Euro-Minnesota citizens who were benefiting from the stolen Dakota land and resources, that the Dakota were not being paid for the stolen lands, and that the Dakota People were not benefiting at all from their own lands and resources. Needless to say, the State of Minnesota proceeded to "celebrate" the 150th birthday of the state. No surprise there!

Then in 2012–2013 there was the 150th anniversary of the horrendous, genocidal events known as the Dakota-U.S. War of 1862 and its aftermath (the forced march, concentration camps, and deportations). Again, as in 1987 and 2008, some of the same kind of white people and some with different names and different faces, wanted to have events in which there would be talk of reconciliation, forgiveness, healing, and apologies. Some of them, from Winona, Minnesota, conducted an annual event by different names such as a unity event, or a homecoming event, etc. for Dakota People. Again, some whites, in Mankato, Minnesota, a site of genocide, wanted Dakota People to "forgive" them. The good Christian white folk of Mankato, along with some colonized and Christianized Dakota individuals, even created and named a new park which they called Reconciliation Park, with benches etched with the words, "Forgive Everybody Every Thing."[38]

This was outrageous! Here were people, both non-Dakota and Dakota, who did not want to face the truth, who did not want to engage in truth telling, and did not want to confront and acknowledge the genocide, the bounties, the concentration camps, the massive land-theft, the broken treaties, etc., etc.

The Dakota Horseback Ride

Then, to make a bad situation worse, a Lakota man, who lived in South Dakota, had a dream about the mass execution of 38 Indigenous men in 1862. This man did not even know that this event, this simultaneous mass hanging, happened in Minnesota, let alone the history of the Dakota People in Minnesota. I do not know if he even knew that there were still Dakota living in Minnesota.

This well-meaning man wished to do something to honor the 38 murdered Dakota men, so he organized a horseback ride which started on the Lower Brule Reservation in South Dakota, a place which had nothing to do with the events of 1862–63 in Minnesota. The ride ought to have started on the Crow Creek Reservation, on the east side of the Missouri River across from Lower Brule, which is historic, because it was the final destination for the Dakota People who were forcibly removed from our ancient Dakota homelands in Minnesota.

When these riders stopped in towns such as New Ulm or Mankato, they asked for "forgiveness" from the white people. I could not believe this. It was mind-boggling. Why were *they* asking for forgiveness? If anybody should have been asking for forgiveness, it was the white people. Almost unbelievably the riders were asking for forgiveness in honor, they said, of the 38 Dakota who were hanged in Mankato! If these Dakota horseback riders were really "honoring" any Dakota, they were honoring the Christian and colonized Dakota who did not fight back in the mid-1860s, for their lands and freedom. They were not honoring the Dakota 38, they were not honoring the Dakota who resisted the white stealers and took up arms to drive them from the Minnesota River Valley.

What these horseback riders did, asking for forgiveness, was wrong. The Dakota People did nothing wrong—they were fighting for their homelands and sacred/burial sites, and for our people to have the freedom to live the lives that we had lived for millennia. Second, they fought as any man would fight to protect his home, his property, and his family. In this situation white people were the wrongdoers—they were stealing our homelands, and our Dakota people resisted these land-thieves. Third, our People were patriots—they were truly fighting for their land here in Minnesota, were fighting for their religious freedom, and were fighting for the freedom to live their lives as we had always done. Fourth, the hung Dakota men ought to have been treated as prisoners of war and not as war criminals. By asking for forgiveness from white people, these horseback riders were not honoring the 38 Dakota who were simultaneously murdered at Mankato on December 26, 1862. They were dishonoring them, just as the blood-thirsty whites had dishonored and murdered them.

I just wished the horseback riders had not started the Dakota 38 Ride! They did not help our struggle ("our" referring to those Dakota People who have been working with these issues—moral, historical, justice, reparations—for quite a while); they did not help further truth telling, justice, or respect for the Dakota.

Back to the Euro-Minnesotans and their obsession with reconciliation. It has always amazed, but not surprised, me that Euro-Minnesotans, in the years 1987, 2008, and 2012/2013, could not see that we can't talk about reconciliation, healing, apologies and forgiveness without first talking about truth telling. justice, and mutual respect. In my experience of 80 "winters," I have learned from our black brothers and sisters that without justice, there can be no peace.

When I marched with them in 1992 in Minneapolis, after the brutal beating of Rodney King in 1991 by white racist cops in Los Angeles, and the white cops were acquitted, they would chant "No Justice, No Peace!" Thus, I, too, say my variation of their chant, "No Reconciliation or Forgiveness without Truth Telling, Justice, and Mutual Respect!"

Thus, when the white people were calling for "reconciliation" in Minnesota, I thought they not only wanted our cake but to eat it, too (which, of course, they are now still doing). The State of Minnesota and its Euro-Minnesotan citizenry had engaged in massive land theft, stealing nearly 54 million acres; had force marched our people; had placed our women, children, and elders in concentration camps, had engaged in mass execution of 38 Dakota men; had authorized bounties on Dakota scalps; had imprisoned 400 of our Dakota men in Davenport, Iowa; and had forcibly removed, or "ethnically cleansed," 1300 of our women, children, and elders from our ancient homelands in Minnesota. Then, in 1863, with the genocidal punitive military campaigns led by Sibley and Sully, they killed hundreds upon hundreds of our people in the area now known as North and South Dakota, and engaged in wholesale destruction, by fire, of our villages and stores of food and supplies for the winter. Now, the Euro-Minnesotan descendants of these killers and land stealers want us to forgive them and help Minnesota "heal."

Only a few of our Dakota and other Native Peoples have declared that there must be justice, truth telling (i.e., acknowledging the "sins" listed in the preceding paragraph), reparations, and restitution before there can be any kind of discussion of reconciliation. Dr. George Tinker, an Osage man, said in 2012, at a Methodist Church in St. Paul, Minnesota, "Accept no apologies without land!"[39] The Chairperson of our Upper Sioux Community Board of Trustees, our governing body, Kevin Jensvold, declared, at a conference at Mankato State University, "No Reconciliation Without Reparations!"[40]

Since I have been quoting Bible verses throughout this book, I might as well quote another one which deals with the idea that action must accompany words: James 2:15–17 reads, "If a brother or sister be naked, and destitute of daily food, and one of you say unto them, Depart in peace, be ye warmed and filled; notwithstanding ye give then not those things which are needful to the body;what doth it profit? Even so faith, if it hath not works, is dead, being alone." (KJV). The NAB reads, "If a brother or sister has nothing to wear and no food for the day, and you say to them, goodbye and good luck! Keep warm and well fed, but do not meet their bodily needs, what good is that? So it is with the faith that does nothing in practice. It is thoroughly lifeless."[41] Reconciliation, forgiveness, and apologies without just actions and "works" is useless and "lifeless," and, of course, does nothing to promote "healing."

As for me, I say, "Where is the cash payment for the stolen lands? Where is the back rent? Where are the reparations for genocide? Where is the return of public lands to the Dakota People of Minnesota? And when will the Euro-Americans and Euro-Minnesotans begin to tell the truth about land-theft, treaty violations, and the genocide of the Indigenous Peoples of the U.S.?

Above and Beyond Reconciliation

As I indicated earlier, when unpleasant and inconvenient aspects of Minnesota history come up—such as the genocide of the Dakota People—the Euro-Minnesotans immediately wish to talk about reconciliation. Hence a few more comments about "reconciliation." One definition of "Reconciliation" is taking action "to restore to friendship or harmony."

The Euro-Minnesotans liked this definition of "reconciliation." So did many of our colonized and Christianized Dakota. They, the colonizers and the colonized, wanted "harmony," no unpleasantness, such as talk of payment for the stolen lands, or talk of genocide. However, "reconciliation," without truth telling, without justice, especially economic justice, and without mutual respect, is useless and "lifeless."

When white people and Dakota people have come together, if I began to talk about the massive land theft and the need to make reparations, or if I talked about the U.S. needing to honor broken treaties—of the 400+ treaties between Native Peoples and the U.S. and state governments, I cannot think of a single one the U.S. or any of the states honored—and, for sure, if I talked about the genocide of the Dakota People, and the need for white society to acknowledge that their ancestors perpetrated this genocide, and the need to be held accountable, my comments were, and are, regarded as abrasive, offensive, or totally inappropriate. Or, worse, they, that is, the colonizer and the colonized, might say that now is not the time to talk about this. The question, of course, is, "If not now, when?" (Their unspoken answer is "never.")

If I mentioned that Indigenous Peoples, generally, and the Dakota People, specifically, have a right to be angry over what was done to them, and that, furthermore, anger, resentment, vengefulness, and even hatred, were, and are, appropriate and reasonable responses to enduring historical injustices, then my comments were regarded, as one writer put it, as "an ugly intrusion on a peaceful, healing process."[42] Really?

Genocide, land theft, scalp bounties, forced marches, concentration camps, and mass murder are evil, and the people who perpetrated them were/are evil! Genocide is unforgiveable. Massive land theft is unforgiveable.

There is a phrase, "Righteous Anger," which is appropriate and reasonable. Righteous Anger is "the emotional/psychological response of victims of racism/discrimination to the system of power that dominates/exploits/oppresses them. Righteous anger is *not* racism; rather it is a defensible response *to* racism[43] and blatant injustice. And, to reiterate, the Dakota People of Minnesota, and the First Nations Peoples, not only in the United States but also in all of the Americas, have a *right* to be not only *angry*, but also to be resentful, and vengeful about the colonizers'/settlers' behaviors of invading, killing, stealing, enslaving, occupying, exploiting, and their benefitting from their criminal actions and heinous behaviors against Indigenous Peoples, and not being held accountable.

Dr. Steven T. Newcomb, in his essay, "Critique of a Doctrine of Reconciliation," said several pertinent things. One was "Reconciliation has a history . . . it can be used to maintain a particular kind of reality that benefits states to the continued detriment of Indigenous nations and peoples."[44] Another was, "In my view, it is not possible to 'reconcile' ourselves with a dominator perspective and behaviors, or with the terribly destructive legacy of that paradigm of domination."[45] Newcomb also made a comment related to the residential boarding schools which were, and are, operated by both Church and State: "The boarding 'schools' and residential 'schools' were part of the mission of Apostolic Conquest in keeping with many Vatican papal documents that declared war against our originally free nations and peoples with the goal of instituting a Reign of Domination under the rubric of church and state."[46] Again, it is good to remember that these residential boarding schools fulfilled criterion (e) of the 1948 UN Genocide Convention, "Forcibly transferring children of the group to another."

As for "forgiveness," it always seemed to me that when the Dakota People got together with Euro-Minnesotan to talk about the Dakota-U.S. War of 1862–63 and its aftermath, that they, the Euro-Minnesotans, wanted us, the Dakota, to forgive them. It seemed that they, the good Christians and well-intentioned Euro-Minnesotans, were placing "primary responsibility for forgiveness on the wronged party," i.e., the Dakota People of Minnesota.[47] I thought that this was wrong, but I could not articulate why.

Then, I read a bit about the matter. Primo Levi says that the wronged person who grapples with forgiving evil imposes upon himself "a terrible moral violence."[48] Then, I read what C. Fred Alford wrote: "Almost no Holocaust survivors forgive," instead finding that "for the most part forgiveness is simply irrelevant, a category as extraneous as the moon."[49] Another writer, Sam Grey, says that the ability to forgive is a prerogative underwritten by privilege, while fate confers different standing upon different survivors.[50]

A black South African, Charity Kondile, who testified before the South African Truth and Reconciliation Commission said, "It is easy for Mandela and Tutu to forgive . . . they lead vindicated lives. In my life, nothing, not a single thing has changed since my son was burnt by barbarians . . . nothing. Therefore, I cannot forgive."[51]

Cynthia Ozick, after reflection upon the Jewish Shoah, quotes a rabbi, who said, "Whoever is merciful to the cruel will end by being indifferent to the innocent." This rabbi goes on to say, "Forgiveness can brutalize . . . forgiveness is pitiless. It forgets the victim. It negates the right of the victim to his own life. It blurs over suffering and death. It drowns the past."[52] In my view, those points, that "forgiveness drowns the past" and that "forgiveness negates the right of the victim to his own life," make "forgiveness" an enemy to truth telling, justice, and mutual respect.

I think it would be worthwhile for good Christian white folk, and well-intentioned Euro-Minnesotans, to ponder the statements in the preceding two paragraphs about reconciliation and forgiveness. Also, it would be worthwhile for Christian Euro-Americans and well-intentioned Euro-Minnesotans to meditate on how the wronged, how the victims, in this case, the Indigenous Peoples and Dakota People, might feel and think about having bounties placed on their heads, being burned alive, killed, beaten, raped, bayoneted and shot, hung, dismembered . . . the list goes on, and to further understand that the wronged will look at things differently. In fact, most of the time, the victim's view will be diametrically opposite to the views of those who perpetrated the wrongs.

Another thing—it seems that whites, the Euro-Minnesotans, who talk about the Dakota-U.S. War of 1862, about reconciliation, and about forgiveness, think that the Dakota people should think and talk as they think and talk.

As Thomas Brudholm notes, the whites, as they talk about post-conflict reconciliation, have focused "on a model of an idealized actor who demonstrates a readiness to forgive and reconcile and [has] a capacity to let go of the past."[53] The colonized and Christianized Dakota who are like the "idealized actor" are "good Dakotas." If they are not like the "idealized actor," then they are bad Dakotas. Many times this Dakota writer and speaker has found himself characterized by white folk as unlike the "model of an idealized actor," that I was unwilling to "let go of the past," and, therefore, I was "the bad Dakota man." I would think, by this logic, that those Euro-Americans who said they will "never forget 9/11" are also unlike the "model of an idealized actor," and, therefore, are bad people, too. Right?

What Can Be Done?

The answer is, on the one hand, simple and obvious, and on the other is difficult and probably impossible to implement. For example, Euro-American society simply needs to begin telling the truth about what was done to the Indigenous Peoples of the United States and who did it. White people need to admit that white people perpetrated genocide. They need to pay for the lands their ancestors stole and they still possess, and they need to honor the approximately 400 treaties their government violated. They need to acknowledge that their people put bounties on the scalps of Indigenous Peoples, they have to admit putting Native Peoples in concentration camps, suppressing Native languages, denying religious freedom to the Indigenous Peoples, and a host of other crimes against humanity.

As one can see, what ought to be done is relatively straightforward and should be simple and obvious. Euro-American society needs to engage in truth telling, and to work for justice, particularly economic justice, and to begin to work on developing respect for those who are not white folk, who are dark skinned, and perhaps wear their hair long, speak other languages, or have different religions.

What ought to be done, though, will probably not be done, especially the achievement of mutual respect. Why do I say this? I say this because white supremacy seems to be deeply and firmly embedded not only in the psyche of most Western Europeans and Euro-Americqans, but also indelibly etched in the psyche of most Euro-Minnesotans. White supremacy says, "Our language, English, is the best language. Everybody ought to speak English. Our religion, Christianity, is the best and everybody ought to be Christians. Our economic system, capitalism, is the best and all peoples ought to be capitalists, not socialists nor communists."

Generally, Euro-Americans think they're exceptional and therefore superior to all non-white peoples. Their egos will not permit them to acknowledge their people perpetrating genocide, nor will their vanity permit them to admit to their people breaking *all* of the treaties; most are too greedy to pay for stolen lands, and they will not return public lands to the Dakota People of Minnesota and to the Indigenous Peoples of the United States because they (the Native Peoples) did not obey the "divine injunction" to "subdue the earth" and other similarly stupid commands.

Even though I acknowledge that what I would like to see done is probably never going to happen, especially in my lifetime, for me to do nothing is not acceptable. So, in my retirement years I have focused upon three activities. One is truth telling, and to do so fearlessly. The second is to engage in the pursuit of justice, especially economic justice. The third is to work for mutual respect. These are complex issues. One of many useful statements that I heard in graduate school at the University of Minnesota went something like this, "The problem is multi-faceted—calling for multiple approaches." The issues connected to truth telling; justice, especially economic justice, and mutual respect are very much "multi-faceted issues calling for multiple approaches." To use a sports metaphor, it's a big ballpark and there's plenty of room for plenty of players.

Truth-Telling

And you shall know the truth, and the truth shall make you free.
(John 8:32, NKJV)

Golda Meir, former prime minister of Israel, said this about the trial of Adolph Eichmann in Jerusalem in 1961: The trial "was not, in any sense , a question of revenge . . . but those who remained alive—and generations still unborn—deserve, if nothing else, that the world know, in all its dreadful detail, what was done to the Jews of Europe and by whom."[54]

I share a similar sentiment. As a Dakota man, I would paraphrase Meir's statement by saying, "It is not a question of revenge. Rather it is a question of justice and truth telling. Those Dakota women and men who are descendants of the survivors of the genocide of the Dakota People of Minnesota in the 1860s—and the generations still unborn—deserve, if nothing else, that the world know in all its dreadful detail what was done to the Dakota People of Minnesota and other Indigenous Peoples, and who did it."

Regarding what was done to the Dakota and other Indigenous Peoples, and who did it, Zsuzsanna Ozsvath, a Hungarian Jew, talks about her three years-plus experience at Auschwitz, and about the "obligation to recall the past."[55] She quotes a verse of Scripture to support her point:

Take utmost care and watch yourselves scrupulously, so that you do not forget the things that you saw with your own eyes and so that they do not fade from your mind as long as you live. And make them known to your children and to your children's children."[56]

I say amen to Ozsvath's sentiment, and to her wonderful words and use of scripture.

In my 80 "winters," I have found that the overwhelming majority of Euro-Americans and Euro-Minnesotans whom I have met not only do not want to hear the truth about what happened to the Indigenous Peoples of the Americas, but also do not wish to rectify the wrongs and injustices. Thus, there is, in U.S. academia, and in our society, a willful and deliberate suppression of the truth of what happened and who did it.

Who can be some of the possible players in this truth-telling enterprise about the Indigenous Holocaust? Some potential participants are state education departments and state education committees; education departments in the colleges and universities; teachers and curriculum committees at all education levels, in both public and private schools; state historical societies; museums; state legislatures and their education committees; city councils; publishing houses; and church education committees. Readers can, no doubt, think of other possible participants..

Economic Justice

Let Justice roll down like waters and righteousness like an ever-flowing stream. (Amos 5:24, NOAB)

What can be done about genocide and land theft in addition to truth telling? The main question is that of economic justice. It would be good to have a series of in-depth discussions and dialogues between and among Dakota People, non-Indigenous allies, supporters, legislators, et. al. about what we are talking about, and then, to plan on how to go about meeting the economic obligations to the Dakota People of Minnesota and other Indigenous Peoples. The obligations would include, but not be limited, to the following:

1. Reparations for the stolen land—locally, the 54 million acres which comprise the state of Minnesota;

2. Reparations for genocide of the Dakota and other Indigenous Peoples.

3. Back Rent—For example, the Treaty of 1805 involves land on which St. Paul and Minneapolis are located. This would entail a two-fold process: first, to pay for the approximately 155,000+ acres; second, to pay back rent for the land from 1805 to the present;

4. Land Restitution—to return public lands—state, federal, county, and municipal—to the Dakota and other Indigenous Peoples.

5. Honoring the 400+ treaties and the financial obligations contained therein.

Mutual Respect

Love one another with the affection of brothers. Anticipate each other in showing respect. (Romans 12:10, NAB)

Over the past five-plus centuries, since the invaders and land-stealers came in 1492, when the Great Evil began, I have read, at different times and places, about our leaders saying that these strange white men had no respect for our rights, nor respect for our ceremonies and spirituality, nor respect for our languages, nor respect for our customs and traditions, nor respect for our place names, no respect for our women, and no respect for our very lives. In fact, they called us by derogatory names, called us savages, beasts (remember Jane Swisshelm?), wolves (a la George Washington, Andrew Jackson, et. al.), subhumans, or "children of Satan," etc. Thus, I wish to encourage white people, in general, to not only acknowledge the attitude of white supremacy, but also to begin a series of discussions about it, about "white privilege," "whiteness," racism (racial prejudice plus power), and prejudice.

In addition, it would be profitable for all to begin a series of discussions in which we start talking about ways to develop mutual respect for one another, especially for the white man toward not only the Dakota People but also toward other Indigenous Peoples and to other peoples of color, all of which would be extremely difficult if not impossible.

In Closing

I am reminded of what Elie Wiesel said regarding the perpetrators of the Jewish Shoah:

All the killers were Christian . . . The Nazi system was the consequence of a movement of ideas and followed a strict logic; it did not arise in a void but had its roots deep in a tradition that prophesied it, prepared for it, and brought it to maturity. That tradition was inseparable from the past of Christian civilized Europe.[57]

I'm inclined to agree with David Stannard when he says that Wiesel's observation, that "all the killers were Christian," "is an equally apt beginning for those who would seek to understand the motivations that ignited and fanned the flames of the mass destruction of the Native Peoples" of the Americas, generally, and of the United States, specifically.[58] When we look at the abundance of Bible verses used to justify killing Indigenous Peoples and the stealing of Native lands, then it is not difficult to accept the truth of Stannard's statement. Stannard, also, refers to "a frame of mind that would allow to take place the genocide that was carried out against the Native Peoples of the Americas were in many cases the same religio-cultural traits that buttressed justifications" for the Jewish Shoah.[59]

I, too, say of the perpetrators of the genocide, of the Indigenous Holocaust in the United States, that "all the killers were Christian," and that many of them were good Bible-thumping and Bible-quoting killers, such as the Reverend Colonel John Chivington, Rev. Cotton Mather, and William Bradford. Using Chalk and Jonassohn's "Fourth Motive for Genocide,"[60] I conclude the following: any group—Christians in general, the denominations, churches, seminaries, missionaries, clergy, et. al.—who imposed, or still imposes, the religious ideology of Christianity upon a victim group are perpetrators of genocide.

The genocidal system of the Western Europeans and Euro-American Christians was, indeed, "the consequence of a movement of ideas," specifically, the religious ideas which consisted of the genocidal commands of Yahweh, the Old Testament God; the "chosen people" and "promised land" ideas; the religious imperialism of Jesus Christ; and of the three-cited previously papal bulls of the Roman Catholic Church. These ideas foreshadowed, prepared for, and "brought . . . to maturity" the Indigenous Holocaust. It's also true that this "tradition was inseparable from the past of Christian, civilized Europe."

I am beginning to understand why Vine Deloria, Jr. says, "What distinguishes a Christian from any other person is difficult to determine. The track record of individual Christians and Christian nations is not so spectacular as to warrant anyone seriously considering becoming a Christian. From pope to pauper, Protestant to Catholic, Constantinople to the United States, the record is filled with atrocities, misunderstandings, persecutions, genocides, and oppressions so numerous as to bring fear into the hearts and minds of non-Christian peoples."[61]

I, too, am now asking the same question that my high school classmate and friend asked me, many years ago, "why would any Native/Indigenous person want to be a Christian or be associated with the Christian Church?" (See the Introduction for my personal experiences as a child.)

Finally, to reiterate one last time my litany of lamentations, the United States of America and its Euro-American citizens were the ones to do all the invading, killing, stealing, occupying, dominating, suppressing, exploiting, destroying, criminalizing, discriminating, persecuting, and oppressing of the Native Peoples of the United States in the 500-plus years that they have been here in the Americas. They were the ones who placed bounties on Indigenous scalps, who force marched our Native Peoples, who imprisoned us in concentration camps, perpetrated mass executions; who forcibly removed, or "ethnically cleansed" our First Nations Peoples, who burned thousands of our communities and towns (a literal "holocaust," thorough destruction by fire)[62]; who used our peoples as bait to troll for fish, and who perpetrated genocide on the Native Peoples. They were the basic cause of the sorrow, suffering, and calamities of First Nations Peoples.[63]

What was done to the Indigenous Peoples of the United States, of Canada, of Mexico, the Caribbien, and of Central America and South America, and what was done to the Dakota People of Minnesota, and who did it, comprises a sorrowful, destructive, calamitous, and genocidal history. When the U.S. government and its white citizenry begin to address seriously the above-mentioned issues, including truth telling, mutual respect, and reparations, then, perhaps, justice can "roll down like waters and righteousness like an ever-flowing stream."[64]

What has happened in the past half-millennium to the Indigenous Peoples of the United States and of the Americas, perpetrated by the western Europeans and U.S. Euro-Americans, is Wosice Tanka Kin, "The Great Evil."

I think back to a statement I found in an article in the March 15, 2018 *Minneapolis Star Tribune* headlined in part, "To Rise Above Our Past, We Must Acknowledge It." The article was about *National Geographic* addressing its racist coverage, especially of black people in the United States. Susan Goldberg, the editor in chief admitted that "it hurts to share the appalling stories from the magazine's past. It includes some of the most blatant examples of racism . . ." The full title of the *National Geographic*'s article on racist coverage was, "For Decades, Our Coverage Was Racist. To Rise Above Our Past, We Must Acknowledge It."

The United States government and its Euro-American citizenry, after 500+ years, must now acknowledge its genocidal history in order to rise above its racist and white supremacist past.

Finally, I think of the statement of M. Annette Jaimes, who said, "Ultimately, we must all go forward together or we are lost to the evil which has engulfed the land we mutually inhabit."[65] In that spirit—"all going forward together"—I say that in spite of these bitter truths I have presented, and in spite of the fact that I think my three retirement goals—engaging in truth telling, working for justice, and calling for mutual respect—being impossible dreams does not mean I am going to stop what I am doing. I will keep on writing, speaking, and working for these goals as long as I still breathe, and will continue to address the Wosice Tanka Kin, "The Great Evil."

And, I am hoping that upstanders (i.e., allies and supporters), both Indigenous and non-Indigenous, with a good heart and good will, will join in the struggle in addressing the "Great Evil." And that, together, we can work to honor and protect Ina Maka ("Mother Earth"), to honor and protect our children, our women, and our elders, and to honor and protect our animal relatives, the birds, the fish, the rocks, and all other life forms, and to make a better society, and planet, for all.

Mitakuyapi, owasin wopida tanka eciciyapi do!

"My Relatives, I extend to you all my deepest appreciation!"

How, Mato Nunpa de miye do. "Yes, I am Two Bear!"

Mitakuye Owasin "All My Relatives"

Endnotes

1. "The Demography of Native North America," by Lenore A. Stiffarm and Phil Lane, Jr. *The State of Native America: Genocide, Colonization, and Resistance,* M. Annette Jaimes, ed. Boston: South End Press, 1992, p. 27.

2. Ibid., pp. 36–37.

3. *American Holocaust,* by David Stannard. Oxford: Oxford University Press, 1992, p. x.

4. Ibid.

5. Stiffarm and Lane, op. cit., p. 27

6. Stannard, op. cit., p. 146

7. Stannard, op. cit., p. 256

8. *As Long As The Grass Shall Grow and Rivers Flow*, by Clifford Trafzer. New York: Harcourt College Publishers, 2000, p. 330.

9. *History of the Santee Sioux: United States Indian Policy on Trial*, by Roy Meyer. Lincoln, NE: University of Nebraska Press, 1983, p. 1.

10. *What Does Justice Look Like? The Struggle for Liberation in Dakota Homeland*, by Waziyatawin. St. Paul: Living Justice Press, 2008, p. 61.

11. *Custer Died For Your Sins: An Indian Manifesto*, by Vine Deloria, Jr. Norman, OK: University of Oklahoma Press, 1988, p. 28.

12. Ibid.

13. "Trump defends Putin: 'You think our country's so innocent?'" CNN, February 6, 2017, Updated 3:30 PM ET.

14. Ibid.

15. Deloria, op. cit., p. 48.

16. *Native American Voices: A Reader*, by Susan Lobo and Steve Talbot. Upper Saddle River, NJ: Prentice Hall, 2001, p. 188.

17. "Key Indian Laws and Cases," by Ward Churchill and Glenn T. Morris, in *The State of Native America: Genocide, Colonization, and Resistance*, M. Annette Jaimes, ed. Boston: South End Press, 1992, p. 17.

18. "American Indian Education in the United States: Indoctrination for Subordination to Colonialism," by Jorge Noriega, in *The State of Native America*, M. Annette Jaimes, ed. Boston: South End Press, Boston, 1992, pp. 376, 377, 380.

19. "Kill the Indian, and Save the Man," by Capt. Richard H. A paper read by Pratt at an 1892 convention.

20. "Burning down the house: A little 'teaching moment'," by W. Roger Buffalohead in *The Circle*, publication of the Minneapolis American Indian Center, February 1999, Vol. 20, No. 2.

21. Deloria, op. cit., pp. 28, 42, 48, 49, 51, 52, 255, 256.

22. *Laying Down the Sword: Why We Can't Ignore the Bible's Violent Verses*, by Richard Jenkins. New York: Harper One, 2011, pp. 6, 22.

23. Ibid., p. 6.

24. Ibid.

25. Ibid.

26. The Holy Bible: Giant Print Reference Edition. Nashville: Thomas Nelson Publishers, 1976, pp. 292-293.

27. "The Worldwide Network of US Military Bases," by Jules Dufour, November 14, 2014, p. 3.

28. Floyd Red Crow Westerman, in a presentation at Southwest Minnesota State University, Marshall, Minnesota, in the spring of 2007.

29. Jenkins, op. cit., pp. 22–23.

30. *Divinity of Doubt: The God Question*, by Vincent Bugliosi. Philadelphia: Vanguard Press, 2011, p. 144.

31. Ibid., p. 142f.

32. *The History and Sociology of Genocide*, by Frank Chalk and Kurt Jonassohn. New Haven, CT: Yale University Press, 1990, p. 29.

33. Bugliosi, op. cit., p. 148

34. Ibid.

35. Ibid.

36. Ibid.

37. The Holy Bible, King James Version (KJV, 1976), Nashville: Thomas Nelson Publishers, 1976, p. 1413.

38. "Co-Opting the Memory of the Dakota 38 + 2," by Dr. Waziyatawin, in *Indian Country Today*," January 1, 2013, p. 1.

39. George Tinker in a presentation in October 2012 at Fairmount Methodist Church, St. Paul, Minnesota.

40. Kevin Jensvold, Chairman, Board of Trustees, Upper Sioux Community, at a conference at Minnesota State University, Mankato, in south-central Minnesota, Spring 2010.

41. The New American Bible. New York: Catholic Book Publishing Co., 1976, p. 276.

42. Sam Grey, unpublished essay, "The Ambit of Reconciliation," p. 3 of 19.

43. *From a Native Daughter: Colonialism and Sovereignty in Hawai'i*, by Hannah-Kay Trask, 1993, p. 252.

44. "A Critique of a Doctrine of Reconciliation," by Steven T. Newcomb, *Indian Country Today*, June 15, 2011, p. 1.

45. Ibid.

46. Ibid.

47. Sam Grey, "Forgiveness," unpublished paper (which I received in 2014), p. 2.

48. Ibid., p. 4.

49. Ibid., p. 3.

50. Ibid.

51. Ibid.

52. Ibid., p. 2.

53. Ibid.

54. *A Century of Wisdom: Lessons from the Life of Alice Herz-Sommer*, by Caroline Stoessinger. London: Two Roads, 2012, p. 132.

55. *When the Danube Ran Red*, by Zsusanna Ozsvath. Syracuse, NY: Syracuse University Press, 2010, p. xxiii.

56. Tanakh: A New Translation of the Holy Scriptures According to the Traditional Hebrew Text, p. 280.

57. Stannard, op. cit., p. 153.

58. Ibid.

59. Ibid., p. 184.

60. Chalk and Jonassohn, op. cit., p. 29.

61. Deloria, op. cit., p. 189.

62. Merriam-Webster's Collegiate Dictionary Eleventh Edition, p. 593. Also, Stannard, p. 111.

63. Merriam-Webster's Collegiate Dictionary, p. 433.

64. "The Book of Amos," The New Oxford Annotated Bible With Apocrypha, 1977, p. 1,113.

65. "Introduction: Sand Creek: The Morning After," by M. Annette Jaimes, in The State of Native America: Genocide, Colonization, and Resistance, M. Annette Jaimes, ed. p. 10.

A

BIBLE COMMANDS REGARDING MURDER, MASS MURDER, RAPE, AND ENSLAVEMENT

This is not a definitive list, but it does provide proof that the Old Testament God, Yahweh, commanded his chosen people to commit murder, mass murder, including the extermination of entire peoples, enslavement, and rape. There are many such passages, so, for the sake of brevity, we're listing only their citations; anyone interested can easily look these passages up in a Bible.

Genesis

Genesis 7:21–23

Exodus

Exodus 7:12
Exodus 17:13–14
Exodus 23:23–24
Exodus 23:27
Exodus 34:11

Leviticus

Lev. 20:9
Lev. 20:10–14
Lev. 24:13-14

Numbers

Numbers 21:3
Numbers 21:35
Numbers 25:4
Numbers 25:9
Numbers 31:7
Numbers 31:9–10
Numbers 31:15–18
Numbers 31:35

Deuteronomy

Deuteronomy 2:33–34
Deuteronomy 3:3
Deuteronomy 7:2
Deuteronomy 7:16
Deuteronomy 13:9
Deuteronomy 20:16–17
Deuteronomy 25:16
Deuteronomy 25:19
Deuteronomy 32:42

Joshua

Joshua 6:21
Joshua 8:22–26
Joshua 10:1-43
Joshua 11:6
Joshua 11:8
Joshua 11:11–17
Joshua 11:20–21
Joshua 12:1
Joshua 13:12

Judges

Judges 16:30

I Samuel

I Samuel 15:2–3
I Samuel 15:7

Esther

Esther 8:11
Esther 9:16

A

Bible Commands Regarding Religious Suppression

This is not a definitive list, but it does provide proof that the Old Testament God, Yahweh, commanded his chosen people to ruthlessly suppress the religious beliefs and practices of those they conquered. For the sake of brevity, we're listing only the citations; anyone interested can easily look these passages up in a Bible.

Exodus

Exodus 34:11–17

Numbers 33:52

Numbers 33:52

Deuteronomy

Deuteronomy 7:5
Deuteronomy 7:25
Deuteronomy 12:2–3

Kings

2 Kings 18:3&4

C

Bible Verses on the Chosen People and Promised Land

This is not a definitive list, but along with the many passages cited in the text, it does provide proof that the Old Testament God, Yahweh, defined the Israelites as his chosen people and commanded them to steal the land of victim peoples, and to mass murder, enslave, and rape them. For the sake of brevity we're listing only the citations; anyone interested can easily look these passages up in a Bible.

Chosen People

Exodus

Exodus 6:7
Exodus 19:5–6

Deuteronomy

Deuteronomy 7:6
Deutronomy 14:2
Deuteronomy 26:18

Psalms

Psalm 135:4

Promised Land

Genesis

Genesis 12:6–7
Genesis 15:18–21
Genesis 17:8
Genesis 28:4

Exodus

Exodus 3:8
Exodus 3:17
Exodus 6:4
Exodus 6:7–8
Exodus 12:25
Exodus 13:5
Exodus 19:5
Exodus 23:30–31

Leviticus

Leviticus 14:34
Leviticus 25:38

Numbers

Numbers 13:2I
Numbers 13:27
Number 14:8
Numbers 16:13–14
Numbers 34:2

Deuteronomy

Deuteronomy 6:3
Deuteronomy 9:28
Deuteronomy 14:2
Deuteronomy 19:8
Deuteronomy 31:20
Deuteronomy 32:49

Joshua

Joshua 1:2–4
Joshua 2:9

BIBLIOGRAPHY

Beck, Paul N. *Columns of Vengeance Soldiers, Sioux, and The Punitive Expeditions 1863–64*. Norman, OK: University of Oklahoma Press, 2013.

Bethany Parallel Commentary On The Old Testament. Minneapolis: Bethany House Publishers, 1985.

Bethany Parallel Commentary On The New Testament. Minneapolis: Bethany House Publishers, 1983.

Blum, William. *Rogue State: A Guide to the World's Only Superpower*. Monroe, ME: Common Courage Press, 2000.

Brandon, William. *Indians*. Boston: Houghton Mifflin, 1961.

Brandon, William. *The Last Americans: The Indian in American Culture*. New York: McGraw-Hill, 1974.

Brigham, Kay. *Columbus's Book of Prophecies*. Provo, UT: Religious Studies Center, 1991.

Bugliosi, Vincent. *Divinity of Doubt: The God Question*. Philadelphia: Vanguard Press, 2011.

Chalk, Frank and Jonassohn, Kurt. *The History and Sociology of Genocide*. New Haven, CT: Yale University Press, 1990.

Churchill, Ward. *A Little Matter of Genocide: Holocaust and Denial in the Americas, 1492 to the Present*. San Francisco: City Lights Books, 1997.

Churchill, Ward. *On the Justice of Roosting Chickens: Reflections on the Consequences of U.S. Imperial Arrogance and Criminality*. Oakland: AK Press, 2003.

Danieli, Yael. *Trauma And Recovery*. New York: Basic Books, 1992.

Dawkins, Richard. *The God Delusion*. London: Black Swan, 2006.

Debo, Angie. *A History of the Indians of the United States*. Norman, OK: University of Oklahoma Press, 1970.

Deloria, Vine, Jr. *God is Red: A Native View of Religions (second edition)*. Golden, CO: North American Press, 1992.

Deloria, Vine, Jr. *Custer Died For Your Sins: An Indian Manifesto*. Norman, OK: University of Oklahoma Press, 1969.

Deloria, Vine, Jr., and Wilkins, David E. *Tribes, Treaties, and Constitutional Tribulations*. Austin, TX: University of Texas Press, 1999.

Drinnon, Richard. *Facing West: The Metapysics of Indian-Hating and Empire Building*. Norman, OK: University of Oklahoma Press, 1980.

Eastman, Charles. *The Soul of the Indian: An Interpretation*. Lincoln, NE: University of Nebraska Press, 1911.

Eastman, Charles A. *Indian Boyhood*. New York: Dover, 1971.

Echo-Hawk, Walter R. *In the Light of Justice: The Rise of Human Rights in Native America and the UN Declaration on the Rights of Indigenous Peoples*. Golden, CO: Fulcrum Publishing, 2013.

Fuchs, Estelle and Havighurst, Robert J. *To Live On This Earth: American Indian Education*. Garden City, NY: Anchor, 1972.

Grinde, Donald A., Johansen, and Bruce E. *Ecocide of Native America: Environmental Destruction of Indian Lands and Peoples*, 1995.

Herman, Judith, M.D. *Trauma and Recovery: The Aftermath of Violence, From Domestic Abuse to Political Terror*. New York: Basic Books, 1997.

Hinton, Alexander. LaPointe, Thomas, Irvin-Erickson, Douglas, eds. *Hidden Genocides: Power, Knowledge, Memory*. New Brunswick, NJ: Rutgers University Press, 2014.

Hogan, Linda. *Mean Spirit*. New York: Ivy Books, 1990.

Jacobs, Steven Leonard, ed. *Confronting Genocide: Judaism, Christianity, Islam*. New York: Lexington Books, 2009.

Jenkins, Philip. *Laying Down the Sword: Why We Can't Ignore the Bible's Violent Verses*. New York: Harper One, 2011.

Lindsay, Brendan C. *Murder State: California's Native American Genocide, 1846–1873*. Lincoln, NE: University of Nebraska Press, 2012.

Lobo, Susan, and Talbot, Steve. *Native American Voices*. Upper Saddle River, NJ: Prentice-Hall, 2001.

Loewen, James W. *Lies My Teacher Told Me: Everything Your American History Textbook Got Wrong*. New York: Touchstone, 1995.

Mendoza, Patrick M. *Song of Sorrow: Massacre at Sand Creek*. Denver: Willow Wind, 1993.

Meyer, Roy W. *History of the Santee Sioux: United States Indian Policy on Trial*. Lincoln, NE: University of Nebraska Press, 1967.

Mihesuah, Devon, ed. *The American Indian Quarterly, Volume 27, Winter/Spring 2003, Numbers 1 & 2*. Lincoln, NE: University of Nebraska Press, 2004.

Mihesuah, Devon Abbott, and Angela Cavender Wilson, eds. *Indigenizing the Academy: Transforming Scholarship and Empowering Communities*. Lincoln, NE: University of Nebraska Press, 2004.

Nash, Gary B. *Red, White & Black*. Englewoord, NJ: Prentice-Hall, 1992.

Newcomb, Steven T. *Pagans in the Promised Land: Decoding the Doctrine of Christian Discovery*. Golden, CO: Fulcrum Publishing, 2008.

Ozsvath, Zsusanna. *When the Danube Ran Red*. Syracuse, NY: Syracuse University Press, 2010.

Peake, A.S. *Peake's Commentary On The Bible*. Nairobi: Thomas Nelson, 1962.

Prior, Michael. *The Bible and Colonialism: A Moral Critique.* Sheffield, England: Sheffield Academic Press, 1997.

Smith, Linda Tuhiwai. *Decolonizing Methodologies: Research and Indigenous Peoples*. London: Zed Books, 1999.

Spicer, Edward H. *A Short History of the Indians of the United States*. New York: Van Nostrand Reinhold, 1969.

Stannard, David E. *American Holocaust: The Conquest of the New World*. Oxford: Oxford University Press, 1992.

Stoessinger, Caroline. *A Century of Wisdom: Lessons from the Life of Alice Herz-Sommer.* Holder & Stoughton, 2012.

Strong, James. *Strong's Exhaustive Concordance Of The Bible*. Nashville, TN: Abingdon Press, 1890.

Takaki, Ronald. *A Different Mirror: A History of Multicultural America*. New York: Back Bay Books, 1993.

Thornton, Russell. *American Indian Holocaust and Survival: A Population History Since 1492*. Norman, OK: University of Oklahoma Press, 1987.

Tinker, George E. *Missionary Conquest: The Gospel and Native American Genocide*. Minneapolis: Fortress Press, 1993.

Toland, John. *Hitler.* New York, Anchor, 1976.

Takaki, Ronald. *A Different Mirror: A History of Mlticultural America*. New York: Back Bay, 2008.

Trafzer, Clifford E. *As Long As The Grass Shall Grow And Rivers Flow: A History of Native Americans*. Fort Worth: Harcourt College Publishers, 2000.

Trafzer, Clifford E., and Joel R. Hyer, eds. *Exterminate Them! Written Accounts of the Murder, Rape, and Enslavement of Native Americans during the California Gold Rush*. Lansing, MI: Michigan State University Press, 1999.

Trask, Haunani-Kay. *From a Native Daughter: Colonialism and Sovereignty in Hawai'i*. Honolulu: University of Hawaii, 1993.

Tyler, S. Lyman. *A History of Indian Policy.* Washington, DC: Bureau of Indian Affairs, 1973

Venables, Robert. *American Indian History: Five Centuries of Conflict and Coexistence*. Santa Fe, NM: Clear Light Publishers, 2004.

Vogel, Virgil. *American Indian Medicine*. Norman, OK: University of Oklahoma Press, 1970.

Waziyatawin. *Remember This*. Lincoln, NE: University of Nebraska Press, 2005.

Waziyatawin. *The Eli Taylor Narratives*. Lincoln, NE: University of Nebraska Press, 2005.

Waziyatawin. *What Does Justice Look Like? The Struggle for Liberation in Dakota Homeland*. St. Paul: Living Justice Press, 2008.

Waziyatawin, ed. *In the Footsteps of Our Ancestors: The Dakota Commemorative Marches of the 21ˢᵗ Century*. St. Paul: Living Justice Press, 2008.

Weatherford, Jack. *Indian Givers: How The Indians Of The Americas Transformed The World*. New York: Crown, 1988.

Weatherford, Jack. *Native Roots: How The Indians Enriched America*. New York: Crown, 1991.

Wingerd, Mary Lethert. *North Country: The Making of Minnesota*. Minneapolis: University of Minnesota Press, 2010.

Young, Robert, LL.D. *Young's Analytical Concordance To The Bible*. Nashville: Thomas Nelson Publishers, 1982.

Zinn, Howard. *A People's History of the United States*. New York: Harper Perennial, 1980.

Papal Bulls

Romanus Pontifex. Pope Nicholas V. January 8, 1455.

Inter Caetera. Pope Alexander VI, May 4, 1493.

Sublimus Dei. Pope Paul III, June 2, 1537.

Speeches

Beveridge, Senator Albert J. "In Support of an American Empire," January 09, 1900, "Record," 56 Cong. I Session, pp. 704–712

"Red Jacket's reply to a Missionary," Document No. 35, in Edward H. Spicer's *A Short History of the Indians of the United States*, 1969.

INDEX